Terrorist Cop

Terrorist Cop

The NYPD Jewish Cop
Who Traveled the World
to Stop Terrorists

BY

MORDECAI Z. DZIKANSKY

AND

ROBERT SLATER

Published by Barricade Books Inc.
185 Bridge Plaza North
Suite 309
Fort Lee, NJ 07024

www.barricadebooks.com

Library of Congress Cataloging-in-Publication Data

Dzikansky, Mordecai Z.
Terrorist cop : the NYPD Jewish cop who traveled the world to stop
terrorists / by Mordecai Z. Dzikansky and Robert Slater.
 p. cm.
ISBN 978-1-56980-445-2
1. Dzikansky, Mordecai Z. 2. New York (N.Y.) Police Dept.-
-Officials and employees--Biography. 3. Police--New York
(State)--New York--Biography. 4. Terrorism--Prevention.
5. Transnational crime. I. Slater, Robert. II.Title.
HV7911.D99A3 2011
363.325'17092--dc22
[B] 2010014517

ISBN 13: 978-1-56980-445-2
ISBN 1-56980-445-1

9 8 7 6 5 4 3 2 1
Manufactured in the United States of America

"When good people in any country cease their vigilance and struggle, then evil men prevail."

—Pearl S. Buck (American author, 1938 Nobel Prize for Literature, 1892–1973)

TABLE OF CONTENTS

Acknowledgments xi
Foreword xvii

Chapter 1 Why Is that Cop Wearing a Yarmulke? 1

Chapter 2 Our Jewish Detective: Working
 the Rabbi Kahane Murder Case 23

Chapter 3 Raiders of the Sacred Ark: The Torah
 Theft Cases 35

Chapter 4 I Thought of My Wife and Son 59

Chapter 5 Guys, We Can't Relax 77

Chapter 6 Meet and Greet: Making Contact
 with the Israel Police 93

Chapter 7 Seat Belts, Cell Phones, and Traffic Jams 103

Chapter 8 2003: The Grisly Face of Terror 129

Chapter 9 Istanbul and Moscow: Chasing
 Terrorists in Exotic, Dangerous Lands 157

Chapter 10 Commuter Trains and a Barren Desert:
 Madrid and Sharm El Sheikh 175

Chapter 11 Lessons Learned 193

Chapter 12 How to Identify a Terror Attack:
 A Manual 209

Chapter 13 Chasing the Demons 223

Dedication

To Zachary, Jake, and Talia

It is to you my children that I dedicate this book, hopeful that through vigilance, courage, and conviction, good will triumph and that you will lead meaningful and happy lives.

MZD

Acknowledgments

There is currently no universally agreed upon definition of terrorism. Common explanations refer to violent acts targeting civilians that are meant to create fear and are perpetrated for an ideological goal. My definition would also include the hell it wreaks on its victims, the physical and mental scars it leaves on its survivors and first responders, and the challenges and responsibilities it places on law enforcement and the public.

I never imagined that after spending a fulfilling twenty years with the NYPD fighting traditional crime, I would stay on to become a global terror expert able to contribute to securing New York City 5,600 miles from home.

I saw, learned, and relayed so much, but the fight against terrorism affected me so strongly on both a professional and personal level, I felt compelled to share my story and the lessons that I have learned while combating this evil.

Mine is a story of tradition, chance, perseverance, and purpose. My goal in writing this book is to demystify the terrorist, to empower the public, to stress the importance and value of awareness, and to shine light on the sacrifice and commitment of first responders.

I have many people to thank for helping me along my journey:

First, in loving memory and in tribute to two extraordinary men who shaped my life—

To my father, Rabbi Jekuthiel Dzikansky, whose quiet dignity and steady moral influence guided me throughout. A true gentleman of the Old World, he still skillfully blazed his own path while never forgetting from where he came. From him I learned that service to one's community is a noble and honorable path.

To my brother-in-law, Frank Kutnicki, more like a brother and truly my best friend. His life's example taught me the value of enjoying the simple pleasures in life, the ease of walking with honesty and integrity, and the fact that being a parent is life's greatest treasure. He was the essence of a gentle soul.

I am grateful . . .

That I met a talented, passionate, articulate, and ever-so-patient writer named Robert Slater. His commitment to our project and support from the get-go gave me encouragement to proceed. I thoroughly enjoyed our meetings and working together. And thanks so much to Naomi Ragen for the introduction; you made a great match! A special thank you to Bob's wife, Elinor, whose editorial contributions were very much appreciated.

To my NYPD Intelligence colleagues and friends: Donny P., Ira G., Howie S., Diana P., and Milton L., and all those who assisted me while I was stationed overseas. Keep up the great work; it really does make a difference!

For my Detective Squad partners, my extended "family"— Brian McCabe, Mike Bachety, the late Alex Renow, Mary Kennedy, Eddie Hennessy, Mitch Parker, and Juan J.—thank you for always having my back.

To my fraternal brothers in the NYPD Shomrim Society, the Detective Endowment Association, and the NYPD Chaplain's Unit; your friendship and support throughout my career will always be appreciated. A special thank you to Sam Miller, Ken Cardona, Brian Reilly, and Rabbi Alvin Kass.

To my Torah Task Force partner, David Pollock of the Jewish Community Relations Council of New York; it has always been a pleasure working together.

To the officers in the Israel National Police, including Gil Kleiman, Asher B., Anat G., Osnat H., and Duby Y.; thank you for letting me into your inner circle. I have only respect and admiration for the difficult work that you do. A special thank you to Esther T. and Michael C. from the Israel police Bomb Squad for your guidance and assistance.

To Eyal D. and Rami S. for your commitment and contributions to protecting both of our countries. Your cleverness and friendship are invaluable.

To my sister Adina for always being there for me. Your encouragement, support, wealth of knowledge on Middle East affairs, keen eye, and contacts were so helpful and very much appreciated.

To Liz and Jack R. for always making me feel welcomed and at home. Your love and support mean the world to me and the family!

For my friends despite the physical distance: Scott Flaum, Stuart Austin, and Joel Seidemann; friends for life!

I am in awe of . . .

The men and women of the NYPD whom I witnessed perform painstakingly difficult tasks on 9/11 and in its aftermath. Their selfless heroism and dedication to the people of New York were truly inspiring.

The officers of the Israel National Police who showed incredible strength and fortitude while under the merciless barrage of terror attacks.

I am blessed . . .

And thankful to have the support and love of an amazing wife. Meryl has stood by my side through thick and thin. Her strength, understanding, and encouragement define the true meaning of dedication to one's family.

To have three fantastic children: Zachary, Jake, and Talia. You make everything worthwhile and fill my life with joy. You reminded me how to smile and to treasure life's simplest moments.

Mordecai Z. Dzikansky
April 2010

Robert Slater adds:

When Morty and I spoke about this book for the first time, my gut instinct told me that he had a great story to tell. As we talked more, I confirmed my original instinct: His story is dramatic, colorful, poignant, and unique. I was confident that we would be able to produce a compelling insider's look at what it was like to be a Jewish police officer in New York and later in Israel. Few cops write their memoirs. Morty has. Over the course of the research for this book, Morty and I had numerous conversations about what should go into the book. Our meetings were very meaningful to me.

I have conducted countless interviews as a journalist and an author and often I could tell that the person I was interviewing was holding back certain things. Morty never held back. He felt that it was important to tell his story in its entirety. There is no better example than his brutally honest recounting of the suffering he endured toward the end of his career as his post-traumatic stress disorder (PTSD) set in. To his credit, he believed that it was as important to include the painful part of his career as it was his exciting adventures.

I have interviewed scores of political and business leaders, but never have I sat down with a homicide detective and been able to talk in great detail about his work, his cases, and his attitude toward his experiences. The subject matter was often difficult, but we both developed a certain detachment in regard to the awful events that Morty was describing.

Our attorney-agent, Lloyd Jassin, played a critical role in bringing *Terrorist Cop* into existence, and we thank him for his immediate sense that there was a good book in Morty's story, for his perseverance, and for his simply watching out for Morty and me.

We also want to extend our gratitude to Carole Stuart, Publisher of Barricade Books, who instinctively sensed that Morty's story was a good "fit" for Barricade. We have found her counsel wise in all aspects of the publishing process. Mark Morrell, Barricade's Print Production Manager, has helped to shepherd *Ter-*

rorist Cop through the various stages of publishing, and we thank him. Suzanne Henry has played a major role in promoting our book as widely as possible at Barricade, and we appreciate her contributions.

In both Morty's and my case, it was obvious that we both looked to our wives for their wisdom and their experiences in helping us to shape this book. In providing her keen editorial eye to the manuscript, Meryl Dzikansky became a true "partner" in this enterprise and I want to thank her. Her counterpart, my wife Elinor, fortunately has had direct professional editorial experience, has edited many of my books, and in this case applied her editorial skills to *Terrorist Cop*. Because of her skills, I know that the manuscript reads better, stays on message, and is, in its narrative, crisper. I thank her for all her hard work.

Finally, a word about my family, my three children: Miriam, and her husband Shimi; Adam, and his wife Tal; and Rachel; as well as our six grandchildren: Edo, Maya, Shai, Shani, Matan, and Ben. They are the joys of my life and provide the happiness and love that makes doing a book-length project possible. I want to especially note my fifteen-year-old grandson Edo's unusual, loving interest in my book career. He constantly asks me, "How's the book going?" Or "What's new with that detective book?" I love the questions; I love his expressions of interest in my career. See what I mean? He and the others are the joys of my life.

I dedicate this book to my six grandchildren in the hope and with the prayer that they will grow up in a world free of terrorism—and a lot of other evils.

Robert Slater
April 2010

Foreword

I resisted giving up my mission, my task, my job, even though I knew the time had come.

I resisted because of the adrenaline rush and the feeling that I was truly making a difference. I resisted because of all the praise that had been lavished on me—from my boss, from my colleagues, and most importantly, from the media.

I had accomplished so much. Everyone said so. It was an easy leap for me to read the newspaper articles about my exploits and then to imagine who would be playing me in the film.

PLUNGING INTO MY OWN HELL

And yet, the warning signs that I was plunging into my own hell were all too apparent.

There was the doctor whom I visited, who suggested in all seriousness that if I did not quit my assignment, I would soon be dead. Then there was the time I drove behind a bus and saw an advertisement on its side for a children's festival. My natural instinct should have been to look at the dates so that I could take my kids to it. But the only thing that went through my mind was what a vulnerable spot the festival would be for a terror attack.

I felt something churning inside of me.

I suppose I was burned out from the job. But, in fact, I was obsessed with my work, so obsessed that as my workload diminished, I grew even more obsessed and I entered my own isolated world: My relationship with my wife and children suffered; with

time on my hands for the first time in years. I poured all my anxiety into eating and put on far too many pounds.

I was not suffering the kind of mental collapse that carried a stigma. My ailment was post-traumatic stress disorder or PTSD. Somehow, the emotions that I was experiencing were easier to absorb now that I knew my situation had a rational explanation.

It was all so ironic.

My job was to be the voice of authority; my tasks were to make sure that the awful scenes that I witnessed would never happen again. I suffered pain from our up-close encounter with the victims. And yet here I was, a victim too.

ADRENALINE RUSH

On these pages I will explain what caused that adrenaline rush; much more specifically I will describe who I was, what I did, how I reached the height of my profession, and how I saved many lives.

I will also relate how in the end I became so obsessed with my mission that it consumed me and I sank into my own private hell for a brief period that happily today is part of my past.

Here then is my story.

CHAPTER 1

Why Is that Cop
Wearing a Yarmulke?

One day I would be called the Jewish detective.

As a youngster, I was Jewish, but I showed no indication of becoming a detective. I grew up in Brooklyn surrounded by "my people." My father, Jekuthiel Dzikansky, born in Minsk, Russia, in 1918, was a rabbi, as was his father. Because my father lived the life of a modern Orthodox Jew, as a child I did too: Wearing a yarmulke, not driving on the Sabbath, observing *kashrut* (the Jewish dietary rules). I believed that Judaism would remain a part of my life forever.

But I had no idea then that one day I would wind up an NYPD First Grade Detective. My father wanted me to be a doctor, but he would have settled for an accountant. Most important to him was that I contribute something to society; that contribution, he told me repeatedly, would show my true value, not how much money I made, or how many houses and cars I accumulated.

As a child, I had no specific career ambitions. I did think fire engines and the pole on which the firefighters slid down were cool.

I was born in the fall of 1962 in the mixed community of Canarsie in Brooklyn. I call it mixed because it was populated largely by Italians but my housing projects were a melting pot: white, black, Hispanic, Jewish, and Italian.

My name at birth was Mordecai Zev Dzikansky, so formally I would be known as Mordecai, but most people would call me Morty.

My father worked at raising funds for Yeshiva University. One of the hardest-working people I had ever met, he believed so strongly in raising funds for Jewish education that he never complained about commuting to work three hours back and forth every day via public transportation, a bus and two trains.

My mother was a housewife and a volunteer for Jewish causes.

WE WERE THE POOR ONES

Only a handful of Orthodox Jews lived in the projects. The upper-middle-class Jews in Canarsie dwelled in nearby private houses. I guess we were the poor ones: We did not own a car (my father never learned to drive), but we did have a black-and-white TV (rarely watched). Despite their financial hardship, my parents insisted on sending me to a yeshiva, an institution devoted to Torah study.

When I was seven years old, I suffered the most traumatic experience of my life: My mother died of cancer at the age of forty-three. Our household then consisted of just my father, my three older sisters, Shoshana, Navah, and Adina, and me; in truth, home was not very stable, since my father was often not around because of his long commute. I often had to fend for myself.

My teenage sisters tried hard to take care of me, but I was more than a handful. My mother's death had a profound effect on my ability to concentrate. I was street smart but scholastically challenged; I probably would have been a good candidate for Ritalin, but who knew about such things back then?

In 1971, when I was nine years old, my father took Shoshana and me on our first visit to Israel. It had been over thirty years since he had seen his older brother, who had fled Europe and gone to Israel just prior to the Holocaust; his other surviving siblings escaped to America. That trip with my father and sister had implications for my future that I could not begin to understand at the time.

A SPECIAL PLACE

We flew to Tel Aviv. I saw a good deal of family, felt their warmth, and never forgot my first visit to the Western Wall, the holiest site in Judaism within Jerusalem's Old City. I knew that I was in a special place. In 1979, at the age of sixteen, I graduated from Adelphia Academy, a yeshiva boarding school near Lakewood, New Jersey.

I could not know it at the time, but all that yeshiva training proved wonderfully helpful later when I became a police detective; as I learned the ins and outs of detective work, the yeshiva "way" taught me to ask a lot of questions and to look at a situation in depth. The yeshiva also taught me to read and speak Hebrew.

At age seventeen, as a freshman in college, I began a year in Jerusalem in the Yeshiva University Israel program. Many Orthodox Jewish families sent their children to Israel as part of this program.

While in Israel, I had my own personal experience with Arab terror against Israelis. Between September 1979 and June 1980, while I was studying in Jerusalem, seventeen terror attacks were carried out against targets in Israel. Each time an attack occurred, the college did a head count to make sure that we students were all safe and accounted for. The image of those head counts remains with me to this day. Those were the first of my many encounters with Arab terror.

During my year in Israel I visited Sinai in 1979 when it still belonged to Israel. For the Passover Seder I was chosen by my school in Jerusalem to assist the Israel Defense Forces (IDF) in spiritually leading a Seder at the IDF's base near Sharm el Sheik. I could not know it at the time, but ironically I would return to Sharm in 2005 under far more difficult and dangerous circumstances as an investigator.

After returning to New York in June 1980, I began my sophomore year at Touro College in mid-Manhattan, an offshoot of Yeshiva University, and majored in accounting. Accounting, I soon

learned, was not my cup of tea. But what was? I had no idea. Unhappy at Touro, I wanted more of a party school.

I MIGHT AS WELL HAVE FUN

In September 1981, after a year at Touro, I looked for another college with a "party" lifestyle and discovered Stony Brook University on Long Island, New York. Uncertain what to do with the rest of my life, I thought I might as well have fun. But I was definitely ripe for a suggestion of what I should choose as a career. When the suggestion came, it came out of nowhere.

I never did get to Stony Brook: One Sunday morning in January 1982 I had one of those moments when I suddenly realized what I wanted to do with the rest of my life. Basketball, as it turned out, provided the catalyst.

I was a basketball enthusiast; I loved the game, watched it, and played it Sunday mornings at the Jewish Community House in Bay Ridge, Brooklyn. Leaving the court that day, I noticed some papers lying on a desk off to the side and picked one up out of curiosity.

It was a recruitment flyer for the New York Police Department, distributed by the Shomrim Society, which sought to enlist Jews in the NYPD; the flyer aimed specifically at recruiting members of the Orthodox Jewish community. At that time only two Orthodox Jews were members of the NYPD.

Until the 1970s the NYPD suffered from a reputation of being exclusive, dominated by officers who came primarily from two ethnic groups (Irish and Italian), who did not reflect the melting pot of ethnic groups they served.

To resolve the issue, the NYPD sought to become more egalitarian, encouraging minorities, such as Orthodox Jews, to join the force. Thus it was that I benefited from the more flexible schedule of exams that the New York City Civil Service offered.

At first the NYPD entry exams were given only on Saturday, making it impossible for an Orthodox Jew or a Seventh Day

Adventist to apply to become a police officer. Then the Shomrim Society affected a change in the Civil Service rules so that Orthodox Jews could take the exam on a Friday; the test became known as the Sabbath Observance Exam.

As I read through the flyer, it sounded very heroic, exciting, cool, appealing—and different. Not coming from a typical two-parent family, I already felt "different" and so the questions asked in the flyer really tempted me:

"Are you looking for an exciting career? Are you eager to help the public? Are you looking to get involved?"

The questions reminded me of those army posters that urged you to be all that you could be—all you had to do was join the U.S. Army. At the bottom of the flyer was a word for Orthodox Jews, assuring us that we could take the exam on a Friday.

NEVER IN A MILLION YEARS

I had never given the idea of becoming a policeman an ounce of thought. Never in a million years would I have dreamed that this was what I wanted to do. I did not grow up watching cop shows on television, idolizing their antics. I never dreamed of carrying a gun or wearing a badge. But I liked the idea that becoming a cop would take me away from office work (well, not completely!).

Growing up in Canarsie, we did not need the police, and we had none of the fear that others had of them. They were an enigma to me, sort of a nonentity in my life. I knew nothing of the reputation of the New York Police Department. In time, I decided that it was the finest police force in the world.

Orthodox Jewish youngsters were encouraged to pursue respectable Jewish-oriented careers such as being a rabbi, a cantor, or a teacher at a yeshiva. Or, they could enter the outside workforce and become a doctor, a lawyer, or an accountant. Becoming a policeman was not considered an option.

But as I stared at that recruiting flyer, the far-fetched idea of joining the police force sounded interesting.

OUT OF THE BOX

Had my mother lived, I most likely would have never finished reading the flyer. Had she lived, our home would have been far more stable, I would have been a much better student, and I would have never entertained such an "out of the box" notion as joining the police force. With my mother there, I would have gone to college, become an accountant, or entered one of the other traditional professions.

But she was dead; my father was frequently absent from our home. I felt I was free to pursue almost any career of my choice. I decided to take the battery of tests—physical, medical, psychological—for entry into the Police Academy, keeping Stony Brook as an option should I not pass the exams.

Strangely, none of the police officers who asked me why I wanted to join the force asked why an Orthodox Jew, wearing a yarmulke, would want to become a policeman. Instead, their only concern was that I was young (I was twenty years old) and largely devoid of what they termed "life experience," which really meant work experience. It was true that other than minor part-time jobs—I had been a busboy and waiter—I had never taken on work that might have demonstrated that I was ready to bear the responsibility of being a cop.

I took the Friday Sabbath Observer Police exam with fifty other Orthodox Jews and Seventh Day Adventists. I can't say that I was overly confident that I would be chosen. As it turned out, I received two acceptance letters on the same day in June 1982. Both Stony Brook and the Police Academy offered me a place on their admission lists. Out of the fifty people who took the Police Academy test with me, one other Orthodox Jew and I got offers to join the NYPD.

Stony Brook would have probably been fun, but I still could not imagine what I might study there that would give me a career I wanted. I was, however, intrigued at the thought of becoming a policeman, and so the Police Academy was my obvious choice.

I entered the Academy in January 1983. I decided to maintain a low profile at first; I did not wear my yarmulke during classes.

MY SON THE COP

Until then I had not told my father that I was planning to join the NYPD. It was not that I feared his opposing my career choice. He had always had a great respect for the police. But I knew that this was not a career he had imagined for his son. He had never imagined introducing me to his friends, as "my son, the cop."

I had a lot of respect for my father, and the last thing I wanted to do was upset him. So I decided to proceed gingerly, to wait and see if I got into the Academy.

Once I entered the Academy, I let him know that his son was going to become a cop. His first reaction was shock. "Oy," was all he whispered. But, realizing that I had grown up and would be doing something positive with my life, he acknowledged that he was proud of my decision.

Of the two thousand students at the Academy, half worked from 7 AM to 3 PM, half worked from 3 PM to 11 PM. For me the only problem arose when I was assigned the 3 PM shift: How could I observe the Jewish Sabbath, which began at dusk Fridays, if I was expected to work during the Sabbath?

Fortunately, allowances were made, and on Fridays I was permitted to work the first shift, which ended at 3 PM, giving me plenty of time to get home for the start of the Sabbath. Some of my fellow students were jealous that I was able to worm out of the less desirable 3 PM shift. But I was pleased with the arrangement, even though juggling my schedule meant that I had to finish up my required exercises at the gym on a Thursday night at 11 PM and return to the same gym for more exercises the following Friday morning by 7 AM.

For others at the Academy the semi-military regimen was a new challenge; but I had gone through a similarly rigid schedule at yeshiva so I adjusted quite quickly. Still, it was an extremely

grueling six months, both the physical part and the various academic disciplines. But when I graduated, I was in the best physical shape of my life.

THE COP AND THE YARMULKE

In June 1983 I graduated from the Academy and became a New York City policeman. It was agreed that I could wear a yarmulke on the job and that I would not have to work on the Jewish Sabbath, which lasted from sundown Friday to sundown Saturday. For any amount of money I would not work on a Friday night or a Saturday. The only exception would be if I were in the middle of a major crime investigation where lives were at risk and I played a key role in the investigation.

Starting police officers are known as "rookies" for the first eighteen months of their careers. I was assigned to the "neighborhood stabilization unit," number 12, or in NYPD shorthand, NSU12. We were forty rookie cops who trained together with seasoned officers in a specified section of New York City. The NSU12 included the 63rd, 67th, 69th, and 71st precincts. I was assigned to Crown Heights in Brooklyn, where the Chabad Lubavitch ultra-Orthodox Jewish community, one of the largest of the Hasidic movements, had a strong presence. Canarsie, where I grew up, was also in NSU12, so it was like going home.

The sight of a police officer can often scare people; but I must have seemed even more intimidating, or at least strange: Here I was, wearing a yarmulke, sprinkling my English with a little Hebrew, a little Yiddish; it was hardly surprising that ultra-Orthodox Jews had trouble figuring me out; was I one of them, confused, or just lost?

I certainly got a lot of stares. Serving with me in Crown Heights was Harvey Hecker, the very first New York policeman to wear a yarmulke. Harvey was the first Orthodox Jew to enter the NYPD; he joined two years before I did. When we walked around the community together, we looked like "Mutt and Jeff;" I was tall and Harvey was not.

MY FIRST COLLAR

On one freezing night in December 1983, assigned to a beefed-up holiday detail in Canarsie and on the lookout for robberies, I patrolled alone on foot. I was under instructions not to vacate my beat—a two-block shopping center containing a department store, jewelry store, and the like—except in an emergency.

To protect against the wind blowing fiercely off of Jamaica Bay two blocks away, I kept my gloved hands in my pockets. I had on layers of clothing underneath my uniform.

I had grown up across the street from the shopping center, so I had probably shopped there a thousand times. This was my first time back in seven and a half years. It was 5:30 PM and getting dark. Moving from store to store, I paid special attention to the stores that were still open.

Searching for a spot where I could hide myself from view yet still have a good overview of the shopping center, I found a place that would allow me to react quickly if necessary. Suddenly, a white male without a mask—later I would learn that his name was Terry Cogswell—emerged from a grocery store with a fistful of money in his left hand and a gun in his right. I would have to act on my own. There was no time to call for backup. My instincts told me to tackle him in much the way a linebacker would pounce on an oncoming halfback.

I moved toward Cogswell and within seconds he and I literally ran into each other. At six-foot-three and 220 pounds, I had been confident that I could hold my own in any physical encounter. But this was my very first brawl and suddenly the issue had become very real.

This all happened in a flash. Grabbing his gun, securing it in my waist belt, I put my knee into his back and cuffed him. "Oh my God," I said to myself, "Holy shit." I realized that I had just made a solo armed robbery collar, quite unusual for a police rookie.

Noticing that Cogswell was in a state of shock, I imagined he was asking himself over and over: How could a lone policeman,

shivering in the cold, come upon him the second he exited the store? Cogswell could not have known, and I certainly did not let on, that I was in a similar state of shock—over collaring my first criminal!

Then I heard a strange sound off in the distance as if someone were taking pictures. And, indeed, that is precisely what was happening. "What the hell is going on here?" I thought, wondering how a newspaper photographer could have gotten to the scene so quickly.

One of the store owners came outside, and I urged him to call 911. I would have made the call but, because I was holding the perp down, I could not get to my radio. "Tell them that a cop needs help, and give them our location," I shouted, trying to maintain calm and to sound authoritative.

I kept my knee on Cogswell's back, not letting him get up, keeping an eye out for his possible backup car or accomplices. The last thing I wanted was for him to run on me. He tried to get up several times. "Don't you dare fucking move," I screamed at him.

Within minutes, the cavalry arrived, a half dozen police cars, sirens screaming, lights flashing. Never was I more relieved. Hey, I was just a rookie!

The whole episode was quite an awakening for me. Most of the time police work is routine and can be boring; but when something like the Cogswell incident occurs, it made me realize that I had to be ready—and fortunately I was.

Bringing Cogswell to the precinct, I quickly discovered that despite the cold chill outside that grocery store, I felt more comfortable on the beat than inside the paper-laden precinct. It was my responsibility to process the perp, but I needed senior police officers to walk me through the stages: How to fill out the necessary forms, how to voucher a gun, how to find a detective to interrogate the perp.

At one point a detective approached me and asked how I spelled my name, giving no explanation for his question.

"Why does anyone need my name?" I asked suspiciously, figuring that only harm could come from giving up my name.

"Don't worry about it," was the detective's terse reply. Now I was even more suspicious.

NEWSPAPER PHOTO

I had no way of knowing at the time, but the *New York Daily News* had obtained a photo of my holding Cogswell on the ground, evidently from the amateur photographer who had heard of the incident on a police scanner and snapped the photo. Now the newspaper was asking how to spell my name. Had I been told why I was asked to reveal my name, I would have dropped my suspicions and laughed out loud.

By the time I returned to my precinct in Crown Heights at midnight, the news of my collar was all over the community. Everyone, so it seemed, had heard that I had made an armed robbery arrest on my own. I was touted as some kind of a hero.

When our midnight shift ended, it was the custom for a bunch of us police rookies to go to Bay Ridge, another community in Brooklyn, for a few beers. Three hours later we found a diner for breakfast. Getting together like that proved a great bonding experience for us, eager to exchange news about our adventures earlier in the night.

This was my night. I was the guy who had made the armed robbery arrest. At one point, one of my buddies picked up a copy of the "Night Owl" edition of the *New York Daily News,* and there on the front page was a photo of me wrestling the perp down to the ground. I looked at the caption, entitled "Sidewalk drama," and could not believe that that collar had become a New York police story so swiftly.

I read each word, wondering how the report that my senior detectives and I had penned earlier that evening had wound up in a New York newspaper so quickly:

"Police Officer Mordecai Ozikansky puts cuffs on robbery suspect identified as Terry Cogswell, 27, of 1232 E. 92nd St. Wednesday night on sidewalk in front of store at 2130 Rockaway Parkway in Canarsie. Police said Ozikansky spotted Cog-

swell burst from store with handgun in his belt and a fistful of money allegedly taken from register. Cogswell was charged with first-degree robbery, assaulting a police officer, resisting arrest, and criminal possession of weapon."

During that first reading I was so excited that I completely overlooked the fact that the newspaper had misspelled my last name! Naturally I knew that once people who knew me saw the photo, they would recognize me and not think it was some other fellow named Ozikansky. That misspelling was the closest I came to being Irish!

My police buddies were proud of me. One joked that we ought to point out the photo to the bartender so that, upon realizing he had a genuine hero in his midst, he would dispense free beers to everyone.

The best part of my surprise collar and the newspaper coverage was showing the photo to my Dad, enabling me to let him know that I had done something positive. However, recalling how often he had told me, as a rabbi's son, I was not supposed to expose myself to possible danger, I was careful to play down whatever dangers might have existed during my collar. To my father, Jews were supposed to be scholars, not fighters.

To my great satisfaction, Cogswell was found guilty of armed robbery and was sent to jail for a few years.

The Cogswell collar and the newspaper photo made me feel what it was like to be a cop. Hearing those sirens and watching the cavalry arrive gave me great comfort that I was part of a larger organization there to protect the public—and me as well.

I realized for the first time how much I relished the publicity focused on myself. Getting my photo on the front page of a New York newspaper so early in my career had been too much to imagine or expect. I could not have been more thrilled when my bosses asked me to lecture my NSU unit to recount the experience on that freezing cold night.

I began with practical advice based on what I had learned the hard way: No matter how cold it is, do not put your hands in your pockets! If I had kept my gloved hands in my pockets, I could have

allowed the perp to get the drop on me. Had the distance between us been greater, he would have easily been able to gun me down before I even had the chance to go for my weapon. I never had the chance to draw my gun but was glad for my tackling skills!

BIGGEST DECISION

Soon after my "15 seconds of fame" in the *Daily News*, in January 1984, I had to make the biggest decision of my career. I had served for six months in NSU12 and now my bosses were ready to give us rookies our permanent assignments. I would have to choose what location I wanted as my permanent beat. Because my decision would affect my career for a number of years to come, I wondered how I could possibly make the best decision for me.

A senior figure with the Shomrim Society, with the influence to try to get me assigned to any locale of his or my choosing, wanted me to pick Borough Park in Brooklyn, a Hasidic Orthodox Jewish enclave. It would be a good fit for "a nice Orthodox Jewish boy," he suggested, convinced that this beat would enhance my career: I could develop my community affairs skills while eating kosher doughnuts.

To me, however, it would have been a dumb move. The Jewish community there would have relied upon me to resolve intracommunity disputes, a kind of community affairs tsar, depriving me of the time to catch criminals. I wanted true law enforcement. That collar in Canarsie had whetted my appetite for more such action. I gave the Shomrim elder a polite no.

Even though I had rejected Borough Park, I still hoped that the Shomrim fellow would help me get to a beat that I had hoped for. Therefore I was delighted when he asked me, "Well, where would you like to go?"

With a certain *chutzphah*, I quickly replied: "Somewhere in Manhattan, I'd like to be in the big city." He promised to see what he could do about it.

In late January 1984 I was on foot patrol one afternoon in East Flatbush, Brooklyn, still with NSU12. On that day I would

learn my permanent assignment, a beat that might last twenty years until my retirement. I was quite nervous.

One of my bosses, a lieutenant, radioed me to get over to the corner of Nostrand and Church avenues, where I suspected he planned to drop this personal bombshell on me.

I was right.

"Moish," he called to me as he drove up to the corner, "come on over." "Moish" was his nickname for me. It was actually a nickname for someone named Moshe. I was a Mordecai and my nickname was Morty. None of this seemed to matter to my lieutenant.

As I approached his car, I noticed he was looking at a piece of paper, obviously the list of new assignments. Smoking a cigarette, he asked cryptically, "Moish, who did you fuck?"

I was so taken back by the question that I could only think of trying to humor him: "Recently? I can't remember. Why do you ask?"

"Do you know where you're going?"

I remained flustered. "No," I replied, getting even more nervous. "Am I going to the Upper West Side?" Again, I was trying to humor him. Rookies didn't get assigned permanently to the Upper West Side. We all knew that. "I don't know where I'm going. Where am I going?"

Taking another puff, trying to act casual, the lieutenant finally revealed:" You're going to the 79th Precinct."

"Where's the 79th Precinct?" I asked, embarrassed that I had no idea where that was.

"You don't even know where it is? It's at Eastern Parkway and Crown Heights. But you're going to be on the other side."

What other side was he talking about?

"Oh, that's nice," I said, trying to sound pleased.

THE KILLING GROUND

He told me the 79th was in the Bedford-Stuyvesant district and then he did something strange. He began to laugh.

What was I missing? Why was he laughing? Then I found out.

At the time, Bed-Stuy carried the police nickname, "Do or die in Bed-Stuy," from its high rate of murders and daily shootings in the early 1980s.

"I thought you had all the juice," the lieutenant smiled.

Then I understood. The perception endured that any cop wearing a yarmulke must have had the right connections, the political "pull" within the Department to write his own ticket. After all, as one of only three Orthodox Jewish cops out of 40,000 officers, I was thought to wield far more power and influence than I actually did.

Well, I had said no thank you to Borough Park and instead of getting Manhattan I had gotten Bed-Stuy. Okay, I'm up for it, I thought. I like action. This could be fun.

Starting in February 1984 I began my assignment in Bedford-Stuyvesant. I served there for a year. Joining me were seven fellow rookies, good friends who made the assignment, socially at least, a lot of fun. I began working the 12 midnight to 8 AM shift.

I learned quickly why Bed-Stuy, or at least parts of it, had an awful reputation for the cheapness of life. On one of my first nights there I got a sudden preview of what it could be like. We got a call that a teenage boy had committed suicide by jumping from the sixth floor of a building. It was the middle of the winter and I remember snow on the ground. The fact that it was the middle of the night made the whole scene surreal.

As the first responding officer, I had to do all sorts of things to preserve the "crime scene" and to interview people to confirm that he had indeed committed suicide; to make sure that he had not been pushed or had not struggled with someone else; to identify the body; to make sure his closest relatives knew what had happened. I did all this while a number of distraught relatives were screaming hysterically.

GRAB HIS SNEAKERS

All of a sudden I heard a voice from a window upstairs shouting down to the relatives, "Hey, go get his sneakers." The apparent

suicide victim had been wearing brand-new sneakers; the person yelling down wanted to make sure that the family retrieved the "valuable" sneakers before the medical examiner's office hauled the body away.

I thought to myself: "Oh my God! This kid has just taken a leap off a building and all this relative can think of is getting his sneakers." This was a new world to me. Bed-Stuy was like the Wild West. Normally if you heard loud noises, you thought fire-crackers, but in Bed-Stuy you knew it was gunshots.

What I saw nightly, most police officers would not see in weeks, months, or years. A routine night could go from stabbings and shootings to a woman giving birth. It was constant. They called upon the police for anything and everything. The majority of the time I was on the scene a few seconds after the crime was committed.

As a twenty-one-year-old rabbi's son, serving in Bed-Stuy was very exciting, I loved it. But let me be clear: Bed-Stuy was not for the meek of heart; serving as a cop there was like watching an action movie, but instead of watching, you were participating. You were chasing bad guys, at least so it seemed, every two or three minutes—and they all had guns.

Bed-Stuy had many good people, but it had a bad element as well. Drugs were the rule and the bad guys had never heard of living by rules of engagement. It wasn't as if there was a tacit un-derstanding not to shoot at cops.

My time spent in Bed-Stuy proved to be a true career-maker. Here I was, serving in one of the highest crime areas in the City of New York, a rookie cop who was quite the oddity with his yar-mulke atop his head. Believe me, my life would have been a lot easier had I not worn the yarmulke that "invited" people to stare at me and wonder just what kind of cop I was.

But I had been wearing a yarmulke since the age of three, and though I knew that there would be those odd stares, I wanted to keep it on my head even while on the beat. The NYPD respected this religious practice and did not turn it into an issue. Wearing the yarmulke gave me self-confidence. Wearing it showed that I

was proud of my religion and proud to be known as a Jew. I could have chosen to fit in, to dissolve into the melting pot and hide my Jewishness, but I was going to be who I was—and take the consequences.

I served in Bed-Stuy until January 1985 and then I worked another year as a patrolman in midtown Manhattan.

When I became a cop, my goals were very limited and I actually felt that I had reached them when I became a patrolman in midtown Manhattan. This time members of the Shomrim Society helped me transfer out of Bed-Stuy. A friend of mine from the Shomrim told me that a midtown Manhattan police unit needed someone willing to work Sundays through Thursdays rather than Mondays through Fridays. Since I was Sabbath observant, I was the perfect candidate. Manhattan was calmer, and the light weekend requirements permitted me to cover for colleagues who wanted Sundays off.

BUSTING DRUG DEALERS

In what seemed like no time I was honing my skills as an investigator, beginning to work cases that took me off of patrol and into the world of the detectives. The more I took part in that world, the more I liked it. In 1985 a joint Drug Enforcement Administration task force made up of NYPD cops and federal agents was working a case against big-time Israeli drug dealers. Because I was relatively fluent in Hebrew and had a passing knowledge of Yiddish, I was on a list of police officers who knew foreign languages. Task force members found my name on the list and asked me to help with the case.

I would not be needed for ongoing translation, they explained; instead, I would be placed in a van near a car where a confidential informant and an Israeli drug suspect were likely to converse from time to time in Hebrew. The informant would be wired and I would be needed to translate the Hebrew on the spot to other police in the van.

I volunteered in a heartbeat, and I was given a car, a credit card, and a small expense account. I became part of the task force for the next three months. It was my first taste of the life of detectives, and I found it quite exciting. That case led to my working other cases involving Israelis.

In my next Israeli-related case, a *New York Daily News* article identified me merely as "Morty, the Hebrew-speaking cop." The reference amazed me, for I had been told that most cops never got their names in the newspapers and few got mentioned in the media with the kind of frequency that I had enjoyed—and so early in my rookie years.

Here I was, a police officer for only three years and I had been in the newspapers already twice. I was only twenty-three years old. That year I was promoted to police investigator, the first step on the way to becoming a detective.

It was March 1986. I began work in the Narcotics Division. Busting drug dealers was hardly what I had aspired to when I joined the NYPD, but it turned out to be a great career move. I knew that my recent rise to Narcotics was due in large measure to the occasional aid that I gave Narcotics catching Israeli drug dealers in New York; translating from Hebrew to English was not as exciting as chasing down criminals, but helping crack those cases gave me entrée to the Narcotics Division.

I was the first to realize that, at age twenty-three, I was still raw and inexperienced; but because my bosses needed a Hebrew speaker, I was able to get an early look into the exotic world of police investigation. Moreover, narcotics was one of the nearly automatic career paths in the NYPD. If I performed well in this new role, eventually I would become a detective.

AN EARRING, BEARD, AND LONG HAIR

The new police work, and a new appearance and dress code that went with it, helped me explain—to my family and to women I was dating—why I needed to wear an earring, grow a beard, and have long hair. I would reveal the true nature of my work only

if I came under great pressure and needed to justify my strange appearance.

Though I knew that my new look was simply a prop for my new line of work, others thought that I had strayed from the basic principles of Judaism! Giving me the once over at Jewish singles events, women asked themselves silently: "Just who is this bum?" Once I explained that I was an undercover cop and that my father was a rabbi, they calmed down.

When I met my future wife in 1991, Meryl persuaded me to remove the beard and the earring. Those were not her type of look. She also "allowed" my long hair to remain for about five minutes!

WAITING FOR MY BLADDER

Not all police work had its John Wayne moments. Sometimes, pardon the expression, you just had to go with the flow. Here is my favorite example from my days in narcotics:

In March 1986, as part of my initial narcotics training, fifty narcotics recruits, including me, were told that we had to adhere to a new NYPD policy of drug testing; the policy required any new narcotics recruit to provide a specimen of urine, and only those who passed muster got to stay in narcotics. Had anyone refused to take the test, the NYPD would have required the person to take it anyway, since the refusal raised all sorts of suspicions as to why the recruit would not want to take a drug test.

One day we boarded a bus at NYPD headquarters, where the Narcotics Division was located, and traveled to the NYPD Health Division. It was made clear they wanted us to do the drug tests quickly, only adding to my nervousness.

The fifty of us who piled into a small auditorium at Health Division represented a new beefed-up influx of undercover investigators devoted to catching drug dealers peddling crack cocaine, the latest flavor of the month. The crack epidemic had recently shot up to extraordinary levels on New York streets.

We were seated alphabetically. As a "D" I was one of the first to take the test (a male sergeant accompanied each recruit to the

men's room; a female sergeant did the same with women recruits). Maybe it was the plea to hurry up, or the idea of performing the chore in public, but my bladder went shy at the crucial time. I was forced to wait for all the others to take the drug test.

Meanwhile, the other recruits gave me all sorts of useless advice: Drink water. Focus. Think good thoughts. Nothing helped. With all others having completed the test, I had fifty people agitating for me to finish the task. They could not end their day until I did. Another fifteen minutes or so passed and I finally felt the urge. Raising my hand, I told the sergeant that I was ready. At last, I provided a specimen. As I walked out to the waiting crowd, a smile of satisfaction on my face, all fifty recruits burst into a standing ovation—for me. Now we could all go home.

If there was a moral to the story, it was that although I would always enjoy attention showered on me for police work, no matter how dangerous, I did not savor the spotlight shining on me when I finally "went with the flow!"

As a rookie narcotics investigator, I soon discovered that not every case got resolved overnight nor did every case make me look like Super Cop. I was still new and inexperienced, trying to learn and, in the process, not make too many mistakes.

WHERE ARE MY KEYS?

That spring of 1986 I was doing investigating work as part of a team chasing down Israeli drug dealers. We were investigating a $1 million-a-week cocaine and heroin operation. Working out of an undercover safe house in Staten Island, we transacted business with the bad guys there, trying to gather enough evidence to nail them.

One day we were about to do our largest transaction yet: A "purchase" of $50,000 worth of cocaine and heroin. With two hours still to go, four of us walked over to a nearby pizza place to grab some food. As I was leaving, I realized that I'd left my car keys inside the car, a car that I had been assigned to conduct surveillance with while the drug sale took place in the safe house.

Embarrassed for me, the others shook their heads. Our only option was to break into the car; but doing so might lead to our being identified as cops. Still, we tried to "Slim Jim" the door open—but with no luck. As a last resort, we called the NYPD SWAT team, who opened the car door.

Needless to say, it was the last time I left my keys in the car. In the end, NYPD treated me leniently, chalking up my carelessness to a certain amount of rawness. On August 19 of that year, despite my forgetfulness, we arrested the five Israeli drug dealers.

Meanwhile, my narcotics lieutenant and I were not getting along. He had made a personnel move at one stage, and impulsively I questioned his judgment. Lesson number one in cultivating good relations with your boss: Don't question his decisions. Punishment will follow, and it did. My "punishment" came in June 1987 when I was "banished" to the scandal-ridden 77th Precinct, in the heart of that old killing ground, Bedford-Stuyvesant. I was back again! Oddly enough, during my eighteen months there I did not have too bad an experience. Because it was Bed-Stuy, the shootings, stabbings, and other mayhem kept me busy. You couldn't go to pick up dinner without seeing or hearing gunplay. Then there was the job satisfaction: Knowing that each time you collared a bad guy, hopefully you deterred further crime, thus making the good people of Bed-Stuy that much safer.

In 1988 I was transferred to midtown Manhattan to work as a robbery detective, in my view a dream assignment; I was hopeful that this posting would last my entire police career. I could not imagine any further promotions or any work beyond my robbery assignment. While there were a few other Orthodox Jewish cops in the NYPD, I was the only Orthodox Jewish detective, a feat that made me quite proud.

ARMED WITH AN ICE CREAM CONE

In October 1988 I was transferred from Bed-Stuy to the Midtown North precinct into its Detective Squad. I was assigned to the robbery unit. On October 20, 1989, at 790 Seventh Avenue

at an A to Z Luggage branch a robbery took place that was to be engraved in my memory.

Before this, there had been several robberies of A to Z Luggage branch stores around the city with a few hundred dollars taken each time. The robber had always used an automatic weapon.

A former employee named Markieth Boyd was a natural suspect, since he knew the operations of the store, but he seemed far too articulate and calm to be our perp. He was currently a receptionist at a Wall Street firm. We tracked Boyd down from a license plate taken from the rented car that the robber had used for his getaway and then returned to the rental company. Brian McCabe, my coworker, got the license plate from interviewing a witness. Learning that Boyd had rented this car, we then discovered that he had worked for A to Z. I decided that someone had "lifted" Boyd's identity and then carried out the robberies. It seemed absurd that anyone would work for a Wall Street firm and commit robberies during his off hours!

One would think that at this point my rawness as a cop had become a thing of the past. There I was on this hot summer day, about to seek out Boyd at his Wall Street firm, when I spotted a Mr. Frosty ice cream truck outside his building. I couldn't resist; nor could my partner. Emerging from the elevator, Mr. Frosty in hand, I noticed a man who fit Boyd's description. I silently decided: "He's not going to believe we're cops. Instead of holding a gun, I was holding an ice cream cone!" Quickly finishing the ice cream, I accosted Boyd and quietly took him away to the precinct. He confessed to the robberies, was convicted, and was sentenced to prison for five to ten years.

Those were some of the best years of my career, and it never occurred to me that there was any other part of the NYPD that could be more exciting—and fulfilling.

CHAPTER 2

Our Jewish Detective:
Working the Rabbi Kahane
Murder Case

I remained a uniformed patrolman until April 1985, when I was transferred to the Narcotics Squad and officially became an investigator, giving up the blue uniform for casual clothes.

It was also during that year that I abandoned my yarmulke while on the job. Co-opted to the Drug Enforcement Administration's Joint Task Force, I was working undercover on an Israeli-related drug case. As an undercover cop I could not allow myself to be identified as a Jew, especially since my job was to translate what Israeli suspects were saying. Had I worn a yarmulke, they might have assumed that I knew Hebrew, blowing my cover.

Two years later, in 1987, I was transferred from Narcotics to the 77th Precinct Bed-Stuy Robbery Squad, and I usually wore a coat and tie, though part of the time I dressed in casual clothes. The following year, October 1988, I was transferred to the Midtown North Robbery Squad. Once there I began investigating robberies but moved on to all crimes. The usual practice is that investigators are promoted to the official rank of detective after a few years.

And so six months later, on April 25, 1989, I was promoted to Detective Third Grade, remaining with the Midtown North precinct for the next decade until 1999. There I worked in the Robbery Squad for two years and then in the general Detective Squad for eight years.

HEBREW-SPEAKING DETECTIVE

Even without the yarmulke, by the early 1990s senior NYPD officers thought of me as their "Jewish detective." From the time I had been hired, I had permission not to work on the Jewish Sabbath. During the 1980s I became the Hebrew-language translator for the NYPD. The *Sunday New York Daily News*, writing an article on the 1985 Israeli-related narcotics case, had called me "Morty the Hebrew-Speaking Detective." Neither the nickname nor the fact that the NYPD exploited my Jewishness for police work bothered me.

It did not help my ambition to rise within the ranks that some of my fellow police officers felt that, when I wore plainclothes, I did not look like your average cop. My face was too friendly, open, and boyish.

I very much wanted to move upward in the NYPD. One incident, in November 1990, gave me that chance as I became involved in my very first high-profile case as a general detective. I first learned of the incident while on a dinner break in my office at the Midtown North Detective Squad, 54th Street between Eighth and Ninth Avenues. I was watching "Monday Night Football" with my partner, Robbery Detective Mike Bachety, while we ate some takeout. Suddenly, we heard calls for help on our police radio.

Shots had been fired and people had been hurt at the Marriott Hotel on Lexington Avenue between 48th and 49th streets. That was all that was reported—not whether anyone had been shot or what the names of possible victims were.

Our first instinct was to find out whether the shooting had occurred in our Midtown North precinct. It turned out that the incident had occurred just outside our precinct, which bordered the western side of Lexington. The shooting was on the east side and thus within the jurisdiction of the 17th precinct.

But, given the proximity to our precinct, we supposed our boss, Lieutenant Barbara Sicilia, might want us to get to the Marriott anyway. When she learned who the victim was, she asked me

to head over to the scene with her. The lieutenant told us that a man named Meir Kahane had been shot and killed at the Marriott.

COME WITH ME

"Morty, you're coming with me," Lieutenant Sicilia announced, and I must admit that I was pumped up because I felt I could really contribute. She knew that Kahane was an infamous Jewish personality and automatically turned to me, her "Jewish detective."

Of course, I had known of Rabbi Meir Kahane. He was one of the most controversial Jewish figures of our time: Founder in 1968 of the New York-based and militant Jewish Defense League (JDL), three years later he had gone to Israel, where he founded and led an ultra-right political movement known as *Kach* (Hebrew for "Only thus").

One of Israel's most extreme right-wing, anti-Arab figures, he created a political platform for *Kach* that called for the annexation of all Israeli-conquered territories from the 1967 Six Day War and the forcible removal of all Palestinians from those territories. Elected in 1984 to the Knesset, Israel's Parliament, Kahane was unable to run four years later when his *Kach* Party was barred from participation in the election on the grounds that it incited racism.

Unprepared for this assignment, I was uncomfortable in what I was wearing. With no suit and tie in my locker, I would be forced to arrive at the crime scene, where senior NYPD brass and politicians were sure to congregate, dressed in jeans, sneakers, and a gray-hooded shirt—typical robbery detective attire.

We had to be ready in an instant to chase after robbers, and a suit and tie would only slow us down. Still, I would have preferred showing up at my first big case dressed in something that didn't make me look like a Central Park mugger!

When the lieutenant and I arrived at the Marriott, she introduced me to the Chief of Manhattan Detectives.

"Chief," she began, a certain pride in her voice, "I don't know if you're aware of this, but this is Morty Dzikansky. He comes

from an Orthodox Jewish background, and he's a robbery detective in our squad. He's a good guy. If you need any help with this, I'm sure he'd love to help you out."

WHO THE FUCK IS THIS KID?

With a thousand other things on his mind, with officers waiting to speak to him, the chief gave me the once over. His eyes glazed over. I had the feeling that had we been anywhere else other than a crime scene, he might have burst into laughter. I could tell for sure that he was saying to himself: "Who the fuck is this kid?"

"Sir, it's nice to meet you," I said politely. I had lots to say to him about Rabbi Meir Kahane, but I had no idea what he knew of the shooting victim or whether he wanted a fill-in from a twenty-eight-year-old junior robbery detective whose dress made him look like he had just competed in the New York marathon.

Aware that I had something to offer, but also aware that the chief would listen to me for only a minute at best, I suggested to him that the Kahane killing had nothing to do with his JDL or New York period; it had everything to do with his extremist anti-Arab stance in Israel.

"This is not a New York thing," I told him, working hard to show confidence in my words. "This has all the earmarks of an Islamic hit."

I doubted that the chief took me seriously: Too little gray hair, I guess, and then there was the hooded shirt and sneakers. He looked at me as if to say, "What are you babbling about?"

I had more luck a few minutes later with the lieutenant of the 17th Squad, my old Sergeant Ed Norris, under whom I had worked at Brooklyn South Narcotics in 1986. After hearing my conclusions on the Kahane killing Lieutenant Norris stated that he also believed that the killing of the rabbi had more to it, and he asked me to look at some notes in Hebrew, presumably notes that Rabbi Kahane used for his speech that evening. After a quick perusal, we decided that they contained no investigatory value. Still, I was glad to be asked to help out.

Eventually, I was proven correct that Kahane's assassination had to do with his extremist anti-Arab views. An Egyptian militant, El Sayyid Nosair, was charged with Kahane's murder. When Nosair's apartment was searched, forty-seven boxes of documents in Arabic were found, which proved that he was part of a worldwide terrorist network.

DAMAGED CASE

Oddly enough, the case against Nosair was damaged seriously by a combination of bad luck and poor police work. First, not one witness came forward to identify him as the killer. Second, with no autopsy performed, crucial physical evidence was lost forever. Third, the Arabic documents slipped through the fingers of the FBI, having been deemed unimportant.

In the end, despite numerous potential eyewitnesses, a jury found Nosair not guilty on the Kahane murder charge. The judge, Alvin Schlesinger, was shocked at the acquittal. He insisted that it was against the overwhelming weight of evidence and was devoid of common sense and logic. "I believe," he stated, "the defendant conducted a rape of this country, of our institutions, of our laws, and of people seeking to exist peacefully together."

Nosair was convicted of assault and possession of an illegal firearm and of related charges, including the shooting of a U.S. Postal Service police officer. The judge sentenced him to the maximum allowed term, 7-1/3 to 22 years in prison. In the spring of 2010 Nosair remains at the Federal ADX Supermax prison in Florence, Colorado.

The New York City Police Department in 1990 was not capable of investigating a case like the Kahane assassination. It was way over its head in dealing with cases involving global terror. That situation would change in due course, starting with Commissioner Ray Kelly's taking charge in 2002.

But most senior NYPD officers at that time saw the Kahane murder as an isolated incident, and no thought was given to digging into Nosair's past, searching for a motive, or culling the

Middle East for accomplices. Such intelligence gathering, routine in later years, was beyond our ken back then.

Of course, back in those days the NYPD was best at hunting down criminals and solving homicides, and it did so frequently. Its intelligence arm, however, was aimed at catching local bad guys, not at bringing to justice international terrorist groups, who until then had caused no serious damage to New York.

We had done a complete murder investigation at the time but given what we had to work with—especially the lack of eye-witnesses willing to testify—we came up short. Even had the case been tried in 2010, the NYPD cannot make bad witnesses into good ones.

It's hard to say whether we would have been able to build a better murder case if we had investigated for possible conspiracies. From what I had heard at the time, once the NYPD brass saw that we had an arrest for the murder, they did not let us get involved with other aspects of the investigation and we were relying on the Feds for follow-up.

I do not know what the Feds relayed back to the brass or to the District Attorney's office. What I can say emphatically is that the brass of the NYPD post-2002 would have investigated all aspects of this case.

A BAD TASTE

The Kahane case left a bad taste in my mouth. I wanted the NYPD to succeed in bringing international terrorists to justice, especially when a crime had been committed in New York that had a Jewish or Israeli dimension. I wanted to contribute to that success, and it gnawed at me that I had not been able to. But to contribute, the NYPD would have to recognize the perils that were looming thousands of miles away.

The case did have a major impact on my role within the NYPD, solidifying me with the brass as the detective who should be called in on all significant Jewish cases citywide. Because I knew the Jewish/Israeli community from the inside, it was gener-

ally acknowledged that I possessed special skills and knowledge. I knew how people in these communities operated, it was my natural environment, and I was confident that I could produce.

Like other police officers, I wanted to be where the action was. But the action that intrigued me the most was happening in the State of Israel. My dream had been to do twenty years with the NYPD, then retire to Israel. Neither a fervent Zionist nor the victim of continuing anti-Semitism, I was simply proud of being Jewish and felt a strong affection for the Jewish state.

SIGNING UP FOR "COMBAT"

Make no mistake, I loved America and especially loved New York City. But, as a Jew growing up in the United States, I always felt something was missing, that I was part of a minority and, for that reason, less in control of my destiny than had I been in the majority.

I must say that I encountered no overt anti-Semitism within the police ranks. I always felt that if you are proud of who you are and what you are, and you combine that pride with competence, people will respect you, even if they don't like you.

By 1991 I had visited Israel four times and each time there I loved the feeling that I was part of the majority. Sure, I could have moved to Borough Park (or some other purely Jewish community in New York) where I would be part of the majority, but my personality would not have fit in with that kind of *shtetl* (a traditional Jewish small village from pre-Holocaust Europe) life.

Feeling affection for the State of Israel, I suffered through each and every anguishing event that occurred there. At times I became so absorbed in Israeli events that I wanted to get on the next plane to offer my services to the beleaguered nation. When war seemed imminent in the Middle East during the winter of 1990 and 1991, as an American military response to Iraq's invasion of neighboring Kuwait seemed more and more likely, I decided to spend my month-long vacation side by side with the Israelis, hoping to play a small role in their next battle.

Israel was once again facing a life-and-death situation. Iraq's Saddam Hussein, with his troops occupying Kuwait, threatened to deliver chemical weapons, using his Scud missiles against Israel should the United States attack Iraq.

Some of my fellow police officers undoubtedly thought my talk of wanting to take part in Israel's next war was mere bluster, and so they were probably shocked to learn that I had volunteered to serve in Israel in January 1991 to help its military in its likely conflict with Iraq. But, to their credit, none of them questioned my loyalty to America or to the NYPD.

Did they think I was nuts? I'm sure some of them did. After all, while they were vacationing on cruises in the Caribbean, I was heading for a war zone. The most dangerous threat to them would be a bumpy ride on an ocean liner while I might face Saddam's Scud missiles and the chemical warfare products on board. My vacationing colleagues would have pills for their seasickness. I would have only a gas mask to ward off the lethal effects of the chemical warfare.

THE SCUDS AND ME

The war broke out on January 17, 1991. For the first time, Arab chemical warfare against Israel seemed a distinct possibility. Sirens that warned of incoming Scud missiles sounded frequently, sometimes three or four times a day. Issued gas masks before hostilities broke out, Israelis, upon hearing the sirens, dashed to so-called "sealed rooms" in their homes or offices to seek protection from the Scuds.

Not since Israel's 1948 War of Independence and the Six Day War of June 1967 had Israelis in all parts of the country been continuously exposed to physical danger.

I arrived in Israel on February 3, 1991. To give me the feeling that I was contributing as directly to the war effort as I could, I volunteered for the IDF's Sar-El program, which integrated international volunteers like me into Israeli army bases.

Permitting soldiers to devote 100 percent of their time and attention to the war effort, I would don an IDF uniform and take

on tasks such as lifting and moving things around an army base near Beersheba—no Rambo moves, to be sure, just a tremendous show of support.

To be clear here, I was not joining the Israel Defense Forces. Sar-El is a volunteer organization that is sponsored by the IDF. While American citizens may hold dual citizenship (American and Israeli) and may join the IDF without losing their American citizenship, I was not joining the IDF via Sar-El, just helping out as a volunteer.

Within fifteen minutes after we boarded a bus at Ben Gurion Airport and headed south to our army base, a Scud missile attack occurred. The bus pulled over to the side of the road; we quickly put on our gas masks, waited, and prayed that no harm would come to us. Fortunately, it did not.

At the base, sirens went off daily, signaling an imminent Scud attack. If we had enough time, we rushed to the nearest air-raid shelter, put on our gas masks, and hoped that Saddam Hussein's Scuds could not reach the Beersheba area. When I didn't have time to get to a shelter, I simply put on my gas mask, waited where I was, and prayed.

One incident during what came to be called the Gulf War remains vivid to this day: While I was visiting family one evening in Tel Aviv, sirens went off frequently, sending us to their sealed room. We all took the sirens seriously after hearing from our family that a Scud had fallen only a mile away from their home a few days earlier. Noticing that I seemed nervous, my nine-year-old cousin laughed and asked only half-jokingly: "What kind of a tough New York City policeman are you to be afraid of a little Scud?" From his question I understood why Israelis, adults and children alike, enjoyed a reputation for resilience.

MY WIFE THE ACCOUNTANT

One other dream of mine did come true very soon after my return. In May 1991 I met my future wife. It was Shavuot, the Jewish holiday that commemorates God's giving the Torah to the

Israelites at Mount Sinai. My dad and I, two eligible bachelors, were spending that weekend at Brown's Hotel in the Catskills. Though he did not tell me at the time, my father nurtured high hopes that his twenty-eight-year-old son would find someone and finally settle down.

As it turned out, the "someone" was at Brown's that same weekend, a Brooklyn-born woman named Meryl Markowitz, who was at the hotel with friends. A mutual friend introduced us. When we met, she was working in the audit department of the accounting firm of Coopers & Lybrand, so she certainly found the life of a cop different from hers! My height—six feet three inches—impressed her, as did my cop stories. I made her feel safe—and she liked my wearing a suit and tie. Her confident stature and smile attracted me. We shared a common connection to Israel. She had spent her senior year of high school there, and on our first date we discussed our individual desires to someday move to Israel. She had obtained her undergraduate degree from the Sy Syms School of Business, Yeshiva University's business school, and then became a Certified Public Accountant.

We were married in September 1992 at the Manhattan Beach Jewish Center in Brooklyn and spent the next seven years career-focused and traveling a great deal. And so a cop and an accountant got hitched. If I had not become an accountant, I at least married one!

After we got married, Meryl switched to Lehman Brothers, where she became a vice president in finance, and she worked for them until they disintegrated in the fall of 2008.

I had been a New York cop for eight years and had indeed settled into the job. My father still was in mild denial. When the *Jewish Sentinel* interviewed him for an article on me ("Dirty Harry He's Not"), my Dad proclaimed: "His grandfather was a *rosh yeshiva* (a yeshiva director) in Lithuania. He would never believe he has a grandson who was a detective." I have to admit that being a cop was a far cry from my roots in a family of Orthodox rabbis.

Meeting the woman I would marry gave me more reason than ever to think of New York as my home. I was proud of helping Israel out when it needed it the most, but even that wartime experience did not budge me from continuing to center my life on New York. My dream of moving to Israel remained just that—a dream.

CHAPTER 3

Raiders of the Sacred Ark:
The Torah Theft Cases

If my goal was to provide succor to the Jewish community at large—including Israel, of course—I would soon get a chance to do that, big-time. In the fall of 1992, when a series of fifteen Torah thefts began on the Upper West Side of New York, it was only natural that senior police detectives would turn to their "Jewish detective" for help—and help was needed. This was no easy case.

The first theft had occurred on September 28, 1992, when two Torahs were stolen from the Jewish Theological Seminary, the academic and spiritual center for Conservative Judaism. A rabbi discovered that the Torahs were missing only on a Saturday morning when he opened the ark during services.

THE SACRED TORAH

Rarely did a community exhibit as much sadness and anger as the Jewish community did over the thieves who were brazenly stealing the sacred Torahs. The Torah, the holiest object in Judaism, is regarded as revealing the word of God; it contains the five Books of Moses. Why would anyone be so disrespectful of it by stealing it?

To all Jews, stealing a Torah is the equivalent of maiming or even killing someone. A Torah, if too old or torn, receives a proper burial with accompanying prayers. It is the only religious object in Judaism that requires that the congregation stand when its ark is opened, or it is held.

So appalled were New York lawmakers at the Torah thefts that they devised a more severe punishment for these thefts than the theft, say, of an expensive men's suit from a department store. Torah theft was a felony carrying a four-year jail sentence; the theft of the suit, a mere misdemeanor, would get the perp only one year in jail. Finding stolen Torahs was difficult and complex; I tried to convey this fact to my partners on the task force.

For one thing, they all look alike, making identification of a stolen one virtually impossible. Attractive to a thief but annoying to the police, Torah scrolls are anonymous because Jewish law forbids adding even one character to the 304,805 letters of the Torah text. Therefore, one cannot place a "property of" stamp, or inscribe serial numbers, or add any other visible identifying mark of any kind to it.

After a sudden increase in Torah thefts in the early 1980s, a Torah registration program was created, relying on microperforations that created a unique, indelible mark on the scroll, although the mark was not visible to the naked eye.

Getting people to testify against an alleged Torah thief was also no easy matter, because the Torah forbids a Jew from testifying against another Jew in a secular court. It was not difficult to circumvent the Torah edict: Secular courts do not accept the edict as a reason not to testify and will compel a witness to testify by threatening him with contempt of court.

WHY STEAL A TORAH?

Why would anyone steal a Torah? The answer had to be money, I concluded.

A Torah might cost as much as $50,000 to $80,000, depending on its quality: A religious scribe copies the Torah by hand, a process that can take a year.

Among shady Judaica dealers, a hideous black market had developed: Dealers would purchase a Torah from anyone without asking for its provenance, without wondering why some private

individual had a Torah to sell in the first place. The dealers would buy the Torahs at a relatively cheap price, say $500, and then sell them to a Jewish institution, usually a synagogue, at a much higher price.

I was so appalled by these amoral black market operatives that I proclaimed, "There are certain Judaic dealers from whom I wouldn't buy a ham sandwich."

FORERUNNER

An incident occurred on February 26 of 1993 involving the World Trade Center. Two people drove a Ryder rental van into the public parking garage beneath the Twin Towers, ignited a fuse; and then fled. Twelve minutes later, at 12:17 PM, a bomb exploded, opening a 100-foot-wide hole through four sublevels of concrete. As was revealed, the terrorists had hoped to knock the North Tower into the South Tower, bringing both towers down and killing thousands of people. In the end, the blast killed six people and wounded over 1,000 others. Tragic, but it was a small number of deaths compared to what would follow.

I did not participate in the investigation of that event and, quite frankly, I gave it little thought at the time. I was too preoccupied with other horrific crimes.

THE NEWSPAPER ARTICLE

When the *New York Daily News* ran a front-page article in April 1993 on the Torah thefts, it added pressure on the NYPD to reinvigorate the probe. Until then the Torah thefts had been investigated by individual precincts. Thanks to the article, the NYPD now realized that it needed to create a special task force that would focus on the Torah thefts.

I was still working in Midtown North as a detective serving in a catch-all role, investigating everything from homicides to bad checks, when I got a phone call from the commanding officer of Manhattan South Homicide, Lieutenant Bob Gibbons. Aware

that I was the "Jewish Detective," Gibbons thought I would be ideal to work on the Torah theft case. He had me temporarily transferred to his homicide squad.

Once there I teamed up with a veteran, no-nonsense detective named Walter Harkins. Polished and respected, with the appearance of a U.S. Marine, Harkins looked like he came out of central casting for the role of homicide detective. We worked under Gibbons' supervision.

Upon hearing that Torahs had been stolen, police detectives from other cities might have cynically scoffed at abandoning homicide investigations to chase down Torah thieves. In contrast, the NYPD, responsible for the one-third of America's 6 million Jews who lived in New York, took Torah theft as seriously as it did homicides.

LEAD INVESTIGATOR

The media noted correctly that only the NYPD would have been willing to create the Harkins-Dzikansky Torah theft task force. I had been designated lead investigator. The assignment was a natural for me. I was familiar with Torah scrolls as well as Jewish customs, I knew Hebrew, and I knew the market for sacred religious objects, including the insular world of the second-hand Judaica shops in various parts of New York. Walter and I attached great importance to the case, as did the NYPD senior brass.

However rich their experiences had been as homicide detectives, Gibbons and Harkins understood that "this young Jewish detective," as the lieutenant called me, had the knowledge and resources to kick-start the case. No other NYPD detective would have known where to begin. I appreciated their confidence in me, especially since I had yet to begin the probe.

Joining as members of the Torah theft task force were two men who advised us throughout the lengthy probe. One was David Pollock, the point man within the Jewish community. Pollock, associate executive director of the Jewish Community Relations Council, had taken a strong interest in the Torah thefts. He be-

came a kind of watchdog for New York Jews, involved in all security issues regarding the Metropolitan areas' Jewish community. The second man was Joel Seidemann, senior trial counsel in the office of District Attorney Robert Morgenthau; Seidemann had taken a special interest in the Torah thefts.

A CERTAIN PATTERN

By assigning two homicide detectives to the case, the NYPD clearly wanted to send a message that we treated Torah thefts as seriously as we did homicides. I detected a certain pattern among the Torah thefts. There had been no break-ins; no force had been used for entry. My conclusion: The thief had simply walked into the synagogue unnoticed!

Although many synagogue leaders had already undergone police interviews, we decided to re-interview them in the hope of learning some pertinent detail that might have been missed earlier. Those re-interviews yielded nothing of value. So we next turned to Judaica store owners, who were all ideal fences for the stolen Torahs. We wanted to enlist them as our "eyes and ears." They politely took our business cards; we urged them to notify us the second anyone tried to sell them a Torah.

It had always been our assumption that we were tracking down a gang of thieves, perhaps three or four people. Then we experienced our first break: One day in the summer of 1993 we received a call from a Judaica dealer in Brooklyn who told us that some youngsters from Sullivan County in upstate New York had phoned him to say they wanted to sell him a Torah. They sounded suspicious to the dealer. Unbeknownst to the dealer, they had stolen the Torah from the Woodridge Synagogue in South Fallsburg, New York.

Walter Harkins and I decided to stake out the Judaica dealer, not by sitting in a car outside the premises; instead, the two of us hid in a closet in the dealer's study. We were quite the pair: Walter, in his mid-fifties, the poster child for first-grade detective, and I, thirty-one years old, a still wet behind the ears junior detective.

HIDING IN A CLOSET

As we secreted ourselves in that tiny closet, the deal went down. Suddenly we emerged from the closet, pounced on the two religious youngsters, Aaron G. and Bernard W., and arrested them. They had stolen a Torah from an upstate New York synagogue and were trying to sell it to the dealer. We recovered the stolen Torah on the spot.

Though the theft had occurred upstate in South Fallsburg, we wanted Joel Seidemann, our highly competent Assistant District Attorney, to prosecute the case. For that to happen, a case had to be made that the trial should be held in Joel's home court of Manhattan rather than where the arrest took place in Brooklyn. By asserting that the Torah thieves had driven the stolen Torahs through Manhattan, Joel was able to assert that they could be prosecuted for criminal possession of stolen property in Manhattan. Quite clever, I thought!

I was never called to testify in the case, because on May 5, 1993, the thieves pled guilty to being in criminal possession of stolen property. They were ordered to make restitution with a conditional discharge. They had to repay any financial loss incurred by the synagogue. The court showed them leniency, since they did not have a criminal past.

I felt great pride when, after the two arrests, my father told me that I had done a *mitzvah* (a good deed). As the Bible says, he told me, "Wipe out evil things among your people." And that is exactly what I had done. Although we had recovered a stolen Torah and arrested two thieves, the Jewish community, while grateful, acted as if it was in deep mourning over the other missing fourteen Torahs.

But our investigation was in limbo. For a while, the Torah thefts stopped. What did this mean? Were these two youngsters the masterminds of the entire Torah theft ring? Might there be more Torah thieves out there? We had no idea.

THE SINGING DETECTIVE

A cop might have to race after a suspected thief, or get physical with a perp resisting arrest, or even draw a gun in rare circum-

stances. But never would anyone have imagined a cop having to take "action" the way I did on November 15, 1993, in a case involving a robbery.

At the time I was working with Alex Renow, an old-time detective, one tough Jew who taught me much about police work and life. Be fair—but be firm: That is a phrase that I have never forgotten. The robbery had occurred at a video distribution warehouse on 43rd Street between 10th and 11th avenues. Early that morning, as the owner was returning from his bank, where he had withdrawn a few thousand dollars in cash to meet his payroll, he was robbed outside the warehouse.

Suddenly from behind him someone struck his skull with a hammer and made off with the cash. The perp had covered himself with a hood, so he was impossible to identify. Close to death, the owner was taken to St. Vincent's Hospital.

Alex and I managed to speak with the owner, and we deduced that the robber had known that the owner had lots of cash on him. It had to be an inside job.

Had the owner fired anyone recently? I asked. Yes he had, a certain Renaldo Perez. We tracked Perez down, put him in the backseat of our police car, and drove to the precinct, where we planned to formally question him. For the first few minutes in the car, no one said anything. Then I got an idea. Some might say it was brilliant, others that it was crazy.

I began singing, admittedly rather off-key, "If I Had a Hammer."

Suddenly Perez began screaming: "I didn't hit anyone in the head with a hammer." Alex and I smiled. The fact that the victim had been struck in the head with a hammer had not been made public.

That slip of the tongue proved costly. At the trial the prosecutor called me as a witness and asked if I had said or done anything during the car ride.

"I sang a song," I replied.

"You sang a song? What song?" the prosecutor asked.

"If I Had a Hammer," I said proudly.

"Would you sing it?"

I began singing, my eyes fixed on the jury. Justice had prevailed. Perez was convicted and given a seven- to fourteen-year jail sentence.

WANNA BE A HOMICIDE DETECTIVE?

Meanwhile in 1993, after I was temporarily transferred to Manhattan South Homicide for the Torah investigations, a boss there proposed that I stay in the Homicide Squad, a very sought-after position in the NYPD.

The only rational response was to grab at the offer. But something bothered me about becoming a homicide detective at this stage. I knew that I had had only two years of experience doing general detective work. Even if my bosses felt the opposite—and it thrilled me that they did—I did not feel ready for the position.

I suspected they merely wanted someone Jewish around the Homicide Squad. Maybe there was no problem with this motive, but I felt I was too young. I did make it clear that if and when senior officers needed me on specific cases, I would gladly help. So in 1993 I remained a generic detective at Midtown North.

THE KILLING OF ARI HALBERSTAM

Meanwhile, NYPD cases with a Jewish angle did not stop. One of my most memorable experiences was investigating the murder of Ari Halberstam by a terrorist in New York City.

On March 5, 1994, the sixteen-year-old Halberstam, affiliated with the Lubavitch movement, had visited its ailing spiritual leader, Menahem Mendel Schneerson, and then returned to his Brooklyn home in a van. Unbeknownst to Halberstam, a Lebanese national named Rashid Baz had been scouting the routes that the Lubavitch youngsters were taking to and from the hospital.

While Baz and Halberstam were on the Brooklyn Bridge, Baz opened fire on the van, fatally shooting Halberstam and wounding four other passengers. Admitting to the shooting, Baz

argued that the van had tried to cut his car off and he had done the shooting as an act of road rage, not terrorism.

But there was strong suspicion that the attack on the van was an act of terror and that Baz sought to avenge a massacre the previous week carried out by an extremist Jewish settler in Israel named Baruch Goldstein against twenty-nine Muslim worshipperss at the Cave of the Patriarchs in Hebron.

Ever since the Kahane case, we NYPD investigators were expected to dig deeply, not to take anything at face value. It was no longer enough just to lock up a murderer; we were supposed to search for the broader picture, especially if we suspected any terror connections.

I was part of the investigative team that followed up on background leads on Baz. We looked at his associates to see if there might have been coconspirators. We conducted interviews with anyone in the New York area with whom he might have been in contact. But our probe yielded no new information.

One of my ongoing tasks in the case was to serve as a point of contact between the Halberstam family and the NYPD, updating them on our investigation.

As for Baz, who had escaped from the scene of the shooting, he was arrested later that day elsewhere in New York after a garage mechanic working on his car became suspicious of him, noticing that his car windows appeared to have been blown out in a shooting. The mechanic reported his suspicions to the police who arrested him. Baz was convicted of murder and sentenced to 141 years without a chance for parole.

SHOOTING OF A RAPPER

When the bosses got excited, when the media was on full alert, I got pumped up too. But not every high-profile case was a thrill. The one that I caught on November 30, 1994, was high-profile all right, but when I learned who the victim was, I wanted no part of it long-term. One night would be enough.

It was my turn to catch the next homicide at Midtown North. A shooting had occurred after midnight at the Quad Recording

Studios on Seventh Avenue between 48th and 49th streets. With my partner, Eddie Hennessey, one of NYPD's best detectives, a real natural, we rushed from our office at 54th between 8th and 9th avenues to the scene. Upon arriving, we were met by a uniformed sergeant, who promptly declared to us, "You got a nightmare on your hands."

"What do you mean?"

"The victim is Tupac Shakur."

I knew of Shakur vaguely, a rapper with an infamous past; an incredibly famous human being who could not keep from scraping with the law. He was twenty-three years old, and had become one of the best-selling music artists in the world. He had sold 75 million albums. His songs, spiced with all sorts of anti-police rhetoric, told of growing up amid violence and hardship in the ghettoes, of racism, and most pertinent to this evening, of conflicts with other rappers.

The shooting had happened on the ground floor near the lobby. We asked the sergeant to secure the crime scene. Then we asked where the victim was.

MEETING THE POSSE

He was upstairs in a studio with his "boys," his "posse." We headed upstairs and found ambulance workers doing triage on Tupac. I had seen many shootings and stabbings, and usually the victim felt fear or denial or both. But Tupac was cool as a cucumber. He had been shot five times—twice in the head, twice in the groin, and once through the arm and thigh.

Looking up from Tupac, we noticed his "posse," some fifty people who did not look police-friendly. These were potential witnesses, and Eddie and I would have to interview each of them. Calling around to other precincts, I asked them to send any spare detective to help out with the interviews.

My partner went with Tupac to the hospital, hoping to get a dying declaration from him on who committed the crime. Phoning me, Eddie noted that Tupac had told him that he had been

robbed. This made robbery a prime motive for the shooting, one reason why robbery would get the case, not homicide. This was great news to me. I had already decided that I didn't want to handle this case.

It would not be an easy murder case to solve, what with hostile, uncooperative witnesses. Also the shooting of rap stars had been ongoing for years, and I didn't remember hearing that anyone had ever been convicted of killing a rapper. It seemed that rappers solved their differences through personal vengeance, not by using the court system.

Taken to Bellevue Hospital, Tupac was going to live. That was another piece of good news. This would definitely not be my case, even though homicide had assigned it to me at first. My plan was to turn the case over to the morning shift at robbery. Astonishingly, three hours after surgery and after being shot five times earlier that evening, Tupac left the hospital, against doctor's orders.

Arriving at 8 AM for their morning shift, the robbery boys heard good news and bad news from me before they could get their coffee: The bad news was that they had a case waiting for them. The victim was Tupac Shakur. The good news is that Eddie and I had done a thorough initial investigation and were handing off a good product for them to start with. The other bad news is that Tupac has not been the most cooperative victim, to put it mildly; he has had a reputation of intensely disliking the police.

Shakur's shooter was never caught. But Shakur became suspicious that others in the rap industry had known that someone was planning to shoot him and failed to warn him. The controversy sparked a long feud known as the East Coast–West Coast hip-hop rivalry.

Nearly two years later, on September 7, 1996, Shakur was shot four times in a drive-by-shooting in Las Vegas. He died six days later.

PROSTITUTES AND A SERIAL KILLER

I can't say my career as a homicide detective had me dealing with prostitutes and serial murderers on a constant basis. But I got

a taste of such crimes in a case on June 29, 1995. It began when I received a phone call that a white female had been found dead in a room at the New York Inn on 8th Avenue and 47th Street.

When the call arrived, I knew I would miss the annual office picnic the next day but police work always trumped office picnics. Upon arriving at the hotel, I found the woman lying facedown, her hands bound. She had been strangled to death. She was a known prostitute, Wendy Hoffman Rivera, mid-thirties.

My Torah thefts buddy, Walter Harkins, was sent to help me out. The case took a strange turn when we learned that Wendy had been the daughter of a deceased NYPD Jewish cop. Out of respect for Wendy and her father, I decided to intervene in the funeral arrangements. No one else would.

The only living friend or relative who came forward for Wendy was her pimp boyfriend, who tried to help. Contacting the Shomrim Society, I confirmed that Wendy's father had been a Shomrim member and thus she was entitled to a Shomrim-sponsored Jewish burial. I followed up to make sure that the funeral arrangements went smoothly.

Meanwhile, Walter had discovered a similar homicide case from a few weeks earlier: A female prostitute had been tied up and choked at the St. Marks Hotel on the Lower East Side. Semen was found at the scene and tested. It matched the semen found at the Wendy Hoffman Rivera crime scene. The same perp had done both murders.

As time progressed we came upon a rash of cases of prostitutes who over the past year had been choked and raped in that order after being approached by a black male. The man, asking for a sex act that the prostitute would not agree to perform, choked her and then raped her after she had passed out. Two of his seven victims had died, Wendy Hoffman Rivera and the woman at the St. Marks.

We got a break when we learned that the murderer had used the name of a childhood friend. The friend was currently serving time at the Rikers Island prison complex, so we knew he could not have been the murderer. From the prostitutes who had survived

attacks, we put together a composite sketch and showed it to the Rikers guy and to prostitutes, but with no quick results.

Finally, on February 17, 1996, a uniformed patrolman received a tip from a prostitute that she had seen someone who resembled the sketch. We picked up the suspect, James Jones, and brought him in to the precinct. He was armed.

Giving us no trouble at all, he admitted to committing all of the crimes in question. I sensed in him relief. He wanted to tell his story. He was cognizant of the crimes he had committed but, he said, he was acting from uncontrollable urges.

What were the uncontrollable urges?

During childhood, a female relative had teased him constantly with her ballerina moves. He developed a fetish. He had to seek out ballerinas. Though an army veteran and post office worker, he retained his fetish toward ballerinas. By picking up prostitutes, he was playing out his childhood fetish. Despite his crimes, which were horrific, he seemed a decent fellow.

The gun we had found on him, he said, was for personal protection; he had never thought of using it during the attacks on prostitutes. After pleading guilty, he was sentenced to twenty years to life.

A WALDORF BURGLARY

Finally in 1996, there were developments in the Torah theft case. We had put the Brooklyn Torah theft to bed; but there was still the matter of those fourteen other stolen Torahs.

It was February 6, 1996. My partner, Detective Eddie Hennessey, and I were working a 4 PM to 1 AM shift, the only two detectives covering the Midtown North Detective Squad office that night. We had just returned to the office after dropping off a prisoner and getting some dinner. It was 12:30 AM when a young police officer arrived and explained that he had just made an arrest connected to an attempted burglary at the Waldorf-Astoria. He had the alleged thief downstairs. He was caught carrying burglar tools trying to break into a silver display in the hotel.

Our ears perked up. Any attempted crime at a New York land-mark like this grand hotel was instant news. We told the officer to bring the man to our office. He turned out to be a white forty-eight-year-old former public school teacher named Richard Stevens. He was Jewish but not Orthodox. Richie, as he was called, was a professional silver burglar, seemingly a nice guy, someone you might invite to your home—but with one caveat: Hide your silver!

I took him through the standard debriefing process: His name, date of birth, previous arrests, and I made sure to read him his Miranda rights. Then I offered him what I called my "Monty Hall" offer, referring to the old game show "Let's Make a Deal."

"You just got arrested for attempted burglary," I began, speaking slowly and calmly. "Do you have any information on a little bit bigger crime? This is the time to speak up, because maybe we could help you out. We could talk to the DA. We can't make things go away. But we'll see what can happen."

"What if I knew about some synagogue burglaries?"

It had taken Richie Stevens a nanosecond to think of me as Monty Hall.

I sat there staring at him, trying to remain calm and collected. Had I heard correctly? Had he just used the phrase "synagogue burglaries?" I was on the edge of my seat and couldn't believe my luck. While I wanted him to get specific, I figured it was best if I acted somewhat indifferently, if I let him think that I was not all that interested in synagogue burglaries.

Often, if a police detective is too aggressive at the start of an interview, the person might panic and shut down. It is better for the detective to let the person keep talking and listen to what valuable information he or she is willing to volunteer, then at a propitious moment, to focus on the truly critical questions.

STUFF IN THE PAPERS

"What are you talking about?" I asked quietly.

"You know. There was stuff in the paper about this."

When Stevens asked us what if he knew about some syna-gogue burglaries, I tried to remain calm.

"Really?" I offered, trying to sound indifferent, hoping that he would not hear my heart pounding. "Holy Moses," I whispered to myself. What a turn for the better. I could already feel the excitement that would swell in the Jewish community.

I explained to Richie that for us to forget about his activities at the Waldorf, we needed to know who the fence was and where the Torahs were. It never dawned on him that, in giving us information about the Torah thefts, Richie would incriminate himself.

Since Torah theft was considered a more serious crime than the burglarizing of the Waldorf, we could not promise Richie that he would get a lighter jail sentence by telling us all he knew about the Torah thefts. But I felt we had to try to get him to talk.

He then made a full confession, taking responsibility for fourteen Torah thefts, explaining that he would simply walk into a synagogue during the day, ask if it was okay to pray, and join others in prayer. My hunch that the Torah thief or thieves had simply walked into synagogues had just been proven correct.

Stevens confessed that he then waited for the people to leave and then, when no one was around, broke into the ark, sometimes using a screwdriver. Or he would ask a clerical or custodial worker at a synagogue to permit him to enter the chapel to pray. Strolling out casually, he carried a Torah and silver adornments stuffed into a duffel bag that he had carried in.

One of his biggest revelations was that there was not really a Torah theft ring: There had been only one burglar (himself) and one fence involved in all fourteen Torah thefts. Armed with his revelations, we were getting ready to cut Richie Stevens some slack. But suddenly he got cold feet.

"I can't give up the fence. He's a friend of mine, and he has a family."

DO YOU KNOW HOW MANY ARE CRYING?

I had come so far. I would not let Richie keep his secret. But how could I pry the information loose? He was not going to be brow-beaten. And I could no longer promise him a shorter jail

sentence. I needed another tactic. I thought of giving him a strong dose of good old Jewish guilt.

Keeping those Torahs from the Jewish community, I told him pleadingly, was a crime against his religion and against God. "Do you know how many people are crying at the fact that their Torahs are gone?" I laid it on heavy—every Jewish grandmother would have been proud!

Let's be clear. Richie was in a state of shock. He had never imagined that the detective who knew the Torah case the best would conduct the interview upon his Waldorf arrest. His mistake—and our good luck—was that he had inadvertently "chosen" my home precinct of Midtown North to try to commit a crime.

Later, David Pollock called it *beshert* (Yiddish for "meant to be") that I happened to be questioning Stevens. I was increasingly confident that he would break. And eventually he did. My "Jewish guilt" strategy paid off. What I wanted from Richie was the name of the fence.

"His name is Markus Fogel," a.k.a. Morty, Richie explained. He was a forty-three-year-old Hungarian-born Hasidic silversmith who was the owner of Restore-All Silversmiths on 47th Street in New York. He lived in Monsey, New York, a religious community north of New York City. Stevens confessed that he had stolen all fourteen Torahs for Fogel.

If convicted, Stevens could have been sentenced to six months for the Waldorf burglary. He wound up being sentenced to two and a half years. Thus, he did not ultimately benefit from disclosing information about the Torah thefts, because the Torah crime carried more jail time than did an attempted burglary at the Waldorf.

We needed Stevens' further help in incriminating Fogel. We planned a sting operation within twelve hours of Stevens' confession in which Richie would try to sell an alleged stolen Torah (obtained for us by David Pollock) to the 47th Street fence. Wearing a wire, our "sting" guy walked into Fogel's store.

Fogel agreed to pay $50 to Richie for a Torah, valued at $50,000, that he said had been stolen but had in fact been borrowed from an Upper West Side congregation. At one point Fogel

suggested to Richie that, inasmuch as stolen Torahs had become increasingly difficult to sell to synagogues, they should lay low and just focus on Stevens' burglarizing silver for the time being.

To that end, Fogel told Richie that while visiting his father in a Brooklyn nursing home, he had noticed expensive silver on display that was worth stealing. To me, that proposition alone made Fogel the scum of the earth.

Having gotten Fogel on tape, we went in for the arrest. Interviewing Fogel after the arrest was remarkably different from my interview with Stevens, who appeared to have a soul and showed remorse. I remember Fogel's cold, shark eyes.

Fogel was indicted in State Supreme Court in Manhattan on October 3, 1996. He was arraigned on seventeen counts, including charges of possessing stolen property and criminal solicitation—fourteen Torah scrolls and their silver ornaments—that was valued at $213,150. He pleaded not guilty.

A judge told Fogel that he faced a maximum sentence of two to six years but could obtain a sentence of less than two years if he promised to return all of the Torahs. So Fogel promised that he would have the stolen Torahs delivered to the District Attorney's office on Centre Street. On the appointed day, all of us involved in the Torah theft probe gathered at the DA's office along with Fogel's attorney.

A BOX OF TORAHS

As Fogel had arranged, a box of Torahs was delivered by messenger to the office. I opened the box and found the fourteen Torah scrolls. I was thrilled. We seemed on the verge of performing fifteen *mitzvoth*, including the South Fallsburg Torah recovery, for the Jewish community. But then our hearts sank. Carefully examining the Torahs, David Pollock noticed that only one had the proper registration.

Fogel had tried to pull a fast one, believing that he could get away with "returning" thirteen unstolen Torahs and only a single stolen one. He assumed that we were all novices and would not bother checking on the authenticity of each Torah—but we did.

In the end the judge sentenced him to two years. Had he kept his side of the bargain he might have been given a considerably lighter sentence. The one stolen Torah that was recovered from Fogel's box was returned to the Jewish Theological Seminary in Manhattan, in a very emotional and moving ceremony on November 7, 1997, in which the Torah Task Force was honored.

On November 7, 1997, I was quoted in the *Jewish Community News* of Northern New Jersey as saying that Fogel's associates believed the other thirteen missing Torahs were in Israel and that negotiations were ongoing to have them returned.

I urged synagogues to take the security of Torahs very seriously and pay attention to strange visitors. In this case, I noted that the thief was able to blend into the crowd; he chose synagogues out of the phone book and pretended to pray. "This wasn't a crime of desecration; this was a crime of greed," I said. "From the get-go, we thought the thief was someone who was familiar with Torahs and had the market to sell them." The remaining thirteen Richie Stevens Torahs had not yet been recovered. We still had a lot of work to do to try to retrieve them.

All trails led back to Fogel. He had fenced all fourteen of the Stevens Torahs; he was the only one who knew where the trail led. Had he been capable of retrieving the Torahs that he had stolen, he would have returned them then to shorten his sentence.

The Torahs had already passed through too many hands and could no longer be tracked down. The only chance of recovery at this stage was for the current owner independently to check the Torahs' history via the registry.

The media loved the story. The *Jewish Community News* of Northern New Jersey wrote on November 7, 1997: "It could be a caper made for the big screen—a robbery, a thief who confesses under pressure, the guy who put him up to it, the quick-thinking detectives, the returned stolen goods, a bit of luck, and maybe even a little divine intervention." And I have to admit that I enjoyed the fact that the media seemed to love me.

A little over a year later the *Boston Sunday Globe* wrote on December 6, 1998: "Only in New York could there be a cop like Mordecai Dzikansky. Whenever anyone steals a Torah in this town, Dzikansky is the guy who roams the rambling backstreets of Brooklyn and the Lower East Side, goes undercover, snares the thief, and recovers the missing treasure." *The Globe* made me sound like a Jewish Superman. My dad loved it.

After the JTS Torah was recovered, I assumed that no more Torahs would be stolen. I was wrong.

THE ENGLEWOOD TORAHS

On October 18, 1998, at 3 AM on a Sunday morning, two Torahs were stolen from Temple Emanu-El, then in Englewood, New Jersey, the synagogue where Meryl's aunt and uncle were prominent members. The synagogue was led for almost thirty years by the noted historian, Rabbi Arthur Hertzberg.

The thief had entered the Conservative congregation's sanctuary and broke the lock on the Holy Ark, where eight scrolls were housed. When a burglar alarm sounded, the thief fled, leaving three scrolls on the floor but stealing the two largest Torah scrolls, valued at $100,000 altogether, as well as their handmade silver breastplates which depicted scenes from the Holocaust and Noah's Ark. The stolen Torahs had been used from the time the synagogue was founded in 1924.

Police officers from the Englewood Police Department had heard of my work on the earlier Torah theft case and called to ask if I could spend a few days helping them work the case. My then partner Mitch Parker and I tried to shake the tree once again by speaking to local Judaica dealers.

We got a great lead from the synagogue itself when a synagogue official called us after receiving a phone call from a Manhattan-based Hasid who was inquiring about the history of the Torahs. The synagogue gave us the caller ID and we were able to track down the Hasid.

It turned out that a thirty-one-year-old career criminal named Charles Jones, from the Upper East Side, a non-Jew (though unconfirmed reports had him converting to Judaism) had contacted a Hasidic man and asked him if he knew where Jones might sell two Torahs. Of all the Torah thieves, Jones was by far the most dangerous, with a violent past.

Mitch Parker and I, along with two New Jersey cops, knew just where to go to find the Hasid. The caller ID had helped us get his address on the Upper West Side. We knocked on the door and were let in. To our amazement, there in the living room were two stolen Torahs and a Torah breastplate. On the covering of the Torah scrolls was the name of the Englewood synagogue!

This was fabulous. The cops from Jersey were doing cartwheels. We knew how much pressure the Englewood Jewish community had been applying to its local police, perhaps even more than in a murder investigation.

Though he had not yet formally purchased the Torahs, the Hasid explained that he had been holding the two stolen Torahs for Jones until he could determine their pedigree. Jones had not minded turning over the Torahs to him even before a deal had been secured: He was quite happy to separate himself from the stolen property.

The Hasid eventually testified against Jones; no charges were brought against the Hasid. I phoned David Pollock from the Hasid's house: "Guess what? We found the two stolen Torahs from the Englewood synagogue."

"Where are you?" he asked excitedly.

I gave him the Hasid's address and he nearly fell over. Pollock lived two floors above the man!

Having recovered the two stolen Torahs and a breastplate, we were still only partly home: We still did not have the actual Torah thief in custody nor had we found the second breastplate. The critical thing was getting the thief. If we got the breastplate also, that would be icing on the cake.

We soon got good news from the sharp doorman who worked in the Hasid's Upper West Side building. When we spoke

with him, he recalled that he had become suspicious when the Torah thief delivered the Torahs to the Hasid. The doorman had the foresight to jot down the thief's license plate.

We planned another sting operation to corner Mr. Jones. Posing as a rabbi who owned a Judaica store on East 30th Street in Manhattan, I phoned him and let him know that I wanted to purchase a Torah and breastplate. He asked to meet us after store hours, an arrangement that pleased me, because it would be easier to carry out the operation without customers or employees, who could have been put in danger.

THE RABBI AND THE STING

As part of the sting, I dressed like a rabbi, with a large black yarmulke on my head, a white button-down shirt, black pants, and *tzitzit* sticking out of my pants (these fringes, worn by observant Jewish men, hung from the corners of four-cornered garments). All of these clothes and Jewish add-ons of my "rabbi uniform" belonged to me.

I looked like I could definitely run a Judaica store, though the store was actually a front. One detective in on the sting joked with me: "Morty, you look more comfortable dressed as a rabbi than you do as a detective." But, in fact, with my yeshiva background, this was one of the easiest disguises for me. All I had to do was put on my yarmulke and my *tzitzit*, and I was ready to go.

Still, I realized that all I had to do was tuck the *tzitzit* into my pockets, slide off the yarmulke, and I could have passed as a waiter in a fancy restaurant!

As we prepared to greet the thief, an unmarked police van was outside the "store" with a camera and microphones. I was wearing a wire in order to get enough evidence to convict the guy. When I thought I had enough evidence, I was supposed to use a code to alert the "cavalry" that it was time to come in and make the arrest.

Into the store walked the Englewood Torah thief. We sat down facing one another. I reiterated that I wanted to buy two Torahs and a breastplate for $20,000. He seemed most accommodating,

unaware that he had just confessed to committing a crime to a (disguised) New York City homicide detective. The crimes that he had committed were possessing and selling stolen goods.

Now that I had the evidence, I was supposed to use the word "cavalry" to alert my backup. But at the crucial moment I forgot the word! All I could do was to jump him myself. I grabbed him and held him in a bear hug. "I'm a New York City cop," I shouted. "Don't move. Don't move. Don't move."

On November 5, 1998, Jones was charged with possession of stolen property. He claimed that he had bought the Torahs at an estate sale, but we believed that he had been planning to burglarize the Englewood synagogue for two years. Jones had been on parole for a 1990 conviction for possessing a loaded gun and robbery at the time of the Torah heist. Searching his apartment, we found a high-powered 9 mm automatic handgun, so Mr. Jones was also charged with illegal possession of a weapon.

Needless to say, I was ecstatic. After the arrest, I told the Newhouse News Service that "This is a crime that touches me very closely. Stealing a Torah is like putting a knife through the heart of the congregation. But I think people of other religions can relate too. I could relate if a chalice were missing."

The Englewood police too were ecstatic, and the synagogue was overwhelmingly grateful. Congregants had feared that the stolen Torahs had been whisked out of the country. Learning that Jones had been caught, Rabbi Geoffrey Haber of Temple Emanu-El in Englewood commented tersely, "In the Torah, it says, 'Thou shall not steal.'" The custom-made Torah sculpture that the synagogue presented to me at a special ceremony is proudly displayed in my home today.

In a makeshift ceremony the same day as the Jones arrest, NYPD's Chief of Detectives William Allee personally decorated me and my team with special "CD" (Chief of Detectives) pins given for major investigation success. Adding to the joy of that day for me, the *New York Times* called our Torah theft task force a "little known but highly effective squad."

This praise was a big deal, as was the news conference over which the chief presided. My wife found it amusing that when the

television crime thriller "NYPD Blue" devoted an episode to my Torah theft cases, they cast the heavy-set, unkempt TV detective Andy Sipowicz (played by Dennis Franz) in my role. Meryl would have preferred that the tall, handsome Detective Bobby Simone (Jimmy Smits) play me.

The only negative aspect was that the Hasid was not cooperative when it came to testifying in court; he wanted to limit his involvement. We needed his testimony to explain who had provided him with the Torahs. He did eventually testify, and Jones was prosecuted and convicted. Sentenced on February 25, 1999, Jones received six to twelve years for the criminal possession of stolen property and criminal possession of a weapon.

Perhaps the nicest comment came from Chief of Manhattan Detectives Kevin Farrell, who told the *New York Times* that "the key to this investigation was the uniqueness of Detective Dzikansky. This is certainly a unique crime, and fortunately we had the unique resources to address it."

Unlike the feeling I had after solving a homicide case, where I was not able to return the victim to a loved one, with the Torah theft case, I could return the stolen items to the synagogue.

September 1999 was a very special month for me. Our first child, whom we named Zachary, was born, lighting up our lives, and I finally accepted a transfer to homicide. Six years earlier I had felt too inexperienced to tackle such an assignment. Now, after Kahane, Halberstam, the Torah thefts, and numerous other cases, I knew I was ready.

FINALLY, A HOMICIDE DETECTIVE

My superiors knew I was ready as well: Close to my seventeenth anniversary with the NYPD, my then Sergeant and "rabbi" (police lingo for mentor), Brian McCabe, one of the most respected sergeants in the NYPD, told me he was transferring to homicide and asked if I wanted to join him. Because I enjoyed working with Brian, this time I made the move; the timing was right. We transferred to the elite Manhattan South Homicide, located at the

NYPD Police Academy on 20th Street between Second and Third avenues on the East Side.

My area was Central Park South, 59th Street, west to the Hudson River, east to the East River, and south to Battery Park. Comprising veterans with fifteen to forty years' experience, our team had mentoring responsibilities for detective squads in the various police precincts within our area of coverage.

Two years and two months later (December 24, 2001), just over three months after 9/11, I was promoted to Detective Second Grade.

All of my religious upbringing, my emergence as the NYPD's "Jewish Detective," my investigations of Jewish and Israeli cases, especially the Torah theft affair, put me in a unique position to deploy my special investigative talents. I would never have guessed, however, where those talents were leading me. But I was ready and able to take on even more complicated assignments. As it happened, I would soon get that chance. But it would take a tragedy of unimaginable proportions to push me into the assignment of my lifetime.

CHAPTER 4

I Thought of
My Wife and Son

How ironic. Tuesday, September 11, 2001, happened to be one of those beautiful late summer days, temperatures in the 70s, blue skies, humidity lower than usual. I assumed that this would be another routine day, whatever "routine" means for a New York City homicide detective. I awoke later than usual because I had planned to take the day off. All five members of my homicide team were scheduled to be off that day. Four days on, then two days off—that was the team's workweek.

As I began to dress, it did not occur to me that millions of people were about to have a whole new reality thrust upon them. Nor could I have imagined that impending events would radically alter my career and my life, sending me to far-flung places, thrusting me into a role that, in all frankness, was perfectly suited for me.

The fact that I did not work on the Jewish Sabbath, barring serious cases, meant that I always had a certain number of days to make up. Despite owing make-up days, I could still choose which days to take off and so on that September morning, unless the office needed me, I planned to stay home. We were living in Long Beach, Long Island.

Thinking how nice it would be to hang around with my two-year-old son Zachary and, quite frankly, how much fun it would be to spend an hour catching a few races at the Off Track Betting office in neighboring Oceanside, I looked forward to a quiet, entertaining day. Let me allay doubts: The OTB is a perfectly legal

form of gambling, akin to playing the Lotto. Was I ahead? Not really; I was probably even.

Had I not taken that day off, I would have arisen at 5 AM, as I routinely did, so that Meryl and I could catch the 6:37 Long Island Railroad train for a one-hour commute into New York City. She was then a vice president in finance for the once-powerful but now nonexistent Lehman Brothers.

On days off, I would drop Meryl off at the train station and return home, where our babysitter, Isabella, would be in full swing with Zach. Since my schedule was constantly changing, Isabella helped with Zach as needed. This arrangement gave me the luxury of being able to play with my son on my days off but allowed me free time as well.

And so that morning, I awoke at 6 AM and put on my sweats. I looked outside and noticed what a gorgeous day it already was. Returning home after dropping Meryl off at the train, I had a cup of coffee while browsing through the *New York Daily News* to check if anything interesting had happened overnight connected to my office. You could be sure that if homicide detectives were on a case, the media would sniff it out.

It was 7:30 AM Zach was eating breakfast. Isabella stood nearby him in the kitchen. I told her that I was going back to sleep for a while. Sleeping soundly, I did not hear the telephone ring around 9 AM; nor did Isabella, who was bathing Zach. She did hear the caller leave a voice mail. It was Meryl. Shouting at me, Isabella, solemn and forceful, implored me to listen to Meryl's message. I approached the telephone, still fighting sleep, trying to guess what had happened.

MORTY, I'M OKAY

"Morty," she began, rushing her words: "I'm okay. When you wake up you are going to hear that a plane went through the World Trade Center. I'm out of the building and calling you from a pay phone at the Vista [a hotel across the street]. I do not have my bag or my phone with me. I love you and Zach. Talk to you as soon as I can."

She sounded almost hysterical. As I listened to her frightening words, I grew alert—and frightened for her.

The building from which Meryl escaped was 3 World Financial Center, adjacent to the North Tower, one of the two 110-floor skyscrapers known as the World Trade Center. A walkway connected the North Tower with the World Financial Center.

At 8 AM she had been taking part in a budget meeting with thirty others in a corner conference room on the tenth floor of the World Financial Center. From her seat she had a view of both the West Side Highway and the WTC's North Tower. Suddenly, she watched a large plane flying in the direction of the North Tower.

Seconds later, at 8:46 AM, shockingly, the plane smashed into the North Tower near the top floors. Along with her colleagues, Meryl ran to the window, stunned, watching flames shoot out from the spot where the plane had struck. Was this pilot error or a terror attack? She and the rest of the world wondered. Probably terror, she concluded, because no pilot, with so much visibility, would mistakenly crash into a New York skyscraper.

It would take a few hours for people to fathom the audacity, the scope of the tragedy, and the implications for America. That first plane crashing into the North Tower was just the start of a series of coordinated attacks upon the United States planned and carried out by al-Qaeda terrorists. Nineteen al-Qaeda terrorists had hijacked four commercial passenger jet airliners that morning.

The hijackers had intentionally crashed a 767 jet into the North Tower and would soon crash another into the South Tower. Everyone on board those planes was killed, as were nearly 3,000 people inside the Towers. Within a mere two hours, both Towers collapsed.

Other hijackers crashed a third airliner, a Boeing 757 (American Airlines flight 77), into the Pentagon in Washington, D.C., killing 189 and wounding 106. Still other hijackers had commandeered a fourth airliner that they apparently hoped to crash into the White House or the Capitol, but passengers and the flight crew caused the plane to crash into a field in Pennsylvania, killing everyone aboard.

Early estimates of fatalities at the Towers disturbingly put the number at 50,000, but, since the attacks came early in the morning, the numbers inside the buildings came to "only" 14,000.

The attacks were unprecedented. The nearly 3,000 people killed at the Twin Towers were more than those killed in the Japanese assault on Pearl Harbor that effectively brought the United States into World War II on December 7, 1941; indeed, this was the worst attack on American soil ever in terms of the numbers killed.

Meryl's survival instincts took over. Horrifying thoughts entered her mind: The flames from the North Tower might spread to her conference room. Or, the entire North Tower might simply collapse. She knew she had to get out of the building urgently. She and a colleague, Mona Adler, decided to leave together.

Meryl was not in the best shape for a sudden dash. She was still recovering from a broken ankle. Still, she and Mona raced down ten flights of stairs into the sunlight two minutes later. Eager to make phone calls, they entered the nearby Vista Hotel and found a pay phone.

Meryl's first call was to her eleventh-floor colleagues, telling them to get out of the building quickly. As events would prove, her warning was right on the mark. Soon after Meryl and Mona departed their office, her conference room was badly damaged from falling debris. The part of the building near the room looked as if someone had taken a bite out of it.

After that first call, Meryl phoned home with her startling message for me.

Her third and final call was to her father, Howard Markowitz, who coincidentally owned a clothing and lingerie store on the Lower East Side on Orchard Street, two miles from the World Trade Center. She told him that she was okay and was on her way to his store. While Meryl was making those calls, a second plane, another 767, slammed into the South Tower. It was 9:03 AM.

Listening to Meryl's voice message, I was not overly worried, knowing that she was presumably safe on the ground; confused and shocked, yes, but my wife had declared that she was okay and

so I felt a sense of relief. But who knew what was happening in the vicinity of the towers? Might there be more attacks?

I desperately wanted to reach her; but since she was calling from a pay phone, having left her cell in her office, I would have to wait for her to call again. I turned on the television. While Meryl had sounded very much like an eyewitness to a horrific event, I needed the authority that only television could provide, confirming what she had seen, explaining what it all meant.

I have to admit that my first thought was not that this had been an act of terror. From my Long Island home, watching on television, I could hardly draw any conclusion about why the two planes had slammed into the World Trade Center.

I tuned in CNN—it was now about 9:30 AM—and heard an announcer speculate that pilot error was unlikely and that there was a high probability that the crashing planes had been terror attacks. I stared incredulously at the TV screen as flames soared skyward and thick black and gray smoke enveloped the Towers.

As I stared fixated at the television screen, I found my mind strangely drifting away from the horrible event itself. It would have been quite natural for me to focus on the maddening events in southern Manhattan. After all, as a New York City homicide detective, I had been present at hundreds of crime scenes. Mesmerized by what I was seeing on television, I realized that I might well be looking at the largest crime scene in history. My professional instincts should have compelled me to study every possible detail.

THINKING LIKE A HUSBAND AND FATHER

But at that moment, I confess that I was thinking more as a husband and father. Meryl and Zach were my first priorities, and until I knew that both were out of danger, I would have trouble focusing on planes crashing into two New York skyscrapers. One thing was certain: My day off was over; the rest of my day would be very busy. My thoughts turned to the scope of the events and

I wondered what I might contribute to helping solve a crime that appeared an act of terror.

Past terrorist cases that I had worked had certainly gotten my adrenaline pumping. Should this turn out to be terror, I knew that I wanted to be where the action would be. I wanted to help in the investigation of this crime.

The perpetrators of the Manhattan attacks were all dead, but the masterminds who planned the attack were still alive and perhaps planning further assaults against New York. I hoped that I would be assigned to go after the masterminds.

I phoned my boss, Sergeant Brian McCabe of Manhattan South Homicide. Normally if some sudden, serious police-related event occurred while I was out of the office, I would have phoned in and asked my sergeant what to do. If needed, I then made sure to get to the office as quickly as possible.

This time my other homicide detective partners and I did not ask if there was work for us to do, we knew there was. All five of us decided to show up together to avoid being tasked, as a solitary officer might have been, with work outside of our specialty of homicide investigation, such as directing traffic or crowd control. McCabe asked us to gather at his apartment in Lower Manhattan, which was closer to the World Trade Center than was the office located at the Police Academy at 20th Street between Second and Third avenues. I figured we would arrive there by noon.

No one could have imagined that terrorists would employ commercial airliners as weapons of mass destruction. In earlier plane hijackings, terrorists had shown no desire to die, only to bargain for the release of imprisoned colleagues.

As I prepared to leave for Manhattan, I faced a wrenching dilemma: Getting to the sergeant's apartment was an obvious priority, but so was ensuring the safety of my wife. I put my wife first. Frustrated at how little I knew of the horrific events, I kept asking myself, where is Meryl?

Of the thousand other questions that crossed my mind, one tugged at me the most: Why am I at home and Meryl is standing outside a skyscraper that might have collapsed on her? For

a homicide detective to lose his life in the line of duty would be shocking and sad, but not unexpected. But for Meryl to die while working for a major Wall Street firm would be neither expected nor fair.

I began dwelling on a nightmarish scenario: That Meryl had already been killed by the impact of a collapsing tower. The thought that Zach might now be without a mother was killing me. My mother had died of cancer when I was only seven years old and I did not want my son to lose his mother at age two.

Staring at CNN and the large debris field created as a result of the Towers' collapse, I kept asking myself how a building of that size could simply fall apart. It appeared as if the entire lower half of Manhattan had been wiped out.

While organizing for my trip into Manhattan, I heard the phone ring. I raced to pick it up, hoping and praying it was Meryl. It was not. A cousin was phoning from Israel to say that she had just heard from a friend that Meryl and another woman had been interviewed on television as they scampered away from the site of the attacks.

Our cousin was aware that Meryl worked near the World Trade Center and that I would want to hear immediately that, at least up to 9:50 AM, Meryl was alive and well. But her interview took place before either of the two Towers had collapsed. Had she survived those terrible events?

A FRESH SUIT AND TIE

Just before leaving for the city, I put on my usual attire: A freshly pressed suit and a tie. I hated leaving Zach with Isabella now; I preferred to take care of him until my wife arrived home. But my obligation was to get into the city as soon as I could.

I had resisted phoning my father-in-law at his store, fearing that if he had not yet heard from Meryl, my call would only worry him more. I finally decided to phone him anyway. I was confident that Meryl would head for her father's store, so I wanted to check to find out if he had heard from her.

Suddenly, the phone was ringing. My heart began to race. Could it be Meryl?

It was my father-in-law. He had beaten me to the punch. I grew nervous at hearing his voice so somber at first. My mind latched on to nightmarish thoughts: Meryl had not gone to his store; something terrible had happened to her.

I certainly had cause to worry. When the South Tower began to collapse at 9:59 AM, Meryl was on West Street, three blocks from the World Trade Center. Realizing the danger she was in, she and Mona raced away, reaching Canal Street to the north. Then at 10:28 AM she and Mona had actually watched as the North Tower fell.

Her father then uttered the words I was so desperate to hear: "She called me and is on her way up here." At 10:45 AM, nearly two hours after phoning me from the Vista Hotel, Meryl phoned me to say that she was with her father at his store.

That was all I needed to hear. I let Meryl know that I would come directly to the store and drop the car off for her so she could get home as quickly as possible. Though I knew that my day was just getting started, somehow I felt that the worst part of it was past me. At least I hoped so.

Finally, I was heading for New York City. Normally, it took me an hour to travel from my home to the city. This time, I knew I would get in much faster. Every highway leading into the city was closed, and the only cars allowed on the roads were first responders such as the police, firefighters, and members of the Emergency Medical Services. My police permit on the windshield of my car gave me quick passage.

Arriving in New York City at about noon, I headed first for my father-in-law's store, located a few blocks from the McCabe apartment, in order to see Meryl and to drop off our car for her. Without trains running, the car was her only hope of getting home quickly.

When we saw each other, she collapsed into my arms, a look of shock, disbelief, and fear in her eyes. We held each other for a few minutes and knew what we each needed to do next.

She and Mona, who had come to the store as well, described what they had seen as they fled the site—how they had started running when the South Tower started to crumble shortly before 10 AM and how they had managed to get to Meryl's father.

At one point, in one of those surrealistic moments, Meryl and Mona saw a city bus idling on West Street. They urged the driver to start taking people north quickly, away from the Towers. Some passengers searched for the correct fare, focusing on the routine, not the nearby ghastly reality.

Leaving the bus at Canal Street, she and Mona hailed a cab but advanced only a few blocks, because traffic had come to a grinding halt. Exiting the cab, they watched in shock and tears as the North Tower collapsed, then somberly walked the rest of the way to the store.

I LOVE YOU, SEE YOU SOON

Both women commented at the contrast between my clean suit and the white, soot-covered clothes of the thousands fleeing Lower Manhattan. For Meryl and me, few words were necessary, just an "I love you" and "See you as soon as I can."

I wanted Meryl home so that she could hold Zach and take care of him. With no idea how many hours or even days I would be working near the World Trade Center, I was sure that knowing Meryl was on her way home would ease things for me. I encouraged her to point to the plaque, the police permit, on the car windshield when necessary. If stopped by a police officer, she should point to the plaque and explain that her husband was an NYPD homicide detective who was helping at the site. And she should add that she was driving home urgently to take care of her two-year-old son. Pointing out the irony of her relying on the permit, I suggested that she might well be the only driver that day using a police plaque to get *out* of the city. Police were using their plaques to get *into* New York.

I then left on foot for Sergeant McCabe's apartment, which was a half-mile from the site. Within a matter of minutes of my arrival, the other four members of our team showed up.

What raced through my mind was an alternate scenario for that morning: Had I reached work at 8 AM, as was my routine, I would certainly have gone to the Towers upon learning of the first plane. Most of my colleagues were already at the site, and I worried about their safety.

Sergeant McCabe suggested that one of us phone the police "mobilization point," comprised of police supervisors who were dispatching police to the Towers and other parts of the city, and ask what they wished us to do.

One supervisor told us that we should get over to the "shaping up" center located in a commercial building lobby on Church Street, three blocks from the Towers.

CLOUDS OF SMOKE

Walking over to Church Street, I looked down toward where the World Trade Center had stood only a few hours earlier. Clouds of smoke and confetti-like paper swirled around the skies, giving the appearance of snow. But snow falls downward; this "confetti" was circulating through the air. It was an eerie, almost supernatural site. I was staring into a complete haze.

Arriving at the "shaping up" center, we met colleagues from our office who had just returned from the site. Their clothes and bodies were white, head to foot. Their mood was unmitigated disbelief; though we knew the headlines—two planes had brought down the World Trade Center, probably killing thousands of people—none of us had any good answers for what had happened.

Each of our colleagues had a story to tell. Perhaps the most poignant concerned a police detective heading for the Towers, who decided to use the restroom at Syms clothing store on Trinity Street before reaching the site. Had he not gone into Syms, he would likely have been pulverized when the first Tower collapsed.

We began asking the obvious questions: What could we do? Were our colleagues okay? Hundreds of other detectives, most

in clean suits and ties, waited for directions. Not getting answers quickly was frustrating to many of us, but given the chaos and bedlam, we had no choice but to wait. At some point we were asked to go to our offices and continue to wait for instructions.

With terrorism the most likely explanation for the attacks, I was eager to help out in the investigation. Fearing that the morning's assault had not been a one-time event, I worried along with many others that more attacks might occur very soon against the city.

We stopped off at Cabrini Hospital, across the street from our office, eager to check on the status of colleagues. The hospital had quickly been converted into a "check zone" for first responders—police and firemen—who had been at or near the site and who therefore required hosing down to rid themselves of toxic material from the Towers. Since we had not yet been at the site, it was decided that we did not need hosing. Only those carrying visible residue were stopped for hosing.

Once back at our office, the five of us grew impatient. Standby mode is anathema to a police officer who wants to help out. Finally, someone brought us a "temp log" which contained incoming phone messages from so-called tipsters. They had been asked to report on a neighbor who disappeared around the time of the attacks; or anyone acting suspiciously that morning.

CHASING THE TIPSTERS

Our job was to follow up on the tips. I had done just that, talking to two tipsters before the five of us, all chasing down tipsters in different locales, had been asked to head back to the office for a new assignment.

Not surprisingly, the two "tips" proved imaginary. Suffering from paranoia, the tipsters had no grasp of what was real and what was not.

In between the two visits, I snuck in a phone call to Meryl at home. What a relief! Now, I felt, I could give my full attention to the job at hand.

GET TO GROUND ZERO

Five of us were told to get down to the site of the attacks. We were being sent to check out information that someone, acting on his or her own, without authority from any official, had ghoulishly set up a makeshift "morgue" at the spot where the Twin Towers had fallen. Who was this person? What was he trying to accomplish? Was he just seeking attention? Was he some lunatic with no motive whatsoever?

The five of us had already pegged the person as crazed or crazy, or both. We were asked to locate and verify the makeshift "morgue" and learn more about the person. Information on the nut case was sparse as no one knew where the "morgue" was located or if it even existed.

It was nearing 10 PM and I headed to the site along with the team. Although I had not eaten since breakfast, I figured I would eat and drink later.

Heading for the site, we stopped on the way at Beekman Hospital's emergency room to pick up masks and protective gloves. A teenager wearing a yarmulke approached our car at the entrance to the ER and asked for a ride through the Brooklyn Battery Tunnel.

We felt sorry for him; he was obviously just trying to get home after what had to be a horrible day for him. He had volunteered to come in from Brooklyn to help out. He seemed exhausted and wrought with emotion, but we had to say no to him.

We told him that we were on official business and had to get to the site quickly. Under normal circumstances we would have helped him out in a heartbeat, but we felt the pressure to get to our assignment as soon as we could. Proceeding, we saw only emergency vehicles, and we parked the car near the Battery Tunnel entrance, several blocks from the site.

We began walking. The air was filled with grayish smoke, water had accumulated on parts of the street, whether from fire hoses or from the Towers themselves. The scene could have come out of a horror film.

At 10 PM we walked the short distance to the dreadful site. As we got closer, we stared in utter disbelief: Before us was overwhelming devastation. We saw crushed fire trucks and police cars that looked like Tonka toys. The ground was covered in soot and ash. The towers had been reduced to jagged steel girders. First responders, covered with white soot, searched and dug for survivors.

The only lighting was from emergency generators, which contributed to the otherworldly nature of the scene. None of us could speak. It was all so hard to digest. An eerie calm prevailed. One minute I felt anger, another simple incredulity.

Some of my police colleagues had been at the World Trade Center attack in 1993, so to them this was *déjà vu*, a nightmare magnified a thousand times beyond that previous event. But for me, 9/11 made terrorism shockingly real. Seeing it in person was different from reading or hearing about it. I could not know then, but this would be the first of many suicide attacks that I would see and evaluate over the next few years.

As we approached the Marriott Hotel near the site, we came upon a young uniformed police officer who instantly identified us as NYPD detectives. On any other day, he might have thought that we were stockbrokers, dressed as we were in suits and ties, but by now all civilians had been cleared out of the area, so anyone wearing a suit and tie was most likely a police detective.

The police officer, who had to be in his early twenties, wore a clip-on tie off to the side—part of the standard NYPD uniform; he also had a cigarette dangling from his mouth. Both the unkempt tie and cigarette constituted minor NYPD infractions, but no one would call him out today. Under instructions not to leave his area of coverage, he stood by himself amid the rubble until replaced by another officer. I admired the young man, embodying as he did true strength and courage.

A solemn look crossed his face. He had something he wanted to show us. He asked us to follow him to a point within his assigned area. His words poured out quickly, machine-gun style. He seemed weary, as if he had been repeating over and over to himself, "This has been one fucking day."

He led us to an alley off West Street, where he pointed to what appeared to be a plane engine, lying on the ground. It certainly looked like a piece of a plane and perhaps an engine. Suddenly the dreadfulness of the morning's events came alive and became real to me. This was a part of one of the planes that had struck the Towers. The police officer now led us back toward West Street, where he wanted to show us something else. There on the ground was a torso, someone's upper body with the head nowhere in sight. The torso had breasts. It was a woman.

All five of us were seasoned homicide detectives; viewing body parts at a crime scene was part of our daily work. We normally would not have found the torso so shocking. But it was a cruel reminder of how many others had met this woman's fate in the attack.

Quite a number of victims, evidently seeking to escape the flames, either leaped from one of the top floors to the ground or were sucked out by the explosion. Meryl later described to me how she had watched people falling or jumping out of the buildings, some holding hands.

One of our team was a very sharp female detective named Irma Rivera-Duffy. She bent down and methodically examined the sweater on the torso, noticing a label with the name of a Boston department store; this suggested to her that the torso had possibly been on the plane that had left Boston that morning heading for San Francisco but had been diverted by terrorists aboard who crashed it into the Twin Towers.

Had this been a "normal" crime scene, with one or two dead bodies, we detectives would have worked it for hours and hours. We would have begun a full investigation—of the torso, of the events that appeared to explain why the torso had been lying on the ground, and so forth. Instead we moved on, leaving the torso for the young officer to secure until a medical examiner could return it to loved ones.

Much as it haunted us, we knew that there was nothing we could investigate regarding the torso at that time. We had been told to find the person with the faux morgue, not to help in investigating the crime scene. As we continued to walk

through the soot and ash, we knew that we were walking on and near body parts, but we could not see them. They had already disintegrated.

FAUX MORGUE

Addressing our main task, we kept looking for the kook who had set up the faux morgue, but we never found the person. We asked those at the site if they knew of this "morgue," but they did not.

From those at the site whom we knew, we asked for information on colleagues and friends. Only later did I find out that a female police officer from our precinct, Moira Smith, had lost her life while heroically evacuating civilians numerous times from the Towers.

Unlike a normal crime scene, limited in scope and relatively easy to control, in the wreckage of the Twin Towers we were confronting the most appalling crime scene in American history, worse even than most battlefields. Indeed, the place resembled a battlefield more than a crime scene. It would take months to go through the rubble at what had been termed Ground Zero, the site of the World Trade Center.

Before we knew it, it was 2 AM. We had been at the site for four hours. The day had started for me seventeen hours earlier. I wondered how long it would take for me to assimilate all that had happened—to all those who lost loved ones and friends, to New York City, to America, to the rest of the world. I wondered too how police business would change. It would have to. Everything was likely to change after the morning attacks.

Too worn out, too numb, and too fatigued to even guess, I promised myself that I would return to these questions at a later date. At that moment, I wanted to get home, to see my wife and son, and to await the police work that I would undertake to protect New York City from further terror attacks.

Before heading for home, we had to go back to the office to get instructions on where to be the next day. A supervisor decided that my four partners and I should return to the office at noon for

further orders. I sensed that everyone was numb. Thinking about the next day was too much of a strain.

A TRAIN HOME

I had no car, and even if I had had one, I doubt that I would have wanted to get behind the steering wheel. My eyes were closing on me. Awful images of death and disaster kept running through my brain.

I was in no shape, mentally or physically, to make the drive. Hitching a ride to Long Island seemed out of the question. New York City remained shut tight as a drum. Nothing was moving on the roads. The only way to get from point A to point B was on foot.

Then I thought, if the trains were running, however slowly, that was my best bet. So I got myself to Penn Station below the world-famous Madison Square Garden; it was just after 3 AM. I knew that I might have to wait several hours before getting on a train; but in the end I managed to board one to my home town of Long Beach at about 4 AM. The journey would take an hour.

I knew virtually everyone on the train, especially the police officers and firefighters who, like me, lived on Long Island. But, however well I knew them, I could only stare ahead, as if in a daze, too sad and worn out to talk to them or even to give a passing nod of recognition.

Arriving at the Long Beach train station, I caught a cab to my house. The place was dark. Meryl and Zach were sleeping. I had no desire to disturb them, though I knew Meryl would have been nervously wondering what had happened to me after we had spoken in the afternoon.

Unlocking our front door, trying to keep as quiet as possible, I knew that my first task had to be throwing my shoes, suit, and tie into the garbage. I could not imagine bringing that suit, now filled with soot and who knew what else, to the dry cleaner.

Hearing the front door open, my wife got out of bed and ran up to me. We just hugged, then went to check on Zach and finally to sleep. We decided to save conversation for the morning.

Throughout that hellish day, I kept thinking that I wanted to be involved in investigating this mammoth crime. I had no desire to sit on the sidelines while my country, my city, and yes, even my religion, had been torn asunder by this assault. If these global Islamic terrorists had acted with the same hatred as those that killed Rabbi Kahane and Ari Halberstam and inflicted so many attacks on Israel, then they were also attacking my religion. I had been unwilling to sit on the sidelines at the time of the 1991 Gulf War: I was unwilling now.

Images of the Gulf War of January 1991 raced through my brain earlier in the day. A month before that war started, I had visited Israel and attended a cousin's wedding, celebrating with them in a Jerusalem wedding hall.

Then the war broke out; Iraq's Saddam Hussein fired Scud missiles at Israeli targets. One month I was hanging out with my Israeli relatives at a wedding; the next those same relatives were wearing gas masks to protect themselves against an unimaginable act of terror: A chemical or biological weapon attached to a Scud missile. As I took all this in, I knew that I had to figure out a way to be in the fight against terror. To me, the kind of terror that rained down on the World Trade Center on September 11 and the radical Islamic terror in the Middle East were cut from the same cloth.

True, one of the worst terrorist acts committed in the United States had occurred on April 19, 1995, when two Americans—Timothy McVeigh and Terry Nichols—detonated a bomb-laden Ryder truck containing more than 6,200 pounds of ammonium nitrate fertilizer, nitromethane, and diesel fuel in front of the Alfred Murrah Federal Building, an office complex in downtown Oklahoma City, killing 168 and wounding another 800 people.

Until the attacks on this day, the Oklahoma City bombing had been the deadliest act of terrorism in the United States. Though initial media reports assumed that the bombing in Oklahoma City had been carried out by radical Islamic terrorists, eventually non-Muslim American McVeigh was discovered to have carried out the gruesome act.

I remember thinking at the time of McVeigh's deadly deed that the Oklahoma City bombing was certainly tragic and mind-boggling in its scope but had no connection to New York City nor was there a proven link to radical Islamic terror, and therefore I didn't focus on the details of the event. When we thought of terror against New York, we did not picture a Timothy McVeigh or Terry Nichols. We thought of religious fanatics emerging from the Middle East.

Radical Islamic terror was the norm, and so whenever I heard that a terror act had been committed within the United States, the Middle East, or anywhere else, I automatically assumed that radical Islamists had been behind the deed. Though at that time I harbored no thoughts of going after terrorists in the Middle East, I always felt that I had an advantage over my police colleagues because I had a good understanding of that region.

I had made a dozen visits to Israel by 9/11; I had family living there who kept me apprised and updated on events there. And I read as much as I could about the Arab–Israeli conflict and its wider implications for the region.

But even when the events of 9/11 occurred, I had no thought that I might actually serve on the front lines in the fight against terror. All that I knew was that I wanted to help root out the 9/11 villains—not the foot soldiers; they were dead; I wanted to get at the demonic masterminds. If I could play even a small role in keeping New York City safe from these evil-doers, I would find great satisfaction in that.

CHAPTER 5

Guys, We Can't Relax

It would take some scrambling on my part, but I was determined to do what I could to help secure the city that I loved so much.

Along with millions of other Americans, I awoke to a new, devastating reality on September 12, 2001. New York City, considered one of the most important cities in the world, and my "beat," had come under deadly attack the day before. For many reasons, I was eager to be personally involved in the follow-up of undoubtedly the worst homicide ever perpetrated against New York, not to mention the United States.

My background and set of interests would not allow me to stay on the sidelines: My frequent visits to Israel had shown me how radical Islamic terror had become an almost daily part of the scene; my continuing contact with the two-million-strong Jewish community in New York, an obvious terrorist target, left me eager to keep the community and all New Yorkers from harm.

I was under no illusion that, like some comic book hero, I would quickly and personally capture the bad guys and bring them to justice. I sensed that my role both in the recovery process and in the pursuit of the 9/11 terrorists, would be small. Given the magnitude of these events, thousands of law enforcement agents and people would have far larger tasks than mine.

I would do what I was asked to do, but at the same time, I vowed to myself that I would look for ways to play a part in the inevitable investigation into what seemed to be a crime without a motive. Few could imagine motives that justified such a deed.

The attacks had to be random, senseless deeds designed only to create mayhem and perhaps to punish the victims for imaginary crimes. Inevitably, in those first hours after the attacks, my thoughts focused on radical Islamist terror organizations as the likely perpetrators.

Indeed, within hours after the planes struck the buildings, the FBI had identified all nineteen hijackers, fifteen of whom were from Saudi Arabia, two from the United Arab Emirates, one from Egypt, and one from Lebanon. Affiliated with the radical Islamic terrorist group al-Qaeda, they carried out the attack with no more specific motive than their ongoing "war" against infidels. Al-Qaeda's leader was the then fifty-two-year-old Saudi Arabian-born Osama bin Laden, who soon became the most wanted criminal in the world.

I was right that I would be a small cog in the investigative effort, at least at first. My task on that "day after" was to go back to responding to tips as I had done for part of the day before. The tip line had become a little bit more active, and we homicide detectives were taking a larger role in tracking down reports, although most arose from the tipster's paranoia.

To the tipsters, people's routine behavior became automatically suspicious. Almost all tips proved fruitless, but each one had to be tracked down; you never knew. So, we had no choice but to interview the tipster, take notes on what he said, and then get that information back to headquarters.

The Jewish New Year, Rosh Hashanah, and Yom Kippur, the holiest day on the Jewish calendar, fell very soon after the New York terror. I had arranged with the NYPD that I would not have to work on Shabbat or the major Jewish holidays. But after 9/11, I chose not to put in for days off for the upcoming holidays of Rosh Hashanah, Yom Kippur, and Sukkot.

An observant Jew will not work on Shabbat or any major Jewish holiday except when his work might save lives. As an Orthodox Jew, I normally would have considered my place on a Jewish holiday to be in a synagogue, praying. But with New York on a war footing after 9/11, I felt I needed to be at work even on *the* High Holidays. Soldiers do not take off during war.

A SUKKAH GETS BUILT

A few days before Yom Kippur, family friend Irwin Koppelman and his son David showed up at my house unannounced to build a *sukkah* for my family for the Jewish holiday of Sukkot, which celebrates the Israelites' Exodus from Egypt as well as the fall harvest. A temporary, fragile hut in which Jews eat during the holiday, a *sukkah* is meant to be a reminder of the huts the Jews lived in while wandering in the desert after the Exodus.

Ordinarily I would have built my own *sukkah* for the family; but it seemed unlikely that I would have the time to build one this year.

I did manage to spend an hour at synagogue during the Kol Nidre service that began Yom Kippur, thanks to my close friendship with Shiya Ribowsky, who at the time was the Director of Special Projects and Senior Medical Legal Investigator for the New York City Medical Examiner's office.

He happened also to be a part-time cantor at the Brotherhood Synagogue at Gramercy Park, down the block from my office. Shiya was one of the nation's most experienced medico-legal investigators as well as a forensics consultant to the television crime series "Law and Order." As a homicide detective, I often met him at crime scenes where victims were dead on site. I ran into him at work in the days just after 9/11, and he suggested that I attend Yom Kippur services at his synagogue.

TEARS IN THE SYNAGOGUE

At 6 PM on Wednesday, September 26, I arrived at the synagogue and soon noticed Shiya entering the building with a police escort. He had been working around the clock, seven days a week. This was his first time off since 9/11.

Until now he and I had kept emotion out of our conversations, though each of us had been dealing with tremendous horrors. Conscious as we were that during Yom Kippur one routinely mourns the dead, and all too aware that our moment-to-moment

tasks involved identifying the dead from 9/11, we hugged, we cried, but we could not say a word to one another.

The moment was powerful and poignant. During those two hours in synagogue, I prayed more intensively than ever before. My emotions got the better of me as I thought of the tremendous loss of life. On that holy day, my belief in G-d was reenergized and I felt strengthened in my desire to fight evil.

Work at Ground Zero was a rescue and recovery operation until September 29, but after that, after all hope for finding additional survivors had disappeared, the sole task was the sad search for bodies.

Once discovered, the bodies had to be identified. Many had been burned sometimes beyond recognition; the chances of identifying their remains through photographs were slim. In addition to bodies, we also searched for personal items and DNA that would confirm someone's presence at the site.

The city set up two recovery locations—one at Ground Zero and the other at Staten Island's Fresh Kills Landfill. Rubble was shipped via barge to the landfill for sifting. Evidence found at both locations was then sent to what came to be the tent city for identification and analysis.

Other detectives who lived in Staten Island were assigned to spend two or three days a week at the landfill painstakingly sifting through debris from the World Trade Center in search of victims' remains or their property.

The Manhattan Medical Examiner established the tent city at the ME's office at 30th Street and First Avenue; it brought together in one place most of the existing technologies used to identify victims' remains. On and off through December, tent city workers would phone our office and ask a supervisor to round up five or so detectives for the tent city for two or three days of that week.

On September 25, two weeks after 9/11, I was sent to work at the tent city, the first of a number of stints there two days a week, twelve to sixteen hours a day. In addition, I continued to track down tips and work homicides not related to the attacks.

In sending us off for that assignment, our bosses worried about keeping our office sufficiently staffed to handle the routine murders and robberies that would crop up (though the crime rate did drop off tremendously soon after 9/11).

TENT CITY

At the tent city I sometimes joined the security detail, which meant standing on rooftops to make sure that no one, especially paparazzi with their cameras, penetrated the perimeters. For us, the site was holy, not a place to be photographed. At other times I helped to process incoming remains and sought to identify them.

My assignments at the tent city were tedious and hardly glamorous, but to me they were of overwhelming importance, a practical act mixed with a touch of holiness. For all the sadness and difficult working conditions there, we knew that those digging at the "pile" at Ground Zero experienced a far worse situation.

Facing extreme danger from toxic elements in the "pile," quite a number of workers either became seriously ill or died as a result of their exposure. No precise statistics are known for those casualties, but they are as much 9/11 victims as those who died or were injured on the day itself.

Had it not been for the paralysis that the city suffered from the effects of 9/11, press releases praising the tent city would have streamed from city offices. But everyone, city officials and the media alike, were too numb to devote much attention to our efforts.

The process at the tent city took on the feel of an assembly line: Once remains had been identified, freezer trucks preserved the body or sometimes just body parts. Bodies and body parts as well as personal items moved through a series of stations, conveyorbelt style, where they were photographed and fingerprinted.

After proper paper documentation, specimens of any item that could be used for identification were then taken for DNA

analysis. When remains were assigned to me, my task was to escort them through the various stations. Everything done at a station had to be logged in and the results recorded. In a normal homicide probe some of these tasks would have taken weeks, but by increasing manpower and working round-the-clock, the ME's office produced results in a matter of hours.

On any given day, we might have had one assignment—or ten. It pretty much depended on the progress of digging at the "pile" itself. Remarkably, I later learned from colleagues that most of the remains that passed through the tent city were identified.

For all of us, police and firemen alike, the worst moments came when the remains of one of our own were brought in to the tent city. As a sign of respect for one of our fallen colleagues, an honor guard was hastily arranged to accompany the remains from the point of recovery to the tent city.

As I think back to the recovery operation—now that nearly a decade has passed—I still get choked up when I try to describe what we first responders witnessed. If my work at the tent city did anything positive for me personally, it whetted my appetite for even deeper involvement in post-9/11 efforts to protect New York from further global Islamic terror.

I continued working in homicide but always hoped that an opportunity to join a police anti-terror unit would present itself. That opportunity came unexpectedly soon after 9/11 and it contained elements of great personal danger. That it was unexpected was easy to deal with. But that it was potentially dangerous and that I lacked prior expertise about the subject matter scared the hell out of me.

I knew guns, knives, fists, and standard "crime-fare." But I did not know anthrax except that it was incredibly lethal: The spores in a letter-sized envelope could kill the person handling the envelope and those in the vicinity.

But the opportunity to join the fight against terror was just what I had wanted. And here was a chance to track down an as yet unknown terrorist bent on committing what we presumed would be further 9/11-style terror in New York.

A CASE OF ANTHRAX

For a period of several weeks starting on September 18, 2001—a week after 9/11—seven letters containing deadly anthrax were mailed to a number of media offices and two U.S. senators. Five people were killed and seventeen others were infected.

The anthrax attacks came in two separate waves: First, five letters were sent on September 18 to ABC News, CBS News, NBC News, and the *New York Post*, all located in New York City, as well as the *National Enquirer* in Boca Raton, Florida. Then two more anthrax letters, dated October 9, were sent, addressed to two Democratic U.S. senators, Tom Daschle of South Dakota and Patrick Leahy of Vermont. At that time Daschle was Senate Majority Leader and Leahy was head of the Senate Judiciary Committee.

Soon after the first anthrax-contaminated letters were sent out, the NYPD set up a citywide task force that would deal with combating weapons of mass destruction; it sought volunteers from among the Department. My partner and I volunteered for the anthrax task force, offering me a chance to play an active role—perhaps too active, in retrospect—in the fight against terror.

But my offer met with stiff resistance from my bosses. They did not understand why a homicide detective, having worked so hard to attain that plum assignment, would take a step backward by joining a task force far beneath his highly prized existing job.

In my view the real reason was that they did not want to lose homicide detectives to lengthy "outside" assignments, further depleting office staff. Task forces could be never ending. What if the letters did not appear again for six months or even a year? My bosses cringed at the thought that I might be tied up for two or three years.

Of course, for me the anthrax task force was the chance to take on an investigatory role in the fight against terror. Without 9/11 I doubt that I would have volunteered for the dangerous assignment of interviewing those who might have been exposed to anthrax. I saw this as a great chance for me to be involved in post-9/11

follow-up. At the time, no one excluded the idea that the anthrax killer or killers might have been linked to those who committed terror against the World Trade Center.

For all my high and mighty eagerness to take on global terror, volunteering for the anthrax cases, in retrospect, seemed an awfully dumb move on my part. Putting on that hazmat protective gear that made me look like an astronaut, and being in an environment that was possibly exposed to anthrax, seemed the very definition of irrational behavior.

However, in the end I never joined the task force. The brass, concerned about depleting manpower, would simply not let me go.

ENTER COMMISSIONER KELLY

At the start of 2002 my luck improved. Michael R. Bloomberg became mayor of New York City, replacing Rudy Giuliani. Bloomberg appointed Raymond W. Kelly as the new police commissioner, one of the new mayor's first and wisest decisions. When Kelly declared that he planned to give the NYPD a proactive role in combating terror, it was music to my ears.

Bloomberg's genius in selecting Kelly was to pick a practitioner, someone who had had military and federal government experience, who had risen through the police ranks, rather than some administrator who might have known how to manage large organizations but little more.

In the aftermath of 9/11 the NYPD was consumed with identifying bodies or remains so that loved ones of the victims would have some kind of closure. The process took six months, and there was other police work to do during that period as well: "Routine" homicides, the anthrax scare, tracking down tipsters. We were so engrossed in 9/11 that little thought was given to preparing New York City for further terror attacks.

Enter Ray Kelly, the man who turned the NYPD upside down.

Kelly decided that the NYPD had to devote ample manpower and resources to protect the city against future acts of terror.

His was an uphill climb, if only because almost all of the NYPD's resources until then had been utilized to deal with conventional crime.

There had been indifference toward terrorism. Until 9/11 the NYPD had regarded terrorism as a phenomenon that occurred thousands of miles from New York City and was irrelevant to the city. Foreign terrorists had rarely targeted an American city. We simply did not believe that such horrors could happen on our shores.

Before 9/11 we had designed intellectual exercises about how we would handle terror in sensitive places, but, convinced that such scenarios would play out only in novels or Hollywood movies, we quickly filed those plans in drawers. Terror, typhoons, and earthquakes—all terrible disasters—did not seem likely to become New York events. We kept chasing after murderers and drug dealers.

Certainly Commissioner Kelly understood that by adding counterterror to the list of tasks assigned to New York cops, he was adding to their burden; but he felt it crucial that the cops chase traditional criminals (those involved in drug dealing, murder, robbery, etc.) as well as search for suspicious people and objects.

After 9/11, those of us who protected New York would have to rise to a new level of vigilance, especially near the vital landmarks of the city. Doing that would not be easy. Local law enforcement in New York and elsewhere in America was not accustomed to guarding the entrances to public buildings, conducting massive drills, or looking for suspicious objects or people.

Of course we had been concerned about crime against our subways and bridges before; but our concern toward those vital transportation links was nothing compared to what it became after 9/11.

What the commissioner understood better than anyone else was that the NYPD could not rely on the Feds or the military to come to the rescue in the event of terror against New York. With all their intelligence agencies, the Feds had not prevented 9/11 from happening. Nor could the army have done much to keep 9/11 from occurring.

To get New York up to speed, Kelly knew that he had to reorient and beef up NYPD counterterrorism and intelligence operations. Perhaps Kelly's greatest innovation was to create the Counter Terrorism Bureau within the NYPD, the first unit of its kind in local law enforcement in the nation.

The new CT Bureau reflected the new overhaul of priorities within the department: If closing cases, dealing with drugs, murders, car thefts, and the like, had been the emphasis within the NYPD in the past, now potential terror against New York became top of mind. In order to minimize casualties in the event of a terrorist act, the bureau saw as its most important task fortifying those buildings in New York that were most vulnerable to terror.

It was generally accepted that the only way of preventing terror was through good intelligence. Kelly certainly realized the value of intelligence. Revamping the NYPD Intelligence Division, Kelly took it from a Secret Service-style operation that mostly escorted and protected visiting dignitaries to one of the most sophisticated and advanced police intelligence units in the world. Among American local police enforcement, it became the gold standard.

BIRTH OF TWINS

While Commissioner Kelly was changing the face of the 40,000-member New York Police Department, I confess that I was off in my own world, devoting myself to helping Meryl out as we prepared for the birth of twins in July 2002. But the little ones had their own surprise: Jake and Talia showed up after only thirty-two weeks toward the end of May. They remained in the hospital for a month while their lungs developed and they gained weight.

JOB OFFER

In mid-June, when the twins were still in the hospital, I received a phone call from someone who identified himself as a member of the NYPD Intelligence Bureau. He had news that sounded intriguing.

The police department was establishing overseas postings for NYPD officers in order to provide on-the-spot intelligence of foreign terror attacks, and to learn as much about the methods of radical Islamic terrorists as possible.

Was I interested in an assignment in Israel? Others would go to Toronto and to Interpol in Lyons, France. My name had come up. I would be, he noted, a perfect candidate for the posting. Was I interested? Did I want to interview for the position?

The Israeli–Arab conflict had been going on since before the Jewish state was founded in 1948, with wars punctuating the six decades since statehood: The Suez War (1956); the Six Day War (1967); the Yom Kippur War (1973); the Lebanon War (1982); the Gulf War (1991); the Second Lebanon War (2006), and the Gaza War (2008–2009).

Though the Palestinian Liberation Organization had been founded in 1964, soon thereafter led by Yasser Arafat, Palestinians flexed their muscles against Israel only when they began the First Intifada, an uprising against Israeli rule in the occupied territories of the West Bank and the Gaza Strip; it lasted from 1987 to 1993. A Second Intifada began in September 2000 with violent events that included a new Palestinian tactic—suicide bombing.

In planning to send a New York police officer to Israel, Commissioner Kelly had only a general idea of what the representative might accomplish. His attitude was: Let's get boots on the ground and then let's see if we can acquire information that would be valuable in fighting terror in New York. The assignment would not be open-ended. It would be for a minimum of three months, but then if too little value was achieved, the liaison would get on the next plane back to New York.

To the Palestinians the Second Intifada was part of their ongoing struggle for an end to Israeli occupation of the West Bank and Gaza Strip and for the creation of an independent Palestinian state. The terror was designed not only to strike fear among the wider Israeli public but also to force Israel to end the occupation and accept a Palestinian state on the West Bank and in the Gaza Strip.

To the Israelis, however, the violence, including suicide bombings, shootings, knifings, and the like, amounted to little more than hate-filled terror against Israeli civilian targets, to which they were determined not to capitulate. Israel was willing to end the occupation and permit a Palestinian state to rise through negotiations but made it clear that Palestinian violence would have to cease.

When I received that phone call in June 2002 asking me whether I wanted to go to Israel, the Second Intifada was at its height.

Israeli security forces had to be prepared for bombings on any given day. For that sad reason, Israel served as a good example of an urban environment coping with terrorism on a continuing basis.

The ongoing terror against Israel was ever-present. From January to June 2002, forty suicide bombing attacks had occurred, often one or two days apart. For Israeli security officials, the fight against terror was relentless. Most of Israel had not become a war zone, but with suicide bombs going off so frequently, it certainly seemed as if the country was under full-scale attack.

I did not blame the Israeli police for the series of suicide bombings against its country nor the Israeli military or intelligence agencies. They are fantastic, working round the clock day after day, not getting paid overtime.

I had never sat in on a cabinet meeting or spoken with prime ministers, so I was not a decision-maker. I was not privy to any political considerations. But I did feel that military action against the suicide bombers could have been taken earlier than it was. Prompted by a particularly bloody suicide bombing toward the end of March 2002 the Israelis had had enough.

The March 27, 2002, Passover suicide bombing of the Park Hotel in the Mediterranean coastal town of Netanya took thirty lives, mostly elderly vacationers. Hamas, the Palestinian terror organization that has controlled the Gaza Strip since 2007, claimed responsibility for the attack. The bomber managed to penetrate the hotel's Seder, where there were 250 guests.

DEFENSIVE SHIELD

Two days later, Israel launched a major military offensive—
Operation Defensive Shield, the largest Israeli attack in the West
Bank since the 1967 Six Day War; its purpose was to take the fight
to the terrorists in the West Bank, in contrast to past efforts to
catch them en route or at a suicide bombing site.

Enough was enough. The hope was that the operation would
put an end to the numerous Israeli deaths from terrorist attacks,
especially from suicide bombings. Finally, the Israelis had taken
the initiative against the terrorists with Operation Defensive
Shield; they had also decided to build a security fence along the
West Bank and Jerusalem to forestall suicide bombers from reach-
ing Israeli targets.

The Israeli incursion into Ramallah put Palestinian leader
Yasser Arafat under siege; assaults then occurred against five other
large cities in the West Bank: Tulkarm, Kalkilya, Bethlehem, Jen-
in, and Nablus.

As a result of the military operation, the number of suicide
bombings dropped in 2002 from twenty-two in February and
March to twelve in April and May, and from the first half of
2002 to the second half the number of suicide bombings dropped
from forty-three to thirteen. The yearly number fell from 55 in
2002 to 25 the following year as the number of Israeli fatalities
from suicide bombings fell from 220 in 2002 to 142 in 2003.

The fence also had an immediate and profound effect on the
number of suicide bombing attacks, giving millions of Israelis a
breather that has lasted into the spring of 2010.

In contrast, from September 2000, when the Second Inti-
fada began, and August 2003, terrorists carried out 73 attacks that
killed 293 Israelis and wounded 1,950. But from August 2003
when the first section of the fence was completed until the end of
2006, West Bank terrorists carried out twelve attacks, killing 64
Israelis and injuring 445.

The intelligence man's phone call caught me off guard, but
I was not surprised that my background and reputation as the

NYPD "Jewish Detective" had led to his phoning. Yet the timing of the call could not have been worse for me.

Ever since 9/11 all that I had wanted was for the phone to ring, asking me to join an anti-terrorist task force, or to use my special knowledge of the Jewish community in New York and of the State of Israel in some other way to help protect New York City.

Now the phone had rung. Destiny was calling, and I wanted desperately to say yes to the intelligence man; but a quirk of fate led me to pause. The timing was all wrong for such a major upheaval in my life.

Unable to believe what I was about to say, I felt forced to give the biggest no I had ever proclaimed in my life. My newborn twins were still in a hospital neonatal unit, I explained to him, and for the time being I had to focus on their recovery.

I did not even suggest that once the twins were safely out of the hospital I would consider the offer seriously. That was precisely what I was thinking, but I was too preoccupied with events at the hospital to verbalize such a thought. So, I basically closed the door to the offer.

While the twins recuperated, I had largely forgotten the phone conversation. In early July my phone rang again. It was the same caller with the same question. By this date the twins were home, but I told my caller that unfortunately their health remained fragile. Again I told him no thanks.

In mid-July Jake and Talia had gone back to the hospital for follow-up monitoring. They received a clean bill of health; doctors had no long-term medical concerns for them and, in fact, predicted that we had future athletes on our hands. We were thrilled and most thankful and ready to go home and enjoy our family.

On the Friday afternoon of that same week the third phone call came; but at this stage my personal situation had changed for the better. Hearing that, the intelligence man renewed the offer, making clear that if I said yes this time, the department would want me to begin the assignment right away. He did not have to say it, but for obvious reasons, I was on the short list. I had to put up or shut up!

Time was of the essence. There would be no prior language training, no briefings on what to look for once in place. I would be flying by the seat of my pants.

Undoubtedly weary from two previous turndowns, the intelligence people were unlikely to keep the offer on hold if I said no this time. They wanted the posting filled at once. Although willing to say yes, I insisted that I be allowed to run the proposition by my wife. My caller grudgingly agreed.

Meryl and I finally had a chance to discuss the offer over Friday night Shabbat dinner. After the untimely death of Meryl's mother from cancer at age fifty-five in January 2002, her pregnancy, the twins' premature birth, their hospitalization, our heads now were clear for the first time in months.

We were brutally honest with each other. It was not a black-and-white matter; there were reasons for me to stay, reasons to go. A big negative was that the department would not let my family join me in Israel. I would have to be away from Meryl and the children for months at a time.

To those who watched CNN and saw the violence coming from Israel, it probably made sense to them for me to leave my family behind. We had watched CNN too and we appreciated that Jerusalem was not as peaceful as Boca Raton and Tel Aviv was not as tranquil as Waikiki.

Perhaps all of us should just stay put. Meryl and I were at a very good point in Long Beach. We were very happy with our life and friends. Our children, thankfully, were healthy. Our careers were going great. As a Second Grade Homicide Detective, I had reached what I thought was the pinnacle of success at the NYPD.

Meryl was doing well at her job at Lehman Brothers. She was also co-president of the Lido Beach Synagogue Sisterhood. We loved where we lived.

But in the end, we decided to go to a war zone. To others, what we were about to embark upon made no sense, but, as it turned out, it was the best decision of our lives.

Then there was the gnawing question of how much cooperation the Israel police would give me. Would they "let me in"?

Would they share information with me? And would I be able to get that information as quickly as New York would want it, which would be immediately after a terror event in Israel?

Unable to answer these questions with complete confidence, I still viewed the assignment in Israel as a calling, as destiny more than coincidence. Given the trajectory of my police career and my deep connection to Jewish and Israeli matters, the assignment seemed to have been hand-picked for me.

SAYING YES TO ISRAEL

We both sensed that this was a special opportunity—for me and for the whole family. If I could just convince the Intelligence Division that my family had to come with me, I would say yes, simple as that. When I urged them to let Meryl and the children accompany me, they predictably balked; and so then I told them I would personally be responsible for their safety. That got them. They agreed and the Dzikansky family was off to Israel.

CHAPTER 6

Meet and Greet:
Making Contact with
the Israel Police

My assignment in Israel, delayed by the birth of our twins, was about to happen. If I was breaking ground for the New York Police Department, my overseas liaison assignment would be equally unprecedented for Israel's police.

To be sure, New York police officers had in the past worked Israeli cases. In the early 1980s I had been part of a Drug Enforcement Administration (DEA) task force that investigated an Israeli drug ring based in New York, whom we later arrested and convicted of dealing drugs.

The NYPD had also attended an occasional seminar on police matters in Israel. NYPD Intelligence was responsible for providing security for visiting Israeli dignitaries and had helped secure the Israeli consulate, as it did all foreign consulates in New York City.

But until I was given the assignment to represent the NYPD in Israel, the New York Police Department had had no permanent physical presence in the Jewish state. Because of 9/11, however, the times had changed. New York had become the most vulnerable terrorist target in the world, and so its main law enforcement agency—the NYPD—deserved to have a presence at the front lines. Certainly Israel was on the front lines.

Other countries had assigned police representatives to Israel, but they were attached to their embassies, not embedded, as

I would be, in the Israel police itself. I became the first person representing another country's police to sit side by side with the Israel police. My counterparts, on the other hand, were considered part of their country's diplomatic staff.

My marching orders from the New York Police Department were not very specific.

Even after 9/11 the notion that it might be possible to mitigate casualties at a suicide bombing event had not been sufficiently understood or appreciated: The only measures that were employed focused on gathering intelligence to prevent suicide bombings; they were not designed to reduce casualties once an event occurred.

Almost no thought was given to what people and institutions could do beforehand to minimize casualties at a terrorist incident. But when Commissioner Ray Kelly took office in 2002, he mandated us in NYPD Counter Terrorism and Intelligence to widen our mission: Not only were we to try to prevent terror, but we had to look for ways to reduce the impact of terror if it occurred.

I did not believe that the commissioner had sent me to Israel only to prevent acts of terror in New York by getting information on terror cells that had connection to the city, though that would certainly be in the forefront of my mandate.

There were times during my stay in Israel when the NYPD would forward a name to me that I passed on to the Israel police— someone, let's say, who had been living in Queens and associated with a global Islamic terror group. The terror suspect just might be planning an attack in New York.

Before passing on a name, I would always ask the NYPD to supply me with some piece of intelligence that the Israel police would appreciate having. Only with this kind of quid pro quo, I felt, would I be able to acquire sensitive material from the Israelis. I am very proud that I developed special Israeli contacts, especially since from time to time my relationship with them paid off beyond anyone's expectations.

The key part of my assignment in Israel would be eliciting from Israeli suicide bombing sites lessons that, once learned and

integrated into the NYPD, could reduce casualties. The NYPD and Israel police agreed that I would not engage in any enforcement role. I would not take part in any police action to apprehend a suspected terrorist; my role would be purely an intelligence one.

The way to learn lessons from suicide bombings, I knew, was to develop as many contacts with the significant Israel police units as possible. The question was: Would those contacts actually cooperate with me and pass on valuable information for the NYPD?

As part of my preparation for the assignment, the NYPD first sent me to Israel in November for ten days, a kind of "meet and greet" with the Israel police.

FRUSTRATED BY A SUICIDE BOMBING

On Thursday, November 21, 2002, the fifth day of my visit there, I had the TV on in my Tel Aviv hotel room while getting ready for the day's meetings. I learned from CNN that there had just been a suicide bombing on a bus in Jerusalem. Eleven people had been killed and fifty wounded. The bus had been filled with Israeli passengers, including schoolchildren, traveling toward the center of the city during rush hour. The terrorist wing of Hamas claimed responsibility for the attack.

I felt frustrated. Here I was, assigned to gather intelligence on Israeli-targeted terror, a suicide bus bombing had occurred while I was in the country, and I could do no more than watch television like any civilian, unable to gather even a tiny morsel of information beyond what TV commentators were saying. Constrained by those limitations, I might as well as have been sitting behind my desk in New York monitoring the Internet.

It was little comfort that I had not been expected to take up the assignment during this preliminary visit, but a part of me asked: "What are you going to do when this happens and you are on the job in Israel? How are you going to go about reporting from firsthand sources rather than what is on CNN or in *Ha'aretz*, the daily newspaper often called the *New York Times* of Israel? You are

going to have to show some real value to the people back home or you'll be headed back there all too quickly."

I laughed when I heard that some Israelis were suspicious of my being sent to Israel. They thought I might have been a spy. Once they got to know me, though, they laughed at this notion too.

It was during that visit that I met someone from the Israel police who would play a crucial role in helping me to perform my assignment well. His name is Gil Kleiman. I believe we got along so well because we both came from the same neighborhood in Brooklyn, and we both shared the same outlook on life, an attitude that has no tolerance for cheaters and liars. We grew up, at different times, one block away from each other but did not know each other during our childhoods.

A YOUNG DE NIRO

Gil, who bore a certain resemblance to a young Robert De Niro, had been born in Flatbush, Brooklyn. He had gone to a yeshiva, then public school, graduating from George Washington University in Washington, D.C., in 1980 as a history major. That July he moved to Israel to join his parents, two brothers, and two sisters.

In November 1980 he had joined the Israeli army, serving as a combat engineer and demolitions expert. Three years later he joined the Israel police; in 1987 he obtained a law degree from Bar Ilan University near Tel Aviv. Back in the Israel police, he spent the next decade in the Violent Crimes Unit, investigating Nazi war crimes, solving drug-related crime, and conducting murder investigations.

In 1997 he moved over to the Security Department of the police, advising banks and the national bus system, among others, how to maximize their security. Four years later he became the police spokesman for the foreign press, staying in that post until 2005.

I was introduced to Gil after he finished giving a speech to foreign security officials from their respective embassies. He was

told that I would be the NYPD's liaison in Israel. Asking each other about our backgrounds, we realized we had grown up in the same neighborhood.

My showing up in Israel did not surprise Gil. The FBI and CIA had a presence there, and now the NYPD would as well; this was the new stepped-up security world after 9/11. Nor was Gil surprised that I had come to Israel; the Jewish state had become a laboratory for terror, so if someone wanted to learn the actual face of terror, the suicide bombings and the way the country responded, he had to come to Israel.

I found the Israeli police officers who hosted me gracious; they made me feel welcome. They all knew my background, that I had family living in Israel, that it was not my first trip there. They also knew what I had come for, not simply to exchange information about crime in our respective countries; I could have done that by visiting Israel once a month or even every three months. They were very much aware that I had come to learn how to combat terror and reduce its impact on New York.

They all loved New York and many had been there and visited Ground Zero. Our 9/11 experience and how we were coping captivated them. My New York roots made me intriguing to them.

During that trip I established contact with the International Relations unit and the Interpol office within the Israel police. Everyone was hospitable but I knew the real test would occur only upon my return to Israel in January. I made no effort to touch base with the American Embassy in Tel Aviv, since I did not have diplomatic status. For me, the only way to do my job was on my own.

HONORING BOUNDARIES

Even during this "meet and greet" visit I would have loved to interrogate one or more terrorists whom the Israelis had captured. But before pursuing that idea, I decided to refrain from pressing my Israel police contacts. I did not want to ask for too many things so early in the game. I felt that I was better off maintaining boundaries.

I wanted to wait until the Israel police grew comfortable with my being around and doing my job. One quick lesson I learned: Knowing those boundaries made it easier for the Israel police to deal with me openly.

One boundary of great importance for me was geographical. For the most part I would have to steer clear of the Israeli-held territories, even though suicide bombings did occur there. I would have to confine myself to such bombings within Israel proper and avoid the West Bank and Gaza Strip, where the Israeli army and not the Israeli police were in charge. Should the Israel police bomb squad enter the West Bank, I could enter with them; but without an armored car, I doubted that I would want to go.

At any rate, there would be little in the form of lessons learned that I could convey to New York were I to venture into Israeli-held territories: The West Bank was not a clear-cut urban environment and hence vastly different from New York City; moreover, the role of the IDF in securing "crime scenes" after suicide bombings meant that I would be sending along to New York intelligence on military methods, not police ones, a case of mixing apples with oranges.

To respect Israel police boundaries even further, I made a point of never taking photographs. I was a guest and no one would want a guest to start taking photos in his home. I vowed that when I was able to visit bombing sites, I would not touch potential evidence. I had to respect that these bombing sites were Israeli crime scenes.

I promised myself that, when at a suicide bombing site, I would listen, keep a low profile and seek briefings from key Israeli security people at a time that would not interfere with their urgent work.

Always, the Israeli police whom I met wanted to know what had brought me to Israel. I gave a two-word answer: "9/11." I told them that I wanted to do my best while in their country to help make sure that we don't have another such attack against New York. If I could make one percent difference in preparing the city in case of another terrorist event, I would feel that I had accomplished my mission.

In general Israelis have no constraint in telling you how to do your job. When they heard that I was a New York police of-

ficer, they felt free to enlighten me on how the NYPD should deal with terror. Over and over again, I heard the same suggestion: The NYPD should organize security guards at every skyscraper, every landmark, every department store, every restaurant, and every theater at Times Square.

I listened politely, but I explained that pursuing that strategy was unrealistic. We wished that we could place security guards at all the sites they mentioned. I knew and appreciated how valuable Israeli security guards had been at suicide bombing sites and how they had heroically saved many lives.

But we did not have an abundance of job-seeking ex-military types willing to work for low pay. With so much terror, Israel had placed security guards at many of its public places because terrorists had been targeting restaurants, coffee houses, railroad stations, and bus stations, frequently several times a week, and sometimes more than once a day. If terrorists began blowing themselves up at our public places in New York, we would urgently have to find professionally trained security guards.

Prior to 2002, the NYPD had based its counterterror strategy on being reactive, not proactive, but it was now trying to change that way of operation.

I was horrified to learn that suicide bombings in Israel had been as frequent as they had been. I wanted to believe that, had they been occurring at a similar rate and with the same level of casualties in New York or anywhere in the United States, those of us responsible for security, including our government leaders, would have gotten sufficiently infuriated to figure out how to stop the bombings.

Back in New York after my November 2002 trip, I began planning immediately for taking up my new assignment. I tried not to be naïve. I knew that the Israel police would not automatically turn information over to me because I seemed like a nice guy, or I was Jewish, or I had spent a fair amount of time in Israel.

I realistically realized that I had to offer them something in exchange for their intelligence, a tit for tat that would be challenging.

TIT FOR TAT

I still asked myself a simple question: How do I show the Israel police that when they see me in the morning at Israel National Police Headquarters, other than bringing a box of *burekas* (baked or fried filled pasty), I really am of value to them?

I racked my brain trying to figure out what would entice the Israel police to cooperate with me. Then it came to me: I sensed that they would be eager to get help with criminal cases involving Israelis in New York. Offering that kind of assistance was a good place for me to start.

My assignment in Israel began soon after the New Year of 2003. I was to go alone at first and my family would come over in a month.

Before arrival in Israel, I set up points of contact within the NYPD so when the Israel police had questions about criminal investigations I was in a strong position to offer that help.

I had a good working knowledge of and great contacts within the various investigative units of the NYPD and District Attorney's office. I knew whom to ask and how to seek and get assistance. I was not limited to just contacts within the NYPD; I would reach out to other agencies in and around New York City such as various District Attorneys' offices and other municipal police departments.

I felt confident that I could come up with information an Israeli police officer needed: And indeed, soon after I arrived in Israel, the Israel police were looking for two Israeli perps believed to be hiding in New York. One was wanted for the murder of an Israeli national in Israel, the other for the physical abuse of an Israeli child.

The Israel police asked me if I could get information and help in locating these alleged felons. It was tough for the Israelis to get immediate information from a "foreign" agency, but an American cop would have a much easier time calling another American cop for help.

I knew that I could break through all the bureaucracy by making the right phone calls to the right contacts and take the information back to the Israelis.

I acted as an investigative conduit, contacting Brooklyn South Homicide for information about the alleged murderer and the NYPD Intelligence's Marshall's Fugitive Unit for the alleged child abuser.

When I learned that the alleged murderer had left New York, the information helped the Israel police refocus their case. And thanks to my contacts in NYPD, the alleged child abuser was picked up in Brooklyn to be extradited to Israel.

I knew after these cases that my Israeli police contacts would look forward to seeing me. I worked about thirty cases like this one during my assignment in Israel, many with positive results. Among them was my helping the Israel police to locate and recover rare Judaica that had been stolen from a Jerusalem library and ended up in New York. The NYPD was able to perform an undercover buy and recover the stolen property.

My actual assignment, of course, was gathering intelligence on suicide bombings in Israel, and the best way to do this was to get to the scene of a suicide bombing as quickly as possible. Neither the Israel police nor the NYPD had set up a concrete protocol for how to do this. I would have to learn on my own.

I was playing beat the clock, because a suicide bombing scene would no longer have relevance for me as an investigator two or three hours after the bomb went off. I would have to arrive at the site within the first ninety minutes in order to get a good look at the crime scene and to garner information from police on the ground. That meant negotiating roadblocks, giving the impression that my car was an official police vehicle.

I grew reasonably optimistic that I would be able to get to suicide bombing sites once someone in the Israel police Special Operations unit was assigned to me as a point of contact. That sounded nice in theory, but in practice it did not work because my assigned contact and I were never near enough to each other to organize our traveling together to a site, so the urgency of getting to the scene quickly took precedence over the coordination of our meeting at some distant point from the site.

I would just get to the site on my own. The Israel police had made clear that upon reaching the site, I would be able to get in and move around. No one would be assigned to me. No one would hold my hand. I would have to observe on my own, ask my questions, and keep a low profile.

Of course, the reality was that if I arrived at a suicide bombing site on my own, I risked the possibility that I would be stopped by Israeli security people who did not know me and who would be unwilling to check with a higher authority.

The trick for me was to make myself known in advance to anybody and everybody who was a critical player, so that once I arrived at the scene, someone would be there to vouch for me as the NYPD's man on the spot.

Gil Kleiman became my best contact and introduced me to many people within his organization.

The one thing I never worried about was my level of enthusiasm for the assignment. Working full-time on curbing terror got my juices going. It was time to get on the plane, fly to Israel, and learn as much as I could about global terror.

CHAPTER 7

Seat Belts, Cell Phones, and Traffic Jams

No place was better for learning about Islamic terror than a nation that had become one of the most active laboratories for suicide bombings in the world. I couldn't wait to begin watching and listening.

On January 1, 2003, anticipating my new assignment, the NYPD placed me in the Intelligence Division. Two days later I arrived in Israel on the day that marked my twenty-year anniversary with the NYPD. Most police officers dream of making it to the twenty-year mark so that they can retire with a full pension. I had other dreams, and to fulfill them I chose to remain with the NYPD.

Upon landing in Israel, the first person I phoned was Gil Kleiman. He and I were fast becoming close friends, which put him in an awkward spot when it came to helping me with police intelligence information.

Gil told me right off the bat that he would not—indeed could not—give me any secret intelligence that would compromise his relationship to the Israel police. I am not your informant, he let me know with an air of finality, adding: I will not pass on inside information to you. My first responsibility is to the Israeli police.

Given Gil's role as an Israeli police spokesman, he enjoyed frequent proximity to police brass who sometimes met with the Israeli prime minister (with Gil attending). At those sessions, Gil gleaned top-secret intelligence on terror that would have unquestionably proven quite valuable to me.

He sometimes possessed details of a terror cell that was the target of an ongoing Israeli investigation—information that I

would have loved to have sent on to New York. Accordingly, it was quite frustrating and disappointing to me to have such a good friend who felt unable to give me the full intelligence picture. Still, I respected that limitation and was able to get what I needed through the proper channels that I developed while in Israel.

Eventually, his willingness to introduce me to everyone who showed up at bombing sites and who was important for me to know provided immeasurably useful.

When I called the National Police Headquarters in Jerusalem the day of my arrival to inform them that I planned to show up for my first day of work on Sunday, a female police officer was on the other end of the line. She seemed startled by my plan to start working in two days. Didn't I want to take some time to get settled, she asked kindly?

I thought to myself that the NYPD had not sent me all this way on such a vital mission just to "settle in" during my first days here. I had a great advantage in settling in: I moved to Ra'anana, the same town where my American cousins Reva and Jeff, who had moved to Israel in the 1980s, lived. They were invaluable in making my and later my family's transition smooth.

No, I told the police officer, I would be there Sunday morning bright and early. I always felt someone was perched on my shoulder, saying, "You didn't go to Israel to be on vacation. This is not a promotion for you where you can goof off. Get to work."

Showing up on that Sunday morning at Israel's National Police Headquarters, a set of buildings in the shadow of the Mount of Olives and Mount Scopus in the northeastern part of Jerusalem, I got in touch with a policewoman who was to be my point of contact in the Interpol section of the Israel police. She made sure to take me around the headquarters, introducing me to a whole variety of police officers. Her English was perfect.

The first Israeli police whom I met did not know what to expect from me. They did not quite know how to interact with an American police officer embedded in their national police organization.

If they thought of Americans as laid back, weak-willed, perhaps even a little soft, I probably surprised them. Even within the NYPD culture I was part of a group of detectives for whom the word "no" was not an option. If asked to perform a task, I did it, no matter how dangerous, how grisly, how unpleasant.

On that first day, with the goal of fitting in, I had dressed casually, button-down shirt, slacks, and a pair of loafers, no jacket, knowing that Israelis rarely wear jackets and ties.

I had brought my NYPD badge but not my police uniform, which I wore only at formal police events in New York. I never wore the badge—just showed it to curious Israelis.

No Israeli police officer suggested that I wear an Israeli police uniform. It was clear that I was from New York City, that I had a separate existence from the Israeli police. The last thing the Israeli police would want me to do was to go native.

In everything I did and said, I had to remember just who it was that I represented. Certainly, I wanted to be a good partner to the Israelis, but the partnership had to be kept at a certain distance.

MY SEAT BELT AND CELL PHONE

I was excited to hear my contact suggest that we leave headquarters and drive to my new office. Getting into the driver's seat of my rented car, not putting on my seat belt (a habit I retained from my police days in New York), I heard my cell phone ring and took the call.

It was once standard operating procedure for anyone with the NYPD not to use a seat belt while driving: At any time you might have to jump out of a car to collar a perp in the midst of committing a crime, or escaping from it.

I looked over at my Israeli contact seated in the front passenger seat and noticed her stern face. She seemed to hint that I had just violated 100 Israeli laws. I had no idea what I had done, or not done!

"What is this?" she said to me quietly but forcefully, as if she were the teacher and I was the guilty student. "We don't use our

cell phones when we are driving, and we don't go without our seat belts." Now don't get me wrong. I believe in obeying the law. I just had no idea that I was in violation of two traffic infractions, and so soon after my arrival at police headquarters.

I put my cell phone away, promising never to use it in my car again (I would get a hands-free gizmo), and I buckled up my seat belt, feeling deeply embarrassed. What is it with these Israelis, I asked myself? Why was this nice young woman acting like a school marm, putting me down for what in New York passed as minor traffic violations?

That was almost certainly one of the first times in my career that I had worn a seat belt. I knew I would need some time to adjust to a different culture, a different way of doing things.

In time I came to believe that using a seat belt was not a bad thing at all, especially considering how crazy Israeli drivers are.

We arrived at my new office, located in a nearby police dormitory. To my utter surprise, I was not being given an office in police headquarters, but one in a building a two-minute drive away—on French Hill, the next ridge north of Mount Scopus. The signal was all too clear: The Israeli police wanted me at some distance from them.

My new office seemed sparse but adequate. The commander of the police dormitory greeted me and began showing me around. His English was competent. He pointed out the lunch room and the synagogue. It was the first time I had seen a synagogue in a police facility. Then he pointed out the men's dormitory, which was separated from the women's.

I decided to make a joke and hoped that this time I did not transgress some other Israeli law! "That's pretty cool," I began. "So let me understand this. First I go to the female dormitory, then to the synagogue to ask forgiveness? Or do I go to the synagogue first to pray to get into the female dormitory?" He was a good sport, with a decent sense of humor. He actually thought my little joke was very funny—or at least he said so.

My police contact left me on my own so that I could settle into my office. Traveling around the country to suicide bombing

sites, I knew I would be on my own; but inside police headquarters I was not going to take many initiatives, at least not at the start. I made a point of going through my point of contact to let her know what I was doing at all times.

There would have to be some "hurry up and wait" time but I was confident, based on the initial friendliness shown me, that I would get the cooperation I needed. The only question was how quickly that would come about and would it be enough to satisfy my bosses back in New York.

One question I did not ask was whether I should carry a weapon. During my November visit to Israel I raised the subject of my carrying a gun with the Israel police. We all agreed that I would not be armed, since I was not going to be in an enforcement position. I did not know the lay of the land and also needed work to perfect my Hebrew. I would just have to be unarmed and rely on my street smarts.

I would do my best to avoid getting into a spot where having a gun would have been handy.

My New York City police colleagues had asked me if I planned to carry a weapon when in Israel. I said no. One officer even said: "Let me understand this, Morty. You're going to be the only Jew in Israel without a gun?"

"You're damned right," I replied. My sense was that the Israeli police would not want me armed; nor would I want to carry a weapon in a foreign country.

But sometimes I wished I were carrying. On several occasions I had to rush home in the middle of the night after responding to a bus bombing in Jerusalem to complete my reports for New York. I drove home via route 443, which is partly in Israel and partly in the West Bank; it was a dangerous road, the target of multiple shootings and tossing of Molotov cocktails. But it was the quickest way to my computer. I certainly would have felt more secure with a weapon on me.

For my twenty years in New York, whether in a dangerous area or a safe one, I had carried a gun. Facing a potentially violent situation, I tended to be confrontational. So it certainly would have proven challenging to confront a terrorist unarmed!

But my reluctance to carry a weapon was confirmed when I learned of an Israeli civilian who had a face-to-face encounter with a would-be suicide bomber at the West Bank Jewish settlement of Ariel on October 27, 2002. The civilian and the bomber wound up struggling on the floor of a gas station.

Trying to do what he thought was the right thing, he did not shoot the bomber in the head, as he should have; instead he shot him in the chest, accidentally igniting the explosives and killing three Israelis. The lesson that I learned from that horrific event was all too clear: You needed training to take down a terrorist. While undeniably a hero, the Israeli civilian who shot at the Ariel suicide bomber had caused a tragedy for nearby Israelis. I knew how to shoot a terrorist, but there were different rules of engagement and protocols here.

That first day of work in Israel had gone smoothly except for my cell phone and seat belt infractions. I hit the road for home at the end of the day feeling good. I still didn't know how the job would develop, but at least I had started to make contacts within the Israel police. For now I just wanted to get home and start unpacking.

TRAFFIC JAM

That was not to be. At 6:15 PM I set out for my apartment north of Tel Aviv. Upon reaching Highway 4, which runs from southern Israel to Haifa, I came upon a traffic jam. Nothing surprising here. Though Israel has "only" 7.3 million people, it seemed as if everyone owned a car and got on the road at the same time.

To my surprise, and disappointment, the traffic was at a standstill, a veritable parking lot. "What the hell is going on here?" I said to myself. Turning on the radio, I heard an anchor speaking nervously and rapidly in Hebrew, most of which I could understand. According to the anchor, there had been a double suicide bombing at the old bus station in south Tel Aviv. It was 6:30 PM.

Like almost all suicide bombings in Israel, this one was unexpected (I hadn't been aware of any warnings); it was also tragic and gruesome. Two Palestinian suicide bombers had blown themselves up at a pedestrian mall, killing 15 Israelis and 8 foreigners, with another 120 people wounded.

The pedestrian mall had been crowded with shoppers and laborers returning from work that day. Just before 6:30 PM the first bomber had set off his explosives at a bus stop on a street parallel to the mall. The second bomber struck thirty seconds later at a coffee house a block from the first bomb.

The double bombing scenario was particularly tragic: One bomber blew himself up in a crowded area and a second one, hoping to maximize casualties, specifically aiming at first responders, detonated his bomb shortly thereafter.

DO I HATE PALESTINIAN SUICIDE BOMBERS?

Though I was stuck in traffic, or perhaps because of it, my mind wandered to just what kind of person could calmly (or even nervously) wake up one morning, strap on a belt of explosives, and head for a place where he would blow himself up, taking as many others with him as possible.

Did I hate these Palestinian Arab suicide bombers? The natural instinct of anyone who values life, including Israeli and Jewish life, would be to say yes. It's hard for me to feel anything but hatred toward anyone who would find pleasure in killing my wife, children, me, or countless others in Israel.

I found the attitude of terrorist leaders particularly galling and hypocritical. These leaders boasted of sending young martyrs to their death but never did they send their own children into the fray as suicide bombers. What was that all about? I could only assume that when it came to their children, these leaders valued life over death, whereas in the case of any other Palestinian Arab's children, death trumped life.

Just as I analyzed the horrific and tragic bombing sites that suicide bombers left behind, I tried coolly to analyze just what kind of person accepted a mission so irrational and unspeakable to any rational person.

Were the suicide bombers, through their deeds, hoping to fulfill something that was missing in their lives? Perhaps they believed that their families and acquaintances thought them unworthy and did not pay them sufficient honor but if they went out with a bang, everyone would pay tribute to their martyrdom. It was all such nonsense, but suicide bombers and their supporters glorified death over life and the worst thing was that there were hundreds of other future martyrs willing to fall on their swords, or to be more precise, detonate their explosive devices.

It was a heavy price to pay for such a reminder, but every Palestinian suicide bombing illustrated, as no other human could, that Israelis and Jews and all other rational people glorified life over death!

For Israelis hearing of this latest suicide bombing in Tel Aviv, their first priority was to reach for their cell phones and try to contact loved ones (often unsuccessfully, because the cell phone lines could not handle so many simultaneous calls).

"What the hell do I do now?" I thought the answer was obvious: Get to the site of the bombings as quickly as possible.

How ironic: Here I was ending my first day as the NYPD representative in Israel, stationed "in country" to learn as much as I could about terror against Israel, and before I could unpack the terrorists had struck. I had to try to get to the bombing site as quickly as I could. There would be much I could learn there; but I was stuck in a traffic jam created by the police diverting traffic away from the bombings.

I weighed my options for getting to the site, none of them good. Had I already been assigned a police contact who could help me get to a bombing site, I surely would have sought him out on my cell phone.

But earlier in the day the Israeli police had spoken only vaguely about hooking me up with a police contact perhaps within

the next few days; he might escort me to the site or, if I showed up on my own, he would give me immediate access, I was told. I knew the person's name but did not have his cell phone number.

So, left to my own devices, I realized that I would have to get to the site on my own. Ordinarily, if the traffic were running normally, it would have taken me thirty minutes to get to the bombing site. But stuck in the traffic jam, I realized I was going nowhere.

I realized despondently that even if by some miracle I managed to get to the bombing site, I had no way of identifying myself once there. I had no Israeli documentation that certified that I was attached to the Israel police. All that I had was my NYPD badge and an ID card that identified me as an NYPD detective working with the Israel police. I doubted that that would get me inside the ropes.

All that I could do was phone the NYPD and tell them that a suicide bombing had occurred in Israel, providing only the details that I had gleaned from listening to the radio. I felt like a rookie all over again. I spoke to one of the higher ups in the Intelligence Division at the NYPD. Surely he could tell the panic in my voice that comes from feeling useless. I felt trapped. I knew in my heart that there was something I should be doing other than sitting in a traffic jam. I was angry and frustrated.

It was one thing to seem like a rookie cop when you were in fact a rookie. When I was a rookie patrolman in Crown Heights, a man once approached me and screamed that he had just seen his car that had been stolen three hours earlier.

Getting on the police radio, I tried to give a description of the car, but anyone listening to me would have known that I was not comfortable speaking over the radio. I did not know north from south. I must have sounded thoroughly confused. But this was twenty years later, and I was supposed to know how to act creatively in order to extricate myself from situations like this one. Still, I felt like a rookie.

Instead of just sitting in my car waiting for the traffic jam to break up, I should have gone on the shoulder of the road and driven as far as I could. Then I should have searched for the first emergency vehicle and driven behind it to the site. If anyone had

stopped my car, I would explain that I was on duty for the NYPD embedded with the Israel police, and that I needed to get to the bombing site. I would have been like the Dalmatian chasing after the fire truck.

So bewildered was I on this day that at a certain point I drove onto an exit ramp and almost wound up in a not-so-friendly Arab village. "Now I'm really fucked," I said to myself. "They're going to hold me captive and demand a ransom." I hastily made a U-turn and got back on the highway.

The traffic remained at a standstill. The one consolation was that by getting off the highway and getting back on, I had somehow wound up moving forward a decent amount. Eventually, I arrived home at 7:30 PM. I felt useless.

I watched the news, read details of the incident on the Internet, and again called the NYPD to let them know that I would send in a basic report, meaning that it would all be from open sources. I was still disappointed with myself and I guess it showed: The voice at the other end of the phone urged, "Morty, calm down." I was not calm.

I was on my first day on the job: It had begun in a police dormitory in Jerusalem and wound up with me almost driving into an Arab village. My assignment from the NYPD was to gather intelligence on terror; here was a major terror incident and I was stuck in traffic.

I promised myself that if in the future I got caught in a traffic jam when a suicide bombing was occurring, I would get to the site by hook or by crook. If I had to commandeer a cab, whatever I had to do, I would get there.

And, indeed after that first catastrophe, on each trip to a suicide bombing site I would get my car to the side of the road, put on my flashers, and find an ambulance, a police car, a news truck, anyone who was going to the site, and drive behind one of them.

The next suicide bombing occurred two months later, on March 5, on a bus in Haifa along Israel's Mediterranean coast. Seventeen people were killed and 53 wounded in the bombing in the Carmel section of Haifa. Bodies lay scattered on the road.

I was in Jerusalem when I heard about the attack. My instinct was to get to the scene as quickly as I could, but it was a three-hour drive. I knew that would have been too late to get there and process the scene.

Although I chose not to go to that scene, I did get very pertinent information.

THE LETTER

By then I had established some good contacts within the Israel police and one faxed me a copy of a letter that was found near the suicide bomber's remains immediately after the letter was discovered, and long before any other U.S. law enforcement agency, including the FBI, knew of its existence.

The note, I was told, handwritten in Arabic, praised the "glorious" 9/11 attack on the "two big buildings in New York." I decided that the NYPD needed to know about the note, especially the suicide bomber's obsession with 9/11.

I sent a copy of the letter to the NYPD Intelligence Division, which then had it translated into English. The translated letter was put into Commissioner Ray Kelly's hands within hours. As a result, the NYPD had information nearly in real time that it could act upon.

And that information could be highly significant.

Let's say that this suicide bomber had come from Hebron in the West Bank. Once we knew that he had been thinking about 9/11 when he blew himself up, we would want to check to find out if he had a relative or friend living in New York or its surroundings who might be planning a similar thing in New York.

If that friend or relative existed, we would want to track him down immediately. I never found out whether the NYPD actually located such a person, but I knew that the matter was thoroughly investigated.

Anything that established a connection between a suicide bomber in Israel and the City of New York was a first-rate piece of evidence. When trying to track down would-be terrorists thousands of miles away from New York, it can be crucial to look

for the minute, granular nexus between a suicide bombing in Israel and New York City.

Having obtained the letter immediately, a feather in my cap, I was able to show the first proof of my value to the NYPD. In time, the note was released to the wider public.

I had been in Israel for only three months when America seemed on the verge of invading Iraq. The Bush administration had become convinced that deposing its leader, Saddam Hussein, said to have close ties to al-Qaeda, would deal a crushing blow to worldwide terrorism.

And so once again there was talk that Saddam would use his Scuds to inflict damage on Israel as revenge for the expected American invasion.

As Israeli officials urged citizens to keep their gas masks close at hand, I was very concerned, persuaded that the Israelis would have issued the gas mask order only if a war was in the offing. The gas masks that were issued for Jake and Talia, who were only ten months old, resembled plastic body bags. The thought of having to use them made my skin crawl.

In 1991 I had been on my own, a bachelor cop helping out the IDF while evading Scud missiles. But this time I had responsibilities I did not have then: Meryl and the children were with me, and we would have to endure the Scuds together.

Why had I exposed my family to this danger? I had no good answer—only that I felt an attachment to Israel. I doubted that, had I been anywhere else overseas, I would have felt obligated to keep my family in Israel despite the impending war. Still, I was very nervous and so was New York.

In the days before the American attack, which occurred on March 20, one of Commissioner Kelly's senior aides told me that if I felt my family was in danger, the commissioner wanted me to know that he was fine with my wife, children, and me returning to New York immediately.

When the Second Lebanon war broke out in 2006, the commissioner, through an aide, made the same offer. In both cases, I asked the aide to thank Kelly for his generous thought but begged off.

When he asked why, I simply said that Meryl and I had discussed our remaining or leaving and she wanted to remain by my side and to keep the children in Israel as well. We promised one another that we would be as careful as possible.

What I didn't say to him was that I might have been swayed by his offer had the Israeli students in my children's classes gotten on planes, but they were staying behind. So as long as their classmates were staying, I felt an obligation for all of us to stay behind. It just didn't seem right to leave.

In the end, Saddam did not fire off any Scuds at Israel. It was widely assumed that he possessed none to fire. Within a day of the war's breaking out, almost all Israelis shunned their gas masks and went back to their normal schedules, pleased that the United States was taking out one of their more dangerous enemies.

MY FIRST SUICIDE BOMBING

It was not until the spring of 2003 that I actually got to a suicide bombing site in Israel. The bombing occurred on April 24 at the entrance to the brand-new Kfar Saba train station northeast of Tel Aviv.

On that day I arose at 6 AM, showered and shaved, and started to read the English-language *Jerusalem Post* and the English edition of the Hebrew-language, *Ha'aretz*. Sometimes the newspapers would carry details and photos that their Internet story did not. All of a sudden at 7:20 AM I heard ambulances going east to nearby Kfar Saba. Hearing ambulance sirens was not a new experience for me. I heard sirens frequently in New York City. I knew immediately that something bad had happened.

The answer came seconds later when my beeper went off. By now I possessed a beeper that provided me with public announcements put out by the Government Press Office, the Israel Defense Forces, and the National Police.

Gil Kleiman, the police spokesman for the foreign press, announced over the beeper that there had been an explosion at the new train station in Kfar Saba. Not knowing at that point

whether this was a suicide bombing or some kind of accident, Gil used the word "explosion." It was only a ten-minute drive to the bombing site.

Driving there, I was optimistic that I would be allowed inside the ropes. By this time I had acquired credentials spelling out that I was embedded inside the Israel police force as a liaison between the NYPD and Israel's police.

Had I tried to get in touch with my contact back in Jerusalem, it might have slowed me up. I could get to the site long before my contact could.

Fortunately, I had my own small network of police friends who were certainly at the site, and who, once I called them on my cell phone, would alert the guard at the periphery to let me in. In this case, I phoned a friend from the bomb squad who was working the scene. He passed the word to the guards that I should be let in—and I was.

In preparing for this, my first suicide bombing site, I had put together a series of questions that I wanted to make sure to put to my Israeli briefers at the scene: Had there been a prior warning of a possible terrorist attack? What was the nature of the explosive device? Was the device camouflaged? What were its size and its contents? What was unique about the device?

Why was the location of the suicide bombing chosen? Were there any obvious flaws in the security at the site?

Had the bomber displayed any new tactics not seen in prior suicide bombings?

What if anything made this bombing different from the others?

How had the bomber positioned himself or herself at the time of the detonation?

Were there any particular behavior characteristics of the bomber? Had he tried to fit in to the scene? If he tried, how did he?

Once at the Kfar Saba site, I learned the details of the incident from a senior Israeli police officer: The suicide bomber, eighteen years old, had come that morning from a nearby Palestinian town, Kalkilya, known as a hotbed for terrorists. He wore a black,

long-sleeved, zippered sweater with a suicide belt attached to his chest, with five kilos of explosives.

At 7:20 AM the bomber stood facing the train station with his back to an open parking area. He wanted to get into the station, where numerous Israelis were waiting on platforms for arriving trains. Sensing that the bomber was suspicious, a security guard refused to let him into the station, demanding to see his identity papers.

The bomber changed his plan and set off the bomb there and then, killing the security guard and wounding nine others. The entire entrance to the station was blown away by the blast. Pieces of twisted metal hung from the ceiling. Glass was strewn some distance.

As it happened, I was familiar with the security guards assigned to protect the brand-new railroad station at Kfar Saba.

Knowing how interested the NYPD was in anything connected to subways—the New York subway system was an obvious target for terrorists—a week earlier I had spent an entire day with a private company that trained newly hired security guards for the Kfar Saba station.

I had watched the guards practice shooting and get briefed on how to examine passengers. The training took place at a nearby site.

TOP-SHELF GUARDS

What I took away from their training was an appreciation of the professional level of these guards. They were top-shelf and Israel was getting them on the cheap. These were men in their twenties who had recently completed a three-year stint in the Israeli army in combat roles. They remained attached to the army, serving in the reserves for one month a year.

In New York the same guy would have had to be paid $50 an hour. Here they were probably getting $10 an hour. The guards were young, in good shape, and really good at their jobs. The day after the attack a photo of the one Israeli killed in the incident—

the security guard at the entrance—ran in the newspapers. I remembered him from that day of training.

It intrigued me that the only person who died in the Kfar Saba attack was the security guard. At first I could not understand how so few people were killed. Had the railroad station been suddenly closed? Was it not crowded outside the station?

Then I thought of the training session I had attended and I realized that the reason for so few casualties was the professionalism of that security guard: He had done his job so well, establishing an aggressive presence outside the railroad station, confronting the terrorist, not permitting him to move one step further toward the train station.

The guard gave the terrorist no other choice but to blow himself up at a time and in an area where few people had gathered.

When I got home after the bombing that day, I sat down at my computer, wrote a report, and sent it off to New York. It took several hours and I knew I was consuming too much time but I could think of no other option at the moment.

The reports that I would write for the NYPD, while detailed from the start, would eventually include lessons that I had learned from my visits to the suicide bombing sites. To properly determine what those lessons were, I made a point of not shooting from the hip during my early reports. As I grew more confident because of what I had seen at the sites, I infused my reports with a whole set of lessons learned.

MIKE'S PLACE

That spring I had little time to relax. Suicide bombings were occurring in Israel one after the other, often just days apart. The next one came only six days after the Kfar Saba train station bombing. It happened on April 30, 2003, at a restaurant/pub called Mike's Place, located on the Tel Aviv beach.

I was eager to find a local tavern where I could entertain people or just go out for a beer with some buddies. Just such a place existed; it was called Mike's Place and was just south of the U.S. Embassy on the Tel Aviv beachfront (The Embassy and Mike's

shared a wall). Except for my not particularly wanting to run into Embassy types there, Mike's would have been perfect: The beer was cold, the music was lively, English was the first language, and I could watch American football there.

The fellows at the U.S. Embassy had not done anything to me other than make me feel unwelcome. It was no secret that U.S. security representatives in Israel regarded my presence in Israel as intrusive, as stepping on their turf. I might have come from the city that experienced 9/11, but to them the problem was that I represented local law enforcement, and New York's counterterrorism issues were supposed to fall under their responsibility.

Paradoxically, by keeping me at a distance, by not offering to cooperate with me, the U.S. Embassy did me a favor and made my job easier. Had I been embedded into the Embassy's operation, I would have had to work within its parameters, not mine. On my own, I managed to develop a close give-and-take relationship with the Israel police that went beyond what I might have expected from "partnering" with the federal authorities.

For reasons that baffled me, most of the Embassy personnel did not socialize with me. I was not brought into their circle as the CIA folks did with me. I was irked when on July 4, 2003, I was not invited to one of the highlights of Israel's social season, the July 4th party hosted by the U.S. ambassador in a large outdoor park in Ra'anana. It was beyond strange. Making things worse, I watched the fireworks at the party from the terrace of my home in Ra'anana. That non-invitation reinforced my conviction that New York City truly needed its own representative in Israel, because if we did not take care of ourselves, no one else would.

Disappointed not to make Mike's Place my tavern of choice, I settled on a place called Molly Bloom's, an Irish pub run by Israelis, just across from the Dan Hotel, also located along the Mediterranean coast. The place had little of the warmth associated with Mike's Place though.

On that April 30 at about 6 PM, after I had put in a long, hard day at Israel police headquarters, I wanted a beer and some French fries before going home to Ra'anana. Seated at the bar, I asked the bartender—rather harmlessly, at least so I thought—to change the

television channel from sports to the Fox News Channel. I had asked them on previous visits to switch channels—always in vain. Maybe they would now, I thought, because the place was almost empty.

A news junkie, I felt the need to stay on top of Israeli and world events, pretty much 24/7. By now I had turned myself into New York's "warning siren" for terror attacks around the world.

Of course, the NYPD had officers sitting at its Operations desk monitoring world events, but since I arrived in Israel, thanks to the lightning-fast work habits of the Israeli media, I was almost always getting information about "live time" global terror events faster than the officers in New York were.

We would keep entire shifts on overtime because of concern for nearly simultaneous copycat attacks. Reaching New York with the vital information could save numerous lives.

And so I politely asked if I could update myself on the latest news.

"We're not allowed to change the channel," the bartender replied, somewhat arrogantly.

"Excuse me?" I asked. "I won't tell anyone," I laughed.

Asking for the manager, I told him that I wouldn't tell anyone that he had violated his rule against changing channels and I would only watch the news for two minutes.

The manager arrived, listened to me, and promptly backed up the bartender. There would be no channel-switching that night. After that incident, I knew I would never go back to Molly Bloom's. And I wouldn't go to Mike's Place, not wanting to bump into U.S. Embassy guys who had been chilly toward me from the time I arrived in Israel. Their cold shoulders actually did me a favor: I was forced to do my job on my own, and that independence gave me far more freedom to maneuver than had I been under their wing.

"GETTING ALONG" WITH THE FBI

The Embassy environment is conventional and structured, and my tasks did not by any means fall into the conventional realm. The *New York Times* wrote on May 15, 2005, that the NYPD's pres-

ence overseas "has strained the department's often tense relations with the FBI, in Israel, for instance, the bureau opposed creating the post for the department's detective, according to American and Israeli officials. At bottom, these officials say, the FBI deeply resents New York's efforts to collect its own intelligence.

Ed Cogswell, an FBI spokesman in Washington, said, "It's a problem for the U.S. government, which needs to have a unified voice in foreign countries; and it's important for the foreign government to know who the official representative of the U.S. government is."

So, to be sure, the FBI felt that I was stepping on their toes, but I genuinely felt that if Commissioner Kelly had decided to send me to Israel, he was sending a signal to all American law enforcement agencies that the city of New York needed its own eyes and ears, and the NYPD was not going to cower in the face of resentment and resistance. I am told that today, in 2010, the relationship between the NYPD and federal agencies both in New York and overseas is much better.

Ironically, the only Americans who showed any warmth to me were the CIA staff in Tel Aviv. I think they understood the out-of-the-box approach, especially in unconventional times.

Once a month the Israel police held roundtable talks with all sorts of Israeli security-related agencies, inviting me to join in. The CIA was included as well, so we got to know one another. When CIA staff began inviting me to their homes for receptions, I sensed they appreciated the need for New York to have someone in Israel, specifically looking out for New York's interests. As for the CIA, I did not work with them on suicide bombings, but I knew there was mutual respect.

How ironic and how trivial all this was—worrying about where I was going to get my next beer, trying to avoid American officials—considering what transpired later that evening of April 30.

Arriving home, I was about to fall asleep when my beeper went off, announcing that Mike's Place had been bombed at 12:45 AM. Prior to the attack, two terrorists spent a night at a nearby hostel, and they reached the scene of the attack from that same

hostel. Searching the hostel later, Israelis found an elastic belt, ex-plosives, and a map of the center of Tel Aviv on which several crowded locales, including Mike's Place, had been clearly marked.

Israel's security forces had vague information just prior to the event that a terror attack was being planned for somewhere in the center of the country; but the intelligence was too vague to prevent the attack.

One of the two terrorists approached Mike's Place and blew himself up at the entrance to the bar, killing three people, including a twenty-nine-year-old French waitress named Dominique Hassa, who was a familiar face to U.S. Embassy customers. Another sixty had been wounded, one of them security guard Avi Tabib, who had blocked the bomber, keeping him from entering the bar and causing more casualties. Tanzim, the militant faction of the Palestinian Fatah movement, along with Hamas claimed responsibility for the attack.

It transpired that two British Muslims, entering Israel from Jordan via the Allenby Bridge, had been dispatched by the Hamas military command in the Gaza Strip to perpetrate the attack. The terrorist who blew himself under the doorpost at the entrance to the bar was identified as Asif Muhammad Hanif, a twenty-two-year-old British citizen from London.

A second British citizen, twenty-seven-year-old Omar Khan Sharif, from Derby, England, had been due to perpetrate a suicide attack at the scene as well, but he fled when his explosive device malfunctioned. He discarded the bomb in a trash bin a few blocks from the scene of the attack and got into a taxi, but the driver real-ized something was amiss and threw him out of the cab.

He continued to flee, and tried to get into the David Inter-Continental Hotel, which had gone into lockdown mode after hearing of the attack nearby. The terrorist was rebuffed by hotel security. As was evident in this suicide bombing, the immediate relay of information between police and private security is one of Israel's best security practices.

From the hotel he ran into the Mediterranean Sea, but swim-ming from Tel Aviv to the Gaza Strip beach would have been quite a swim. The second bomber was found floating in the Mediterra-

nean, dead, ten days later. He had drowned. Ironically, his name was Omar Sharif, the same as the actor. I found it unfortunate that the fish got to snack on Sharif before Israeli Intelligence had the opportunity to interview him.

A million thoughts raced through my head, the chief of which was that, had I chosen Mike's as my watering hole that evening, my fate could have been very different. I might have been killed! I raced to the restaurant, setting off cameras at red lights; I arrived within thirty minutes.

The very first person I ran into at the site was Gil. I had identification that indicated that I was working with the Israel police, but having Gil there obviated the need to show my ID to anyone.

He got me right into the inner circle. I was standing under a shed below the U.S. Embassy. Some Embassy guys whom I had met previously were nearby, nervously waiting for news about whether someone they knew had been a victim. Happily, they discovered that no Embassy personnel had been in the restaurant at the time of the bombing.

The night before the bombing, a large contingent of American visitors to Israel had been in Mike's Place. My theory was that the bombers had done surveillance and, realizing that Americans frequented Mike's often, decided that, as a backup to attacking the Embassy, they could wipe out Americans in Israel—quite a bonanza for them.

I also ran into my police representative counterpart from Russia who lived around the corner from Mike's Place. He had heard the explosion and ran outside to see what was going on. That was the first and last time I would see foreign personnel at the scene of a terror attack. Neither the Americans nor Russians had raced to the scene as standard operating procedure—it was not their job to be there. But it was my job.

I phoned New York convinced that the attack had been meant as a message for the U.S. Embassy. "Oh my God, they've bombed so close to our Embassy," I roared into the phone.

I quickly realized that this evening's terror was different from past events in Israel, at least in terms of its connection to New

York's battle against terror. I kept stressing this point to New York in my initial phone conversation with them. This was not an attack against Israelis per se; it was an attack against the United States, or at least an attempted attack.

The dots became thoroughly connected after this attack: The terror enveloping Israel and the 9/11 attacks were one and the same. The terrorists that night could have picked any restaurant, but they chose Mike's Place.

Piecing together what had happened at the restaurant, I realized that one more security guard had turned into an instant hero by virtue of his quick, accurate instincts and his willingness to "take a bullet" to protect others' lives. He miraculously survived the attack!

It was the guard outside Mike's Place who had properly identified the bomber as suspicious, and, in an act of great courage and professionalism, had kept him from entering Mike's, where many more lives would have been lost.

We don't know what tipped off the guard that the bomber approaching the entrance was suspicious. Every person entering the bar was being searched; that was protocol at the time, and the guard did his job properly. In fact, because the bomber was overweight, he carried the explosives in the small of his back instead of around his chest, the usual practice. Explosives worn in the front on an overweight terrorist might have stood out conspicuously.

The guard faced terrible odds. Even had he put the bomber through a metal detection scanner, the data sheets explosive that the bomber was carrying would have gone undetected. The scanner would have picked up an explosive containing fragmentation, but the bomber did not have fragmentation in his device.

Suspicious of the bomber and thorough in acting on his suspicions, the guard grabbed the man. Suddenly aware that he could not get into the restaurant, the bomber set off his explosives near the entrance, killing "only" three people.

Upon arriving at the scene, I was drawn to the restaurant entrance, where the upper torso of Asif Muhammad Hanif was impaled at the point of confrontation. All that was left of him was

hanging flesh. The bomber's head wound up impaled in the ceiling inside the restaurant's doorway. I had seen plenty of death as a homicide detective, but this was a new and awful sight.

From the outside, the restaurant was totally destroyed, its windows blown out. Cars parked in the vicinity were badly damaged. The scene inside was horrific. The injured had been removed in the half hour it took me to arrive at the scene. Sadly, but fortunately, the Israelis had learned how to evacuate the wounded swiftly. What were left were body parts, and the stench of burning flesh mixed with the smell of sea air.

In the months and years that followed, I brought American visitors to Mike's Place and explained in great detail what had happened that day: Customers had been sitting down, having a meal and enjoying live music. Then suddenly their lives were upended—or just ended.

I had a simple message: This is how Israelis had experienced and coped with terror. It could happen in New York too. There was nothing like a reenactment of that awful day to illustrate the reality of terror.

To this day I can't go to Mike's without visualizing the impaled evil of the bomber. I will always see his upper torso.

I felt a new connection to the place. I saw how quickly Mike's had reopened—within thirty days—and how it had quickly embarked on an expansion of the place. As they say, the music went on. After the bombing, it no longer mattered to me that I might run into U.S. Embassy personnel at Mike's. It became my tavern, my home away from home.

Gil told me that what he admired most about the way I operated was my willingness to get out into the field. He liked to say that I could have sat in an office and waited for the information to come to me. I could have easily written professional-sounding reports and the NYPD might have been satisfied. I was grateful for his comments, but I couldn't imagine operating any other way. I had to be at a suicide bombing scene. There was so much I could learn but only if I were at the site while it was still an ongoing crime scene.

I admit, however, that I was particularly gratified when Commissioner Kelly made a special point of praising my work, telling the media that "We have in-depth information on suicide bombings in Israel within three hours. Morty goes there; he works with the Israeli authorities. It helps us, enables us to adjust, to position our cops here differently."

FILING VIA MERYL

After the Mike's Place bombing, I decided that, to be truly effective, I would need to file my reports to the NYPD more quickly after each suicide bombing.

While in the field I had my cell phone with which I could reach the Intelligence Division, but I couldn't dictate my report to them as a journalist might dictate an urgent story to his home office. I still needed some system to get a written report to the brass immediately after an attack; and to the NYPD bomb squad if there was relevant explosives data that would interest the squad.

How I wished I had arranged for someone with a computer to stand by and wait for my phone call, someone who would key in my report and send it urgently to New York. I thought of Meryl. She had arrived with the children in Israel a month after I had, on February 2, 2003, and we began living in Ra'anana, the same Tel Aviv suburb in which I had been living.

She understood the urgency of my getting information to New York as quickly as possible. And she was my greatest supporter. And so we worked out a system in which I would contact her immediately after getting notice on my beeper that another suicide bombing had occurred. She became my "auxiliary/volunteer."

When I called her, she would rush home, sit down at the computer, and take my phone call; I then relayed my findings and analysis to her, which she quickly whipped into a clear and orderly report. We became a great team. Sometimes I had to scream over the background chaos at the site.

She quickly learned not to get too emotional while listening to me describe graphic and horrific suicide bombing scenes that

would have given seasoned police officers recurring nightmares. She became familiar with terminology dealing with explosives. But far worse, I shared with her photos given to me by Israeli police at the scene—decapitated bombers and victims lying dead.

Thanks to her, my reports arrived in New York in real time. I was so pleased when senior brass in New York expressed gratitude for her crucial efforts.

In Israel only three months, I had already racked up some achievements. But the suicide bombings were coming at such an alarming rate that I wondered whether I would even have time to piece together what was happening, to study carefully what I had learned of terrorist techniques and of Israeli responses to terror.

Would I find the opportunity to make a real contribution to the NYPD's effort to protect New York City from terror? I knew that question still loomed large and was still as yet unanswered.

CHAPTER 8

2003: The Grisly Face of Terror

It was not as if the year 2003 was the first year of Arab terror against Israelis. But somehow its constancy that year, the rapidity with which terror was occurring, and the large number of Israeli fatalities gave those twelve months a uniquely tragic flavor.

Between cable television and the Internet, a terror attack in Israel became almost instant worldwide news, with footage of the event transmitted around the globe within thirty minutes. I felt as if the whole world was watching after each attack, adding to the pressure I felt to do my job as quickly and efficiently as possible.

Less than three weeks after the attack on Mike's Place, I made my next visit to a suicide bombing. The date was May 18, 2003, early Sunday morning. Eerily, this incident happened just two blocks from Israel National Police Headquarters in Jerusalem, and thus two blocks from my office!

Although Sunday was a day off for most New Yorkers, for Israelis Sunday was the first day of the workweek. Many Israelis took buses and trains, stopped in malls, and visited restaurants, ideal behavior for terrorists who wanted to maximize casualties.

A bomber boarded a bus at Pisgat Ze'ev, an Israeli community in the northeast part of the city, and waited until it arrived at French Hill near Police Headquarters. Disguised as an Orthodox Jew, he wore a yarmulke and *tzitzit*. The bomb went off at 6 AM.

Profiling based on appearances is largely ineffective: The image of an Arab terrorist might have him wearing the Arab headwear known as a *keffiyeh*, but in reality a terrorist did not automatically emerge from central casting in some standard uniform.

Robert Slater, who has helped me research and write this book, lives in French Hill and heard the sound of the explosion. Turning on the television immediately to check whether an actual bomb had gone off, he was amazed to find that indeed one had— only a fifteen-minute walk from his house!

My beeper went off moments after the attack. Within ten minutes I was racing to the site, and I got there an hour later. I was very nervous about this attack, spooked by the images I conjured up of the carnage I was about to witness.

Perhaps photos I had seen of previous bus bombings reminded me of the gruesome bloodshed I had seen at the World Trade Center site on 9/11. Driving to the site, I cautioned myself against getting too emotional. I had to do my job.

What first struck me about the bombing site was its proximity to Israel National Police Headquarters. It was just a two-minute drive down the road. Was the terrorist sending a message that he could unleash his explosives under the noses of the police?

Although I had already attended suicide bombing sites, none of them proved as gruesome as this was. Working in the NYPD in New York, I had witnessed my share of corpses and the seriously wounded. I had also witnessed the mayhem and confusion that attends a crime scene.

I arrived on the scene after the dead had been removed and the injured taken to hospital emergency rooms. But the scene that I took in was a gut-wrenching reminder of what had just taken place.

What most tugged at my heart were the mundane everyday items such as book bags, cell phones, and yarmulkes that were strewn about. I wondered to whom these belonged.

Then I noticed men with long beards, yarmulkes, and bright yellow jackets with Hebrew letters on them that spelled ZAKA. These were members of an Israeli group that responds to tragic incidents, engaging in rescue, life-saving, and recovery efforts on the scene.

They were painstakingly sifting through the site looking for any flesh and body parts to remove for proper burial and for any blood to sponge up. I could not help thinking back to the sifting

I myself had gone through at the tent city at the Medical Examiner's Office near Ground Zero as part of the post-9/11 identification process of victims.

Eager to talk with an eyewitness, I rushed to the charred bus, but in my hurry and shock at what I was about to confront, I forgot Israeli protocol and left my briefcase on the side of the highway.

Ever fearful that a second terrorist might have planted yet another roadside bomb aimed at first responders, an Israeli security man, spotting my briefcase, politely explained that it had not been a good idea on my part to walk away from the bag.

It was a swift and very useful lesson. I later stressed to New York the importance of enhanced public awareness of unattended objects. New York has since instituted a program called "See Something, Say Something."

Noticing that the exploded bus was a double one, I suspected the terrorist had deliberately chosen this size in order to cause maximum casualties: He managed to kill seven and wound twenty-six. The seven dead who were sitting in their seats toward the front had gotten on the bus at Pisgat Ze'ev.

As the terrorist mounted the bus, hoping to reach its middle section in order to increase casualties, a passenger who had security training sensed something was wrong. Maybe it was the way the bomber walked or his body language, or perhaps the odd way he was wearing his yarmulke and *tzitzit*.

It would be impossible to check every single religious Jew getting on a bus; the only protection was the person's gut feeling and his quick responses.

The passenger was about to confront the bomber. Realizing that he had been spotted, the terrorist prematurely detonated his explosives.

The bomb that exploded that morning contained much fragmentation, pieces of metal that fly in all directions, making the bomb more deadly. But the alert passenger, who had been severely injured, proved another unsung hero. The hero, Steve Averbach, died seven years later on June 3, 2010, succumbing to wounds he sustained during the bombing.

It turned out that the French Hill bomber was not acting alone. A half hour after his attack, a second bomber in Neve Ya'acov, another northern Jerusalem neighborhood, apparently hoping to blow himself up on a bus as well, was forced to detonate his bomb prematurely when he came to an impromptu Israel Border Police checkpoint, killing only himself.

A few hours later, life at French Hill had returned to a pre-bombing normal. Israelis pride themselves on resuming their routine, day-to-day activities as soon as possible after these terrorist attacks. The return to normal was Israel's way of signaling terrorists that they cannot bring long-term harm to the State of Israel. Thus it was that at French Hill the bus had been towed away. Traffic had resumed. Only the Israel television reporter, holding a microphone and standing in front of a camera describing the bombing, reminded everyone of the earlier tragedy.

My next visit to a suicide bombing site came three and a half weeks later in Jerusalem, on June 11, 2003, toward the end of the day.

Getting dressed for what was billed as one of the better parties of the Israel social season, the annual Russian Independence Day celebration at Tel Aviv's David Intercontinental Hotel, I had one eye on the Fox News Channel; even before I got a beep, Fox reported that a suicide bombing had occurred in the center of Jerusalem at 5:30 PM, a few minutes earlier.

The bombing had happened outside the Clal office building on Jaffa Road, down the road from the local Fox office, so the TV network was able to film the explosion from its window. Fox had gone live immediately after hearing the explosion.

Now, here I was, dressed in a suit and tie, not the attire I wanted to be wearing when I arrived at the Jerusalem bomb site. I changed to casual attire; I wanted to blend in with Israelis, so I would access the scene more easily.

Driving to the site, talking to New York by phone, I noted that makeshift roadblocks had already been set up to locate the bomber's associates.

AN ARAB DRESSED AS A RELIGIOUS JEW

Just as at French Hill, tonight's bomber had dressed in religious Jewish garb. My mind began to wander: Were Israeli clothing stores supplying clothes for Palestinian suicide bombers? I hoped that when an Arab walked into their store and asked for Hasidic garb, the store staff had the good sense to raise a lot of questions and alert the authorities as quickly as possible.

That same year (2003) the NYPD had begun a program called "Operation Nexus," which encouraged store owners to notify police of suspicious purchases or requests. Until then, Israelis had done well in controlling the movement of ingredients used to make explosives. We in New York had taken that a step further, looking at all purchasing angles, not just explosive ingredients.

Seventeen people had been killed and over a hundred wounded on the bus outside the Clal building. Hamas claimed responsibility for the attack, this time in retaliation for the attempted assassination of Abdel Aziz al-Rantiss, the Hamas Islamic leader, which Hamas blamed on the Israelis.

Scoffing at a clear link between the al-Rantiss incident and the Jerusalem bus bombing, Israeli security officials were quick to point out that a suicide bombing takes more than twenty-four hours to plan; the Jerusalem attack had to have been well organized before the attempt on al-Rantiss's life.

The usual right-wing protestors had been shouting "death to the Arabs" at the scene while Israeli Arab Jerusalem employees cleaned up the mess at the site. My mind began conjuring up a bizarre situation: An Israeli Arab from Jerusalem might be cleaning up a suicide bombing scene that his cousin from the West Bank had caused!

At the site someone introduced me to Danny Seaman, the director of the Israel Government Press Office. He was explaining to me that so many terror events against Israelis had occurred on Jaffa Road that it seemed as if every two stores had been hit. I think I shocked him when I told him I knew of every event. How

could an "outsider" like me be so knowledgeable about the terror that Israelis lived with every day?

As I was driving at 11 PM that night through thick fog on the sometimes dangerous Route 443 that connected Jerusalem with Tel Aviv and its suburbs, winding at times through the West Bank, I missed having a partner with whom to shoot the breeze, to allow me to forget the horrors that I had witnessed hours earlier.

Putting the phone on speaker, I contacted a buddy from Manhattan South Homicide. I told him that one more terror incident had happened on Jaffa Street that evening, and I asked rhetorically how Israelis could withstand so much violence and personal tragedy. Neither of us had an answer. We switched over to gossip: Who had been promoted, who had been transferred. These lighter moments took my mind off of the Jerusalem attack and I was grateful to my buddy.

WESTERN WALL BUS

I will always remember the August 19 attack for the lessons that it provided on the need for constant vigilance.

At the time of the bombing, I was usually home, as I was this evening. The beep came within minutes of the attack, and I rushed to the scene, getting there in an hour.

The bombing occurred at 9 PM on a Tuesday on a bus filled with Haredi (ultra-Orthodox) Jews coming back from a visit to the Western Wall. Twenty-one people were killed, eighteen of them on the bus, including many children; another 110 were wounded.

The majority of the passengers came from the ultra-Orthodox Jewish neighborhood of Me'a She'arim. Among the dead was a New York mother of thirteen, forty-three-year-old Goldie Taubenfeld and her five-month-old son, Shmuel, who had been visiting Israel from their home at New Square, New York.

The Taubenfeld murder prompted New York Mayor Michael Bloomberg to visit Israel immediately afterward. During a nine-hour solidarity visit to Jerusalem, Mayor Bloomberg visited survivors and participated in a memorial ceremony at the site of the attack.

What made the attack unique was that the bomber was a religious leader, an Imam, from the large West Bank town of Hebron. Married with two children, he was not the typical Palestinian suicide bomber (single and between the ages of eighteen and twenty-four). Perhaps knowing that he would have relatively easy access to the bus, he did not even attempt to disguise himself by dressing in Haredi garb—a long black coat and wide-brimmed black hat.

On the trip Bloomberg brought his own security team, comprising NYPD officers, and I was assigned by the NYPD to take care of that team while they were in Israel. I was in charge of their logistics; I explained the "lay of the land" to them; how they would operate; and how they would coordinate with Israeli police.

Most people who come to Israel, including the security team, were apprehensive about being in a war zone. My job was balancing their concerns with the reality. I told them that my wife and children were here with me in Israel and that millions of Israelis move freely around the country every day and do not stay "imprisoned" in their homes because of fear over suicide bombings.

I tried to comfort them: "You're not in Kosovo or Afghanistan. Yes, there are suicide bombings, far too many for comfort, but even when they occur, Israelis resume their normal patterns of life quickly and eagerly."

At the end of the mayor's trip, as I raced to Ben Gurion Airport along with Mayor Bloomberg and his security team, I noticed that both of the two lead Israeli police officers in our convoy were volunteers, and one in his civilian life was someone I knew, a certified public accountant!

It seemed bizarre to me at first to discover that the driver might also be able to do my taxes. Yet there were 70,000 volunteer police officers in Israel, more than twice the number of full-time officers. Well trained and highly motivated, the volunteers, like the security guards, go the extra mile and take their role seriously in keeping the country safe from terror.

A few years later on his radio show Mayor Bloomberg noted that he had met this "hulking" fellow whose assignment was

to visit suicide bombing sites in Israel and report back to New York on lessons that could be integrated into the NYPD's counterterror campaign. I was only happy that he didn't describe me as "the fat guy."

Three weeks later, on September 9, 2003, it was the same story but with an ugly twist, two suicide bombings in the same day. It seemed as if the whole country, including me, was on a roller coaster and couldn't get off.

It was a few minutes after 6 PM. I was in Herzylia on the Mediterranean coast attending a conference on counterterrorism sponsored by the International Institute for Counter-Terrorism (ICT). The then foreign minister, Shimon Peres was speaking to a large audience.

Suddenly I noted that a very somber Dr. Boaz Ganor, head of the ICT, was approaching Peres with a note. Something was up. I could feel it. Peres's face turned solemn as if he had just learned that a close relative had died. Might this be another suicide bombing? I wondered, because my beeper had not gone off yet.

Still, my instincts told me to leave at once. With Peres still on the stage, I made a hasty exit and, as I was leaving, my beeper went off, confirming my suspicions. Then it hit me. I couldn't just pick up and leave. I had come to the conference with a special guest, my colleague NYPD Detective Michelle Tege, the NYPD representative in Singapore.

She was accompanied by Dr. Rohan Gunaratna, who ran the International Center for Political Violence in Singapore and had smoothed the path for Michelle's arrival in Singapore.

I invited Michelle along to the suicide bombing, since she was in Israel to study local terrorism. What better way to learn than by getting to a suicide bombing site?

Jumping at the opportunity, she asked if Dr. Gunaratna could join us as well as Dr. Bruce Hoffman, another authority on terrorism from America's Rand Institute. Could I get all three of us into the scene?

Fortunately, I knew I could. I did ask my traveling companions to refrain from asking if anyone else could come along. Taking them

to the bombing site was the right decision; here were terrorist experts getting the chance to visit a terrorist event in real time.

A TRIP TO RISHON

At 6 PM, a few minutes before I was busy analyzing Shimon Peres's face, a suicide bomber had blown himself up at a bus stop filled with Israeli soldiers just outside an army base in Rishon LeZion near Tel Aviv. Nine soldiers had been killed and thirty wounded.

Arriving at the scene, I was able to vouch for my passengers and we quickly began observing, hoping for a quick debriefing.

First reports had erroneously noted that the bomber had dressed as an Israeli soldier, but I learned quickly from police sources that the bomber was wearing casual clothes. Another early report proved to be correct: That a second bomber was preparing to carry out another attack, target unknown.

From a police officer who debriefed us, we learned that prior to the attack two security guards had taken up positions at each end of the bus stop. One noticed the bomber and approached him. It was then that the bomber detonated his explosives. The bomber's lower torso, neck and shoulder were found on the roof covering of the bus stop. A visitor there in 2010 would still be able to see fragmentation holes on the covering left behind as a reminder.

How fortunate that Michelle had been there with me at the site: She made diagrams and took measurements at the scene, allowing me to focus on other aspects of the event. As for my two other "guests," they were certainly going to include this visit in their future lectures; they would probably refer to the techniques the Israeli security people used in order to return the "controlled chaos," as I called it, back to normal. As for me, I realized how much I missed the teamwork I had grown accustomed to back at the NYPD.

Despite the gruesome events we had all witnessed, when I returned my guests to their Herzliya hotel by 11 PM, we all agreed to grab a bite to eat and talk through what we had just witnessed.

Seated at a table in a restaurant near the hotel, I watched a nearby television on which an Israeli reporter was recapping the Rishon LeZion bombing.

THE CAFÉ HILLEL ATTACK

Suddenly I noticed that he had switched topics and was now, at 11:20 PM, reporting on a new bombing that had just occurred at a popular Jerusalem coffee house called Café Hillel; it was located on Emek Refaim Street in the German Colony, the "Soho" of the Holy City. Seven people had been killed and fifty wounded, seven seriously.

The roller coaster continued, and I had to stay on it. But did my guests want to head to Jerusalem with me? Perhaps one suicide bombing a night was enough for them.

"Let's go," I said, making it clear that I was heading for my car and anyone who wanted to join me, could. They all came. We arrived at the scene at 12:45 AM. Again I worried about how I would get our group into a bombing site, but fortunately, I ran into Gil Kleiman early on; I told Gil that I thought it was important that my three guests, all leading terrorism experts, observe this suicide bombing scene. He led the way.

At the site we were told that both bombers (the one in Rishon LeZion, the other in Jerusalem) had come from the same Hamas terror cell and the same West Bank village of Rantis, and they had studied together at Bir Zeit University in the West Bank town of Ramallah. Israeli police believed that a third would-be bomber might still be on the loose.

We also learned that both bombers had deployed the same type of explosives—TATP (triacetone triperoxide)—worn on their suicide belts and packed with ball bearings and nails.

I didn't know how long this night was going to last; there had already been too much action for one day, in my opinion.

Sadly, I discovered a tragic connection between the Café Hillel bombing and the United States. Dr. David Appelbaum, age fifty-one, the doctor in charge of the emergency room at

Jerusalem's Sha'are Zedek Hospital, and his daughter Nava, twenty, both of Jerusalem, had been having a late-night snack in the coffee house at the time of the attack, a day before Nava's planned wedding. They were both killed in the suicide bombing that evening.

Pain and anguish weighed heavily in the air, since many first responders, including Gil, knew Dr. Appelbaum personally.

Ironically, Dr. Appelbaum, a leading expert in the treatment of terrorism-related injuries, had flown to New York earlier that week to lecture on emergency room operations in a terror environment. In New York for just twenty-four hours, he rushed back to Israel to attend his daughter's wedding.

Years later Gil and I came across a young paramedic at Magen David Adom headquarters in Jerusalem. Magen David Adom is Israel's version of the American Red Cross. As we began talking with her, I noticed that she was wearing a unique-looking bracelet. What was the bracelet for? I asked. It was, she said, in memory of the loss of Dr. David Appelbaum and his daughter Nava. Did you know them? Gil asked.

"I am David Appelbaum's younger daughter," she replied quietly.

In March 2010 Israel captured Maher Udda, a senior official of Hamas's armed wing, and Israeli officials said he had planned and directed both the Rishon LeZion and Café Hillel suicide bombing attacks.

THE FEMALE SUICIDE BOMBER

My next visit to a suicide bombing site came on October 4, 2003, on a Saturday afternoon as I was about to head to a park with my family near our home in Ra'anana. Then my beeper went off. If it had been a few hours earlier, I would have been in synagogue.

Congregants were quite understanding, aware that I carried a beeper and a cell phone (both kept on during services). I had to stay in contact in case something happened. I made it through services that morning undisturbed.

But that afternoon the announcement on the beeper went off at about 2:30 PM; it told of a suicide bombing at Maxim, a restaurant located on the beach at the southern entrance to Haifa. This was no ordinary restaurant: It was co-owned by Jewish and Arab Israelis and was known as a symbol of coexistence between the two groups. The Israeli soccer team, Maccabi Haifa, was a frequent visitor to Maxim. Three Maccabi Haifa players were slightly injured in the bombing.

Kissing Meryl and the children goodbye, I raced to the scene, arriving at 4 PM. When I drove up to the site, I saw that blood and flesh were strewn about. Dead bodies were in seats and lay on the floor. A mangled baby carriage was outside the back of the restaurant.

The entire restaurant had been destroyed. Its rear windows were completely blown out, as was the center of the drop ceiling, indicating where the bomber stood at the moment of detonation. Cars parked as far away as fifty feet were damaged.

The death toll had reached twenty-one, including four children; another sixty had been wounded. It was one of the bloodiest of all Palestinian suicide bombings yet. Among the victims were two families and four children, including a two-month-old baby.

The Islamic Jihad Palestinian terrorist group claimed responsibility for the attack; the group aimed to destroy the State of Israel and replace it with a Palestinian Islamic state.

I quickly learned that the suicide bomber had been a woman, a rare occurrence. The bomber, Hanadi Jaradat, had been only the sixth female suicide bomber in Palestinian history. Jaradat, a twenty-nine-year-old Palestinian lawyer, had a younger brother and cousin, members of the Palestinian Islamic Jihad, who had been killed by the Israeli army in June 2003.

What made this incident unique was that for the first time a Palestinian suicide bomber had been a professional woman, not an average Jane. Initially planning to attack Rambam Hospital in Haifa, she discovered that security at the hospital entrance was too tight so, sensing that security at the restaurant was weak, she changed her target to Maxim's.

Hanadi Jaradat's family had been supportive of her when she took a job at a law firm in Jenin after receiving her law degree from Jareesh University in Jordan. Her younger brother, twenty-four-year-old Fadi, was due to marry soon. Palestinians, including her father, commended her for her "martyrdom" and portrayed her as a heroine.

It had been Jaradat's luck that Maxim's had a complete security breakdown that afternoon. For starters, the security guard failed to detect that she was carrying a fragmentation explosive on her. It was apparent that the guard had not been using a metal detector, since it was found in the wreckage of the restaurant far from the entrance.

If the security guard had done his job properly, the bomber would have blown herself up outside; but instead she was able to enter the restaurant, eat an entire meal, pay the bill, and then, standing in the middle of the restaurant, blow herself up, maximizing casualties. Standing, rather than being seated, was important to suicide bombers; her fragmentation explosives were more likely to hit customers in their heads.

Early reports suggested erroneously that shooting had occurred at the scene, perhaps explaining how the suicide bomber was able to enter the restaurant. The reports relied on the existence of holes in the walls believed to be from bullets. But the information I gathered at the scene, and relayed to New York, was that the holes were really fragmentation from the actual explosion. I was able to clarify this fact for New York within five minutes of my being there.

At a certain point Gil took me into the bombed-out restaurant to show me the front portion of the bomber's head, which had been separated from her torso. He also pointed out her legs cut off below the pelvis; the upper portion of her body had been shattered.

For my personal records and subsequent lectures, I obtained a "before" photo of the attractive bomber and an "after" one (just her grotesque detached head). Believe me, the "after" photo is an overwhelming tool at my lectures. No one ever forgets that photo.

Ironically both Jews and Arabs had come and eaten at Maxim's, without dwelling too much on how their solid relations were serving as a model for a peaceful Middle East. But the bombing

was a cruel exception to the rule. Those relations obviously meant nothing to the bomber.

Apart from the sight of the headless bomber, I carried with me other images: The blood, the charred flesh, and one other: A mangled child's stroller. I went home and hugged my kids extra tight that night.

CHRISTMAS DAY BOMBING

The Christmas Day suicide bombing in 2003 in Petach Tikva, a community near Tel Aviv, had great significance because of the day on which it occurred. For anyone doubting that the terrorists deliberately chose Christmas as the date of their attack, let me remind everyone that another attempted suicide bombing, which had been far more massive in scope, had occurred on Christmas Day 2009.

It was then that a Nigerian Jihadist tried to blow himself up on Northwest Airlines flight 253, which had taken off in Amsterdam and carried 289 passengers and crew headed for Detroit.

Fortunately, thanks to the heroics of several passengers aboard, the terrorist was subdued before he could ignite his explosives. But the date he chose was no coincidence; he clearly wanted his attack to occur on one of America's biggest holidays.

I don't believe in coincidences. I believe that what the terrorists care about most is maximizing casualties; but—as they seek to increase the impact of their deeds, they also care about picking certain key dates on which to launch their attacks, sometimes at key symbolic locations. In picking Christmas, they were attacking Christianity, hoping to sabotage one of the most celebrated days in America.

Fortunately, my colleagues in New York were extremely aware of every significant date, whether Thanksgiving, Christmas, New Year's Eve, or New Year's Day. It was not a day to take off. The rest of America took the day as a holiday. We did not. We went on high alert.

I knew from firsthand experience when I worked in New York that we took special precautions at the Christmas holiday toward certain landmark sites in the city, especially St. Patrick's Cathedral, where midnight mass was performed every Christmas Eve. I had spent many a year helping to secure that event. So I knew that when the NYPD learned of the Christmas Day attack in Israel, all previous feelings about the significance of dates for the terrorists would be reinforced.

Christmas 2003 was my first Christmas in Israel. I was used to Christmas being a workday for me. I had always worked on that date so that my Christian brethren could have the day off. When I showed up at Israel police headquarters that morning, some Israeli police officers seemed confused by my presence, assuming that, because the U.S. Embassy in Tel Aviv was closed that day, as an American "official" of sorts I too would stay home.

This was one of those times when I felt the need to remind Israeli police officers that while I was an American/NYPD detective, I was still a practicing Jew, a fact that gave me an admittedly unique status.

I spent the day at police headquarters, then at about 5 PM. I wandered over to Gil Kleiman's office, which happened to be next door to the Israel police commissioner's office. I loved being in Gil's office.

Our banter reminded me of being back in my New York detective office. We spoke the same language and possessed a similar mentality. For over an hour, Gil and I shot the breeze, hanging out together, catching up, and telling one another stories of our police days.

All of a sudden his phone rang. We let it go, hoping the caller would call back later. However, after ten rings or so, Gil and I realized that the persistent caller was not going away. Something must have happened, I decided. Finally answering the phone, Gil listened and then said softly, "Oh, my God." At the other end, someone working in Israel police Operations was telling Gil that a suicide bombing had just occurred at the Geha intersection in Petach Tikva at 6:20 PM.

Talk about access to suicide bombings! Here I was, sitting next door to the Israel police commissioner, able to see and feel the Israeli police kick into high gear.

Gil and I looked at one another and knew that we had to get to the scene urgently. We took separate cars because we both needed our cars at all times. I trailed his car to the scene.

I'll always remember that ride to the site, Gil in his small police car, I in a larger rental. Gil had the advantage over me at IDF roadblocks. Because I did not want to lose him, I followed him into the emergency lane for smaller cars. His car managed easily; but I had a harder time maneuvering. These were the times when my twenty years of chasing bad guys in New York came in handy as I recalled how New York City taxi drivers maneuvered.

Upon arriving at the site, we were told that four Israelis were dead and twenty wounded. The bomber had approached a spot where Palestinian workers from the occupied territories were picked up and returned after spending the day working in Israel, a perfect location for the Palestinian bomber to blend in. I was intrigued to learn that he had blown himself up outside at a bus stop, evidently failing to get on to the bus.

Why hadn't the terrorist gotten on the bus? My theory was that he had panicked after learning that he had been spotted by either an alert bus driver or a security guard. With four Israelis killed, that "small" number suggested that he had prematurely detonated himself.

Once again, as Gil and I walked around the bombing site, we saw the grisly, telltale sign of a suicide bombing: The bomber's head, detached from his body, had flown through the air and landed on the highway's overpass five yards above the spot where he had detonated his device. In a suicide bombing the bomber's head almost always detaches from his body.

At a certain point, I noticed a billboard with an ad for the Amana refrigerator company, and most of the ad was dominated by an American flag! So the last thing the bomber probably saw before blowing himself up was that flag. But of even greater significance was the fact that the bomber's handlers might have chosen this site because of its proximity to the American flag.

Morty and his father, Rabbi Jekuthiel Dzikansky, at Morty's June 1983 graduation from the NYPD Police Academy. *Morty Dzikansky photo collection.*

Morty promoted to Detective Third Grade in April 1989 at NYPD headquarters, 1 Police Plaza, New York City. Then Police Commissioner Richard Condon shaking hands with Morty and unidentified police official (back) appear in photo as well. *Morty Dzikansky photo collection.*

Guests attending a lecture in November, 1990, given by Rabbi Meir Kahane tend to him moments after he was shot dead in a New York hotel. *Freelance photographer Shannon Taylor.*

Morty at Western Wall, Jerusalem, in IDF uniform, carrying Uzi and gas mask while serving with Sar-el in February 1991. *Morty Dzikansky photo collection.*

Morty with son Zachary after Morty's promotion ceremony to Detective Second Grade at NYPD headquarters in December 2001. *Morty Dzikansky photo collection.*

Morty's "partner," and close friend, Gil Kleiman of the Israel National Police in January 2003. *Morty Dzikansky photo collection.*

Inside the bus struck by a suicide bomber on May 18, 2003, at French Hill, Jerusalem. This was the first suicide bus bombing scene that Morty visited. *Avi Ohayon for Israel Government Press Office.*

View from the outside of the bus struck by a suicide bomber on May 18, 2003, at French Hill in Jerusalem. *Avi Ohayon for Israel Government Press Office.*

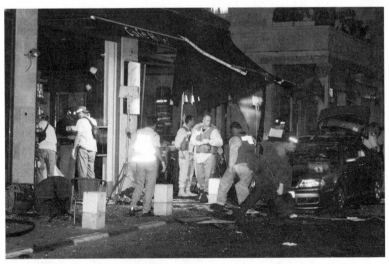

The Israel National Police forensic team analyzes the scene after the Café Hillel (Jerusalem) suicide bombing attack on September 9, 2003. *Moshe Milner for Israel Government Press Office.*

Maxim Restaurant (Haifa) suicide bomber Hanadi Jaradat prior to October 4, 2003 bombing. *Photo released by Jaradat family in the West Bank city of Jenin after the Haifa attack.*

Remains of Hanadi Jaradat moments after she blew herself up at the Maxim Restaurant. *Morty Dzikansky photo collection.*

Turkish first responders gathering evidence after suicide bombing at Neve Shalom Synagogue in Istanbul, Turkey, on November 16, 2003. *Moshe Milner for Israel Government Press Office.*

The inside of a bus after January 29, 2004, suicide bombing near the prime minister's residence in Jerusalem. Though accidentally locked in his house, Morty later raced to the bombing scene. *Avi Ohayon for Israel Government Press Office.*

NYPD Police Commissioner Ray Kelly (left) and Morty on February 23, 2004, at NYPD headquarters at private ceremony where Morty was promoted to Detective First Grade. *Morty Dzikansky photo collection.*

Members of ZAKA, the Israeli group that responds to tragic incidents and engages in rescue, life-saving, and recovery efforts, gather blood and flesh of victims for proper Jewish burial after French Hill, Jerusalem bus stop attack on September 22, 2004. *Amos Ben Gershom for Israel Government Press Office.*

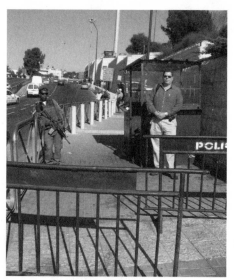

Fourteen months after French Hill bus stop attack, Morty visits rebuilt bus stop checkpoint; to his left is a permanently stationed police officer. *Morty Dzikansky photo collection.*

Morty and New York Mayor Michael Bloomberg at Ben-Gurion Airport near Tel Aviv in March 2005. *Morty Dzikansky photo collection.*

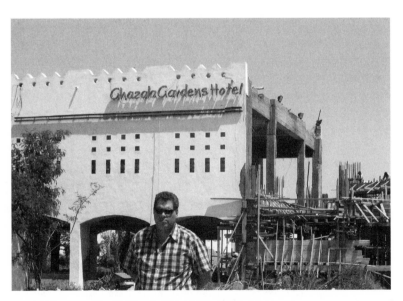

Morty in front of Ghazala Gardens Hotel, Sharm el Sheikh in September 2005, one of the hotels targeted in suicide bombing attack. *Morty Dzikansky photo collection.*

Shwarma I—Inside Shwarma Rosh Ha'ir Restaurant after suicide bombing on January 19, 2006. *Moshe Milner for Israel Government Press Office.*

Shwarma II—Israel National Police bomb squad and forensic team work suicide bombing scene outside Shwarma Rosh Ha'ir Restaurant in southern Tel Aviv on April 17, 2006. *Moshe Milner for Israel Government Press Office.*

What message were the terrorists trying to convey? Perhaps it was that we will hit both Israeli and American targets. We are in a global war against the infidel. But another message seemed apparent: Not only did the bomber want to kill Israelis, but he also wanted to show his hatred for the United States.

The presence of the American flag near a suicide bombing in Israel evoked similar bombings in Israel when there existed an American connection, sometimes even a New York connection.

There had been the note found the previous March on the body of the suicide bomber praising the 9/11 attacks on the Twin Towers; the three American diplomatic personnel killed in the Gaza Strip on October 15, 2003; and the day before the convoy bombing the photo, in the English-language Israeli newspaper *The Jerusalem Post*, of American and Israeli flags simultaneously burned by Hamas youth in the Gaza Strip. The photo depicted Hamas's pure hatred against both Israel and the United States. As a terrorist organization, Hamas was capable of unleashing its hatred in violent terms against both countries.

I theorized that the Petach Tikva suicide bomber or his handlers had staked out the bus stop, had seen the flag, and had decided to launch the attack there. Both the American flag and the Christmas Day timing turned what might have seemed a faraway event to New Yorkers into a very real one. My message to New York was simple: We have to be vigilant. We cannot let our guard down. Every time I called New York from a bombing site, I always felt that I was making a world event more localized.

I wanted my colleagues in New York to feel that my phone calls and my E-mails made events in Israel seem not only more real, but more urgent. I wanted New York to think: Morty is one of us; he should normally be in midtown Manhattan, but he's on the phone, giving us a blow by blow of the event. So I felt I was making overseas terror attacks like this one more relevant for New York. I couldn't have done it sitting in an office.

I felt very good about my reporting to New York: It had put the whole city on alert. Whether the NYPD changed something for Christmas, it didn't matter. The fact is that I had made

a Christmas event in Israel relevant to Christmas in New York. I knew that my reports from this and all bombing scenes I attended were passed on to Commissioner Kelly at his daily briefings and were used to shape operational deployment for the day.

By 10 PM Gil and I were ready to leave the bombing scene. Appreciative of his help at the site and in need of decompressing, I suggested to Gil that I take him for a late dinner.

We found a steak house, ordered our food, and the food arrived. But something was amiss. We both felt it at the same time. We could not take the smell of the steak; it was too reminiscent of the smell at the bombing scene that day. We lost our appetites. It was a very poignant moment, and a very troubling experience.

LOCKED IN MY HOUSE

Five weeks later, on January 29, 2004, Meryl had gone to the gym that morning and I was home getting ready to head to my office in Jerusalem when Gil called to say that there had been another suicide bombing, this time in Jerusalem; a bus had been blown up at the corner of Gaza and Arlozorov streets, with eleven killed and over fifty wounded.

Almost by rote, I got dressed and began looking for my keys. I tore the place apart, but I could not find them. My only guess was that Meryl had mistakenly taken both of our keys.

To make matters worse, I discovered that I was locked in my own house! We had a front door that, if double-locked from the outside, prevented someone inside from opening the door unless he had a key.

I phoned Meryl and asked her to check her purse for my keys. She searched and came up with them. "Please get home now," I said, trying to keep calm. "Don't stop for anything. I need you here as quickly as possible."

Meryl returned home and I raced off to the site trying to make up for lost time.

As if the day hadn't already started on the wrong foot, during my three-hour tour of the bombing site, I received a parking

summons on the windshield of my car three blocks away for illegal parking. With nothing on my windshield that identified me as a police officer, I was like any other Israeli civilian—and I would have to pay the 100 shekels ($25) fine.

I tried to turn the summons into something positive. I would put the incident into the wider context of Israelis continuing their routine lives no matter that hell was breaking loose all around them. This message—that Israelis know how to cope with suicide bombings—had to go into our New York survival kit. If the Israelis could do it, we in New York could also. I still paid the summons!

I will always remember that suicide bombing as the time when an overzealous uniformed policeman noticed a Fox News Channel correspondent reporting live from the scene and then ordered her to move away, insisting that she was blocking traffic.

She did not want to move away. She liked broadcasting with the site as her background. Gil, as the Israel police official in charge of the foreign press, was the perfect mediator for this altercation. He argued with the cop: "No, no, no, this is Fox going live. We need this. We need to get the message out."

LAS VEGAS STORY

I spent eight days in Moscow from February 7 to 15, taking a careful look at the Moscow Metro's security arrangements following a terror attack on those commuter trains on February 4. More on this visit in the next chapter.

After I arrived back in Israel from Moscow, Commissioner Kelly summoned me back to the United States so I could be debriefed. I arrived in New York on Monday, February 16, 2004, and would give a week of briefings.

Once the briefings were over on Thursday, I decided to exploit my long weekend by giving myself a few days off. I needed them. It would be my first vacation in a year. I desperately needed to decompress. I called a good friend of mine, my Vegas buddy, defense attorney Stuart Austin. He quickly agreed to join me for a short weekend in Las Vegas.

We planned to fly to Las Vegas Friday, February 20, and return Sunday night in time for my trip back to Israel.

A few hours before our flight to Las Vegas, I received a phone call from the NYPD Intelligence Division asking me to delay my return to Israel until after Monday. It seemed that Commissioner Kelly had decided to promote me to First Grade Detective that coming Monday in a small ceremony in his private office, a highly unusual setting and a highly unusual promotion for an NYPD cop.

What was so startling was that I had been on my current assignment for only fourteen months, normally far too early for someone to expect a promotion.

Hence, I was heading to Las Vegas on a high, knowing that I would return to New York to receive this wonderful promotion—not bad for a first-generation NYPD son of a rabbi. I was looking forward to putting terrorism out of my mind for a few hours: Playing a little cards, watching sports on television, reading a book, walking around remembering how normal people vacation and relax.

It was 10:30 PM local time Saturday night when my cell phone rang. It was Meryl. While surfing the Internet, she had noticed that a suicide bombing had occurred in Israel. With none of my obsession for monitoring media outlets on the Internet, Meryl still understood that the bombing was something I should be informed about. Because Meryl was married to me, terror had become as much a part of her life as it was mine.

The attack had occurred near the Liberty Bell Park, a landmark in western Jerusalem not far from the Imbal Hotel, both of which were down the block from the world-famous King David Hotel. Eight people were killed and another sixty wounded, eleven of them school pupils.

Here I was a veteran of numerous suicide bombings in Israel. But this time, hearing the news from Israel—with my family there and me in America—was heart wrenching for me. It didn't seem right for me to be in Las Vegas and not at the bombing site. Feeling helpless, and, yes, concerned for my family, I wanted to cry. My hope for relaxation in Las Vegas disappeared.

I have never forgotten that moment when I got Meryl's call and asking myself after I hung up: "What the hell am I doing here in Vegas?" I felt useless, ineffective. Forget the promotion ceremony; I couldn't wait to get back to Israel, to reengage with my family and with my assignment.

But out of respect to the commissioner, and not wanting to miss my own promotion ceremony, I pulled myself together and kept my travel plans so I could attend the great event on Monday.

Phoning NYPD Operations, I was a little surprised to find that they had not yet heard about the attack from open news sources. They knew I was in the United States and had heard through the grapevine about my upcoming promotion.

Again my phone rang. It was Gil Kleiman. He was so good about informing me of suicide bombings, even when I was clearly out of touch, off in America. I obviously couldn't get to the scene back in Israel, but I was able to get some information back to New York about the attack.

A VERY PRIVATE CEREMONY

Having the private ceremony in Commissioner Kelly's office made it seem as if it was a battlefield promotion. Promotions are usually announced formally at public ceremonies for the tiny number of NYPD officers (two to three percent) who ever get promoted to First Grade Detective. "First Grade" was, within the NYPD, the greatest honor that the top brass could bestow on a detective.

Just before the ceremony, I asked the brass at Intelligence: Should I be in full dress uniform or in a suit and tie? I was told that a suit and tie would do fine. They did not say as much but, eyeing my girth, they probably doubted that I could fit into a uniform from earlier years.

My only regret was that Meryl, the children, or my father would not be there for this big personal moment. Inside the commissioner's office I spotted a lot of the senior brass, including Rafael Pinero, Chief of Personnel, who conducted my

swearing-in; members of my Intelligence Division; my sergeant from homicide, Brian McCabe; and Joel Seidemann, my Torah theft colleague.

I was thrilled to be in the police commissioner's office with its historic tradition. A man named Theodore Roosevelt had once held the same title, and though he had not been in this office, relics from his time, including a desk, adorned the Kelly office.

The whole ceremony lasted twenty minutes. There was the swearing-in. I raised my hand and took an oath. I was given a beautifully engraved certificate. And the NYPD's official photographer snapped away.

It had been my activities in Israel and Russia that had earned me the promotion. At the ceremony, the commissioner declared: "Often at great personal risk, Detective Dzikansky has responded to incidents worldwide to improve the NYPD's understanding of and capacity to prevent suicide bombings and other terrorist attacks." He applauded me for getting to Moscow and Istanbul (site of another foreign bombing that I had visited) swiftly, and all I could think of was how difficult it had been to enter those countries.

The commissioner could not have been warmer or more complimentary. An intelligence officer "informed" Kelly that I had been "out in California" the other day when I called in a suicide bus bombing in Israel. I silently forgave the officer for the factual error: How much better it sounded to put me in California than in Las Vegas!

After the promotion ceremony, my star rose meteorically in the media. The next morning (February 24, 2004) a photo of Commissioner Kelly and me at the ceremony appeared in the *New York Daily News* under the headline "One of the Finest." *Esquire* magazine ran a five-page article written by a well-known author, Tom Kelly, in its October 2004 edition headlined "Morty the Cop." The subhead was: "The NYPD could leave counterterrorism to the feds … but it tried that. So New York has quietly extended its security perimeter a bit, including a Manhattan homicide detective in Israel."

On May 15, 2005, the *New York Times* ran a front-page piece by the highly-respected reporter, Judith Miller, entitled "A New York Detective's Tricky Beat in Israel." A photo appeared of me standing tall in Jerusalem's Old City, NYPD badge displayed on the front left pocket of my blue suit—Israeli police to my left, Arabs to my right. Somewhat out of character, I was smiling.

Then, on March 19, 2006, CBS Television's *60 Minutes* interviewed me as part of a piece looking inside the NYPD's Anti-Terror Fight. Anchor Ed Bradley noted that every morning Commissioner Ray Kelly received an intelligence briefing. On the day that a *60 Minutes* reporter attended the morning briefing, Kelly listened to details of a botched suicide bombing in Israel. Bradley noted that I was the source of all those details.

All that publicity might have given me ideas of exploiting my new, illustrious reputation by immediately capitalizing on it, leaving civil service for the higher-paying private sector. But I loved being a cop, and I was going to stay a cop as long as I could.

TWIN BUS ATTACK

My next visit to a suicide bombing site was actually to monitor a pair of suicide bombings that had occurred within minutes of one another on August 31, 2004, in the southern Israeli city of Beersheba, nearly a two-hour drive from Jerusalem.

Seven people had been killed on Bus #6; another five had been killed on Bus # 12. Four people died of injuries later—sixteen dead in all. Another 100 had been wounded. Both suicide bombers, sent by Hamas, had blown themselves up inside the buses, with bus #6 about half a block behind bus #12; the buses were traveling along Beersheba's main six-lane artery, Rager Boulevard, near city hall.

I can only describe the site of the suicide bombing as controlled chaos. It was one of the largest crime scenes that I had been to in Israel. Once again a hero saved numerous lives. The bus #12 driver, after hearing the explosion on the other bus, had the instinct and foresight to pull off to the side of the road. He yelled

to passengers that there had been a terror attack, fearing that a similar event could happen to his bus as well.

His greatest concern was that a second terrorist might be on his bus! Once on the side of the road, he opened up the doors, unquestionably saving many lives.

When the second bomber did explode his device, he was standing at the center of the bus near the rear exit doors. All that I could think of was how does a bus driver go to work every day, worrying that this might be the day his bus comes under attack. Traffic, not suicide bombings, should be the biggest problem he has to face.

These bus drivers were heroes beyond belief. The media made heroes of security guards who performed admirably outside restaurants and malls, sometimes giving up their lives; but little attention had been paid to the bus drivers who were also risking their lives daily. Though Israeli bus drivers are not considered security professionals per se, they are often thrust into that same role when confronted with suicide bombers. What makes these drivers heroic is that they frequently behave as a security professional would, identifying and confronting suspicious people, and evacuating their buses when necessary.

Just over three weeks later—on September 22, 2004—an eighteen-year-old female suicide bomber from the West Bank town of Nablus, dressed in full Arab attire, including a veil on her face, approached a Jerusalem bus stop. While people were waiting at the bus stop outside French Hill, she blew herself up, killing two Israeli police officers, and wounding seventeen others.

The bomber aroused the suspicion of both officers after touching one, a highly unusual gesture for a religious woman. When the officers sought to isolate her, she prematurely set off explosives hidden in her bag.

PLAYING SUPERMAN

I woke up very early Monday morning, November 1, 2004. My youngest son, Jake, two and a half-years old, decided to play

Superman and leaped off his bed. But Jake could not fly and quickly began screaming. He had hurt his leg.

Meryl and I rushed him to a nearby friend who is an orthopedic surgeon. He advised us to get Jake X-rayed, which we immediately did. Fortunately, Jake would be fine, it was just a sprain.

It was closing in on 11 AM when we got home. I exited the car and held Jake in my arms for the short walk to our house. While carrying him, I got a message on my beeper that there had been a suicide bombing at 11:15 AM in the outdoor Carmel market in the heart of Tel Aviv, not far from Mike's Place. Four people had been killed and thirty-two wounded. The Popular Front for the Liberation of Palestine, a secular, nationalist Palestinian police and paramilitary organization, took responsibility for the bombing.

I handed Jake over to Meryl and, knowing that my son was going to be okay, I got back in the car arriving at the bombing site in forty-five minutes. Gaining access to the crime scene, I learned that Jews and Arabs worked side by side at the market, which was in effect a large alley with a metal grated roof, with produce stands and stores on either side of the alley. The blast had gone off at the most crowded point of the market behind a dairy stand.

At one point I was only three feet from the bomber's detached head and I noticed that he had a Marine-like buzz cut. With the clean-looking haircut as a disguised way to blend in, he must have tried to pass himself off as Western.

Finishing my tour of the site at 1:30 PM, with the day only half over, I wondered what else might happen. Fortunately, nothing did.

STAGE CLUB

The date was February 25, 2005. Though it was Friday night, and the Jewish Sabbath had begun, I was browsing the Internet on my computer and noticed that there had been a terror attack in Tel Aviv. I woke up Meryl and I said that I'm leaving. You have to wake up. Drink a cup of coffee. I'll be calling you within an hour to get information back to New York.

The bombing had occurred at 11:20 PM, outside the Stage Club, on the Tel Aviv promenade along the Mediterranean beach. Five people had been killed, and fifty wounded. The Islamic Jihad claimed responsibility for the attack.

I raced to the scene and got there in thirty minutes. On the way, I began briefing New York. When I heard the address, I actually thought the attack had been at Mike's Place again. But I was mistaken.

I realized that terrorists might attack the same place a second time—to take even larger casualties than the first, or simply to scare the hell out of the people who had experienced the first attack.

As I was driving, I recalled that about a week before, one of the managers at Mike's Place came over to me while I was having a bite to eat and asked me if I could speak to someone at the Israel police about a problem he was having. The police were requiring that, in addition to one security guard standing outside the entrance, another be placed at a second, separate entrance.

Thinking of the cost of hiring a second guard, the manager was balking at covering both doors. He wanted me to get the police to leave him alone. My reaction was tinged with anger and amusement: I told him I would absolutely not help him with the police "because the second entrance has to be guarded too." He grudgingly accepted my argument.

At the scene I learned that the bomber had tried to enter another nearby club but was chased away by a security guard. He approached the Stage Club and again could not enter the premises. Turning his back to the security guard, he probably appeared to be leaving. Instead, he detonated his explosives out front.

The body of the suicide bomber was mangled from the area above the knee; a piece of his head was flung twenty yards, indicating a very large explosive.

Sadly, the terrorist knocked out several members of a reserve army unit that was waiting outside for entry into the restaurant to celebrate someone's birthday. That was a great success for the terrorists, who hoped to bring harm to as many Israeli soldiers (even off-duty) as possible in their suicide attacks against civilian locations.

SOMETHING'S WRONG WITH GIL

I'll always remember that Friday night, for it was the day that I noticed signs that Gil Kleiman, by then my closest friend and colleague in Israel, was suffering from Post-Traumatic Stress Disorder.

PTSD is an anxiety disorder that occurs after someone has been exposed to a terrifying event involving great physical harm. It can be triggered by military combat as well as human-caused disasters. Police interacting with terror absolutely fell within these parameters.

Among the symptoms are persistent frightening thoughts, memories of an ordeal, and feeling emotionally numb, especially toward loved ones and close friends.

At a certain point I looked at Gil carefully and felt that he wasn't himself. As usual, he was trying to help me as much as possible, giving me complete access and complete information. As things were winding down, I saw that he wasn't okay. His shirt was out of his pants and he just didn't look right. His speech was okay but he didn't look like my Gil. Something was very wrong.

My first thought was to get him some water or something to drink. He was speaking to the foreign press. He was still functioning, but knowing him as well as I did, I could tell that he wasn't right.

I approached him and said I would get him something to drink. Hustling over to a kiosk across the street, its windows blown out from the explosion, I assumed it would be closed because it was in the middle of a crime scene.

But walking inside, I found someone, perhaps the owner, still behind the cash register. He looked at me, assuming, I guess, that I was a first responder. I thought the man would be in shock but he was strangely composed.

As he gave me a bottle of water he said, "That will be five shekels" ($1.10). I was a bit taken back that he was not prepared to offer a bottle of water free to a first responder. I took his tiny greed as an indication of how quickly Israelis get back to routine and are used to this way of life.

The fact that a kiosk across the street would charge me for a bottle of water; the fact that I could get a summons three hours after a suicide bombing, were messages I wanted New York to put into its counterterror "survival kit." If the Israelis could function "normally" so soon after a bombing, we could do the same in New York.

If suicide bombings like these began occurring in New York, the NYPD would have to encourage New Yorkers to get back to their normal lives as quickly as possible.

Though no one diagnosed Gil as having PTSD that evening, it was clear to me that he had gone to one too many suicide bombing sites. He and I had been to quite a few in the last two years and I wondered if I could be similarly stricken. Meryl had constantly suggested that I was too connected to the violence that was occurring in Israel. I could not detach myself from my assignment for even a moment.

It is sometimes hard to realize that you are suffering from PTSD. When you're busy with your work, you simply don't have the luxury of time to dwell upon yourself. But with a break from responding to terror events, a period of time that is much harder to handle than the work, comes the chance to think about your own personal experience, and what you find may amount to PTSD.

Returning with the water, I realized that Gil needed further help. In time, he recognized what he was dealing with and today, in the spring of 2010, he's doing much better.

I went to two more attacks in 2005, both in Netanya at the Sharon Mall. This was the third attack at the same location in four years, evidence that terrorists can and will return to the same target. At the first Sharon Mall attack, on July 12, five were killed and ninety wounded; at the second, on December 5, five were killed and more than fifty wounded.

While I was visiting suicide bombing sites in Israel, I gained New York's confidence in sending me to terrorist bombings outside of Israel. The challenge of journeying to places that were far less familiar to me than Israel was enormous.

CHAPTER 9

Istanbul and Moscow: Chasing Terrorists in Exotic, Dangerous Lands

By the spring of 2003 I had covered a number of suicide bombings in Israel—from the Kfar Saba train station attack to the one at Mike's Place—and the NYPD was beginning to get used to my "real time" phone calls and reports describing these bombings. I did not realize it at the time, but my reporting from Israel was setting the stage for me to travel to other global terror events for the NYPD.

As my experience broadened, a result of my Israel assignment, I soon became a world terror trouble-shooter above and beyond my reporting from Israel.

With the increase of international bombings, New York felt an urgency to understand those events as well, fearing copycat bombings in the city. It seemed just as logical to identify points of weakness in security at overseas terrorist events other than the ones I was covering in Israel.

Timing was crucial. Terrorist attacks were happening more frequently. We needed urgently to deal with the lessons that could be learned from these international incidents.

For me, the world was becoming one big terror crime scene. With my field experience in Israel, it made sense for the NYPD to send me to international hot spots. I had already proven my ability to glean intelligence from ongoing suicide bombing scenes.

Serving in Israel gave me an unexpected added value: I could benefit from the Israel media's unprecedented rapid response to worldwide terror events. There was good reason for the urgency Israelis attached to world events, especially if Jews were terror victims.

Living with frequent attacks, I gained a different perspective than if I was living in calmer lands. Moreover, Israeli tourists often turned up in countries where these terror incidents occurred, sparking even greater Israeli media interest.

Of course, the NYPD was monitoring overseas terror but mostly via CNN. Televisions were on all the time. But, thanks to the Israel media and the great time difference, I learned of terror incidents overseas long before Americans (or CNN) did. While New York was sleeping, I was just waking up. New York appreciated my news bulletins.

CASABLANCA TERROR

The first international attack outside of Israel that I alerted New York about came on the evening of May 16, 2003. It was on that day that a series of suicide bombings occurred in Casablanca, Morocco, the deadliest in Morocco's history. Ironically, I learned about this attack from a source in the Israel police, who phoned me minutes after the event happened.

The Israeli police officer asked me if I had heard what had just happened in Casablanca, aware that I would be interested, since the main targets were likely to be Jewish. With our own large Jewish presence in New York, we could be vulnerable to similar scenarios.

The most lethal attack in that incident came against the Spanish-owned Casa de Espana restaurant when suicide bombers knifed a guard and then blew themselves up inside the building, killing twenty people, many of whom were eating and playing bingo. Terrorists next attacked the five-star Hotel Farah, where forty Israelis were staying, killing a guard and a porter.

Another bomber killed three passersby near a Jewish cemetery. Two others attacked the Jewish Alliance community center

but, because the building was closed, no one was killed. Another bomber killed two police officers near the Belgian consulate.

The Jewish community had been lucky: Not a single member of the Jewish community was hurt in the attacks, because they occurred on the Jewish Sabbath, when the buildings were empty. Nevertheless, more than a hundred people were injured. Forty five civilians and all twelve bombers perished.

Coming from the shanty towns of Sidi Moumen, a poor Casablancan suburb, the twelve bombers were part of the Salafia Jihadia group, an Islamic terrorist group affiliated with al-Qaeda active in North Africa and Spain.

As soon as I hung up with my Israel police contact, I phoned New York trying to paint a clear picture of the Casablanca attack. I felt handicapped by not being there.

While the NYPD was already quite aware that among the most sensitive terror targets in New York were Jewish sites, my reports to them on the Casablanca bombing served as a grim reminder that terrorists might engage in copycat attacks against New York's Jewish locations.

I got some immediate feedback that Commissioner Kelly was very pleased at getting a clear, concise assessment of the attack from me. For him, my report was a catalyst in his reassessing manpower requirements for all sorts of Jewish sites in the city.

It was not difficult for me to feel that the Casablanca terror was part of my assignment: When Jewish sites are hit, those attacks provide valuable intelligence in the task of protecting New York. If and when the next attack occurred, especially if it was against a Jewish site, I wanted to get on the next plane.

ISTANBUL SYNAGOGUES

The following November two Istanbul synagogues were terror targets.

I was the first to alert the NYPD, again illustrating the great advantage of getting "real time" information. New York immediately

decided to step up patrols and other coverage of New York City synagogues that Saturday morning.

The first of the two Istanbul incidents occurred on Saturday, November 15, 2003, at 9:26 AM; a terrorist hit Neve Shalom, the city's largest synagogue, and five minutes later another bomber attacked the Bet Israel synagogue.

A suicide bomber rammed the entrance of the Neve Shalom synagogue with his explosive-laden Isuzu mini truck, leaving 11 dead and 125 wounded.

Another 12 people were killed at the scene and 220 injured at the Bet Israel attack. Again a suicide bomber slammed an identical explosive-laden mini truck into the synagogue.

In total (including deaths in hospital), 23 people, mostly Turkish Muslims, were killed, and another 300 people wounded in this double suicide bombing. Among the dead were six Jews.

Each truck carried 600 to 700 kilos (272 to 318 pounds) of explosives, hidden in containers wrapped in sacks surrounded by detergent containers. Cable devices were found on the bombers' bodies.

Turkish investigators suggested that World Islamic Jihad had cooperated with al-Qaeda and other terror groups in carrying out the twin blasts. It turns out that the bombers were cousins.

Five days later, on Thursday, November 20, shortly after 11 AM, two suicide bombers detonated their vehicles at the London-based HSBC Bank and the British Consulate in Istanbul, killing 30 and wounding 400 others. Al-Qaeda and the Islamic military group IBDA-C took credit for the attacks.

Most of the victims were Turkish Muslims; among those killed was the senior British official in Istanbul, consul general Roger Short. Turkish police believe that the terrorists may have timed their attacks to coincide with President George W. Bush's visit to England to meet with Prime Minister Tony Blair.

Upon hearing of the second set of bombings in the course of five days, fifty passengers boarding a plane from Tel Aviv to Turkey told the flight crew they preferred to remain in Israel and were allowed to do so.

Since the two Istanbul synagogue attacks were specifically against Jewish targets, I took the responsibility for getting as much information as possible for Commissioner Kelly's daily morning briefing.

My report led directly to a change in the parameters of my assignment to include my responding in person to overseas attacks elsewhere than Israel. Used to getting reports from me two or three hours after an attack, New York had no trouble agreeing that I should get on the next plane when a terror attack occurred in a foreign land. I knew that El Al, Israel's airline, had no planes flying during that Saturday, the Jewish Sabbath. So, I got myself on the first El Al plane to Istanbul early Saturday evening, November 15.

A word about doing my job outside of Israel: I knew I was swimming in new and possibly dangerous waters. Israel had been familiar to me. I had been going there since 1971. I spoke the language, knew Israeli behavior—and I was Jewish.

But Turkey, with 99.8 percent of its 76.8 million population Muslim, anyone coming to this country who was not Muslim could well be misinterpreted as an outsider!

I was definitely leaping into the lion's den. Part of me looked forward to figuring out how to manage; but part of me kept a wary eye for trouble.

Arriving in Istanbul at 9 PM, I was in for one of those unpleasant surprises that you do not want to experience upon landing at a foreign airport. During the six hours that I had to plan this trip, it didn't cross my mind that I might need a visa to get into Turkey.

After all, it was normal practice (with the glaring exception of countries such as Turkey) for an American not to need an entry visa to enter a foreign land. Turkey, as I was about to learn, required travelers to obtain a visa before entering the country, either in advance at a Turkish Embassy or at the airport in Turkey. It was not a big deal to get the visa at their airport, but I was caught by surprise.

Talk about being naïve—I flashed my NYPD badge to the Turkish passport control. That was how I functioned at crime scenes or wherever else it was required.

So here I was, arriving at Istanbul's TAV airport, acting operationally for the first time outside of Israel, holding up my NYPD badge. I then realized with no small amount of panic that this non-English-speaking passport control officer was looking at me as if I had three heads. He began asking me where my visa was. I didn't need to be fluent in Turkish to understand him.

Then he spoke two words in his fractured English: "Twenty dollars." I happily paid the sum and received my visa.

Promising myself that the next time I planned to travel outside Israel, I would check on visa requirements *before arriving*, I began to sense the pitfalls of working as a foreign cop in a foreign place. I was not on an official visit to Turkey. All sorts of weird things could happen—and already had!

The Israel police representative would do what he could to smooth the way for me. He had already driven from Ankara, site of the Israel Embassy, to Istanbul, because of the attack. We met at my hotel where he briefed me.

I made my way to the Hilton Hotel. The Israeli police representative suggested that I stay there, noting that the hotel was a block and a half from the Neve Shalom synagogue, allowing me to get a feeling for the recent terror.

After hearing him go over the basic details of the attacks, I asked if he thought there might be any connection between the terror and New York City. He thought not, but I understood that whatever I could glean from the vulnerabilities of the synagogues' security would benefit New York enormously. I wanted to know what kind of security was in place at the time of the attacks and whether the synagogues had fortified their buildings prior to the terror.

Learning the methodology of the terrorists, while useful information, was often hard to discern. It was possible to piece together some of the terrorists' strategy by learning that both synagogues had special events on that Saturday, attracting larger than usual crowds. At Neve Shalom, a bar mitzvah had been scheduled. At Bet Israel a new day school had been dedicated.

Most likely the terrorists had done surveillance on both places and learned of these special events. They learned too that

on most Saturdays at 9:20 AM synagogue goers took a few min-
utes' break from the services and walked outside. (Because the bar
mitzvah celebration delayed services, leaving most congregants
inside the premises at 9:26 AM, casualties from the attack were
reduced substantially.)

As it turned out, Neve Shalom had been fortified; Bet Israel
had not been.

Seventeen years earlier, on September 6, 1986, Arab gunmen
had entered Neve Shalom and killed twenty-two worshippers. The
Palestinian terrorist and founder of Fatah, Yasser Arafat, had been
blamed.

Because of that attack, all sorts of security improvements had
been put in place: Bullet-proof entrances, security checks of con-
gregants, six large pillars outside the building to act as barriers
against direct hits, video cameras installed to monitor people and
the street. Bet Israel had not made these "improvements."

The pillars worked, keeping the truck from getting closer to
the synagogue, preventing deaths and limiting injuries inside.

The video camera recorded the truck as it came to a slow
crawl and then, while still moving, exploded in front of the syna-
gogue. Heavy structural damage was sustained, but far less than at
the Bet Israel bombing site.

Once a suicide bomber reached a target, it was too late to take
steps to minimize casualties. That had to be done in advance. Inas-
much as suicide bombers were with frightening frequency striking
twice at the same place, fortifying a building made much sense.

Thus, my mantra ever since I began visiting suicide bomb-
ing sites was: Rebuild, fortify, guard. I had noticed early on that
when Israelis strengthened a facility after it had been bombed, it
substantially increased the likelihood of far fewer casualties were a
second attack to occur at the same facility.

Bet Israel, in contrast to Neve Shalom, was left porous: The
street at its main entrance was closed off to vehicular traffic, and
security personnel were stationed at the door. But the street at its
back entrance was open to traffic. Though five security officers and
one police officer were stationed at the back entrance, all six were

killed when the bomber exploded the vehicle on that side of the building.

Nor did Bet Israel have pillars at either of its two entrances, allowing the bomber to get close to the building.

After the briefing, the Israel police representative walked with me toward Neve Shalom. This was a different experience for me. Normally, in Israel, I managed to get to a suicide bombing site as quickly as my car would travel—sometimes fifteen minutes, but at most an hour.

But I arrived in Turkey twelve hours or so after the attack. All that the Israel police representative and I could do was walk close to the site and gaze inside. Still, thanks to the Israel police representative, I had a decent sense of what had transpired, which I put into my report to New York.

In addition to securing major landmarks and high-profile venues, New York considered securing its mass transportation systems as a top priority. Hence, from the beginning of my overseas assignment, I knew that New York would value whatever intelligence I could garner regarding the vulnerabilities of train systems. Terror against mass transit was an acute problem. From 1998 to 2008 more than 250 terror attacks had occurred on rail systems around the world.

The New York City subway system was intricate: 468 stations, 27 subway lines, and 656 miles of tracks. With its large number of lines and underground interfaces with other transit hubs, our subways were among the most vulnerable in the world to terror.

Indeed, starting in 1997 our subway system had come under serious threat. On July 31 of that year two Palestinians threatened to detonate pipe bombs at the Atlantic Avenue subway station in downtown Brooklyn. But the terrorists' roommate tipped off the NYPD.

That incident gave the NYPD a new appreciation that the New York subway system was a prime target of terrorists. But even after the discovery of this plot, it didn't change the general mindset: We were still thinking in terms of traditional crime and not terror. The smell was there but it wasn't being breathed by the average cop.

There were other subway terrorist plots against the New York subway system in August 2004, but the perps were captured before they could cause any human or physical damage.

Having built up a record of reporting on foreign attacks outside Israel, I was in an ideal position to report on any terrorist attack on a subway or train, no matter where. When such an attack happened, it would occur in a tense and dangerous land, many miles from my base in Israel.

RUSSIAN METRO

It happened in Russia, when its subway system was bombed during rush hour at 8:32 AM on Friday, February 6, 2004. For me, Moscow had always seemed ominous, unfriendly. Growing up in America, I had been conditioned to believe that the Soviet Union, Russia's previous government, was our enemy. I saw Russia through the eyes of older American Jews who fought for the right of Soviet Jews to depart Russia; I still remember one of their slogans: "Mother Russia, I'd rather be an orphan."

In 2004 I felt ambivalent about post-Communist Russia, but it was also the home of Dostoyevsky and Chekhov, so it seemed not only distant, but exotic. I was thrilled that I might get the chance to visit.

Learning of the Moscow attack from the Internet, I called New York right away with what was frightening news for them: Their immediate thought was that some al-Qaeda terrorist might decide to blow up our subways in a parallel attack. With the identity of the Moscow terrorists still unknown (they turned out to be Chechen), it seemed plausible to the NYPD that an al-Qaeda cell in America might turn copycat on the New York subway system.

Though I knew my work regarding Istanbul had been appreciated in New York, it had not yet been the established routine that I would get on the next plane to an overseas city where terrorists had just struck. In fact, with regard to Moscow, New York preferred to send someone from the bomb squad there, eager to get immediate technical intelligence on the effect the bomb had

had on the Metro cars and perhaps, armed with these findings, to recommend fortifying certain structures in New York City.

But the NYPD did not get Russian approval to send a delegation over at that time. I became "Plan B." I was told: "You have to get there and you have to get information for us. Get on the next plane to Moscow."

I think the senior NYPD brass was reading the same Russian spy novels that I had read. They told me to make no phone calls from Moscow because of the likelihood that my phone conversations would be intercepted.

Therefore I could only report to New York upon my return to Israel—not the speed with which I was used to working, but I understood that I would have to adjust to these new barriers.

I was going to Moscow, and though I should have been trembling, I only thought of how exciting it would be in a land so out of the ordinary, so intriguing, the land from where my relatives had come to the United States. My fear grew, however, when an Intelligence guy suggested that I "be very careful there."

The explosion had occurred in the second car of a train leaving the Avtozavodskaya station.

The attack was the bloodiest on Moscow's subway, the world's busiest, averaging 8.5 million riders a day (larger than the Paris metro, which carried 6 million; the New York subway system, at 5.2 million; or the London Underground, at 3.4 million).

In that Moscow bombing, forty-one people were killed and more than 140 injured. With probably 200 people on the targeted train car, the driver's quick thinking—he got off the train and asked controllers to switch off electricity on the tracks so that passengers could safely leave the train—kept countless others from being harmed in the aftermath. Overall, 700 people were evacuated safely from the two train stations.

My dual tasks, as I perceived them, were to provide New York with the basic details of the bombing (name of bomber, type of weapon used, tactics and methodology) and to give a complete understanding of the Moscow Metro system's security arrangements: What steps had been taken to lower casualties and whether those

steps had worked; also what security measures had been implemented as a result of the bombing that we should consider for our system.

I hoped to board a flight from Tel Aviv to Moscow early Saturday morning via Turkish Airlines, and the Istanbul visa imbroglio came to mind. If I needed a visa in advance for Moscow, it would be impossible given that it was the Jewish Sabbath and the Russian Embassy was surely closed. I would just have to work things out at Moscow's Sheremetyevo airport.

But a very patient Turkish Airlines clerk explained to me that the Russians would not let me in if I did not show up with a prearranged visa. Obtaining one might take a week, I thought. At least this time I knew about the problem before leaving Israel.

I informed New York that I would be delayed in departing Tel Aviv because I needed to wait until Monday to obtain a visa from the Russian Embassy. How long the delay would be, I did not know. I certainly did not tell them it might take as long as a week. My bosses thought that was fine. I was relieved.

Perhaps, I thought, wisely as it turned out, that the Russian police representative could expedite my getting the visa. He did, but I realized that in asking for his help, I was tipping the Russians off that I planned to go to Russia. I would not be able to begin reporting on the terror attack by slipping under the Russian radar. My anonymity would disappear before I even landed.

But I had no choice. I needed a visa. The Russian police representative told me that he was happy to expedite my visa but he could not—and he emphasized this—persuade his bosses to turn my visit into an official one that would have enabled me to interview the Russian police. There would be no Russian police interviews for me, he said pointedly.

Bright and early Monday morning I showed up at the Russian Consulate in Tel Aviv and obtained my visa.

I guess the Russian police representative felt guilty about leaving me on my own because he promised me that toward the end of my visit he would arrange for me to sit down with a Russian Interior Ministry official, who would brief me on the subway attack. I wondered if I would really meet this guy.

There I was, heading to the Russia of Tolstoy and Pushkin but also of Stalin and Khrushchev, without an official invitation, without official status, unprotected in a kind of no-man's land.

I had read enough Russian spy novels to know that an American homicide detective poking around a Russian crime scene might land in a lot of trouble. Yet I did not want to lie. I decided that I would be vague in talking about the exact nature of my visit to airport immigration officials without directly lying.

I wouldn't lie, but I wasn't going to be stupid. I planned to keep my work as an NYPD cop and my religion a secret. I left my NYPD business cards and badge behind in Israel because I was not going to Russia as an NYPD policeman. I also did not take my *Chai* (Hebrew for "life") necklace that I normally wore every day.

In Istanbul, whose residents were practically all Muslim, I had done nothing to disguise my Jewishness. But in Moscow I preferred being unidentifiable. I switched to a four-hour El Al flight to Moscow after missing the Turkish Airlines one because of the visa delay. As the plane began to land, my supercharged paranoia kicked in again, only this time the cause was unfortunately quite real. I double-checked my carry-on to make sure nothing could identify me as an NYPD cop or as a Jew.

To my horror, I found a bunch of courtesy cards on which were written NYPD Shomrim, the Jewish fraternal organization of police officers. As a member of the organization, I always tried to spend time with them.

Not long before my visit to Moscow, a group of twenty or so had met with me in Israel as part of their annual visit and had given me their latest membership cards. I panicked. What could I do? I had to get rid of them, but how?

Leave them in the seat pocket among the magazines? No way. The cleaning crew could easily find them and "turn me in."

Put them on someone's seat on the plane? No, I might get someone else in trouble.

Then I came up with a solution, a little too secretive and sneaky for my blood, but a solution: Feeling and acting more like a

bank robber than a homicide detective, I wiped my fingerprints off the cards and put them in a garbage bin in the bathroom.

I landed in Moscow early Monday evening. I was nervous. I had just wiped my fingers off an "incriminating" set of courtesy cards.

I feared how immigration officials would react when they reviewed my U.S. passport with its many exotic entry and exit stamps along with my work visa to Israel that linked me to the Israel police. I would have felt better with the standard NYPD backup but I was on my own.

Looking out the plane window, I saw the ground covered in snow; I also saw a military-like vehicle with armed soldiers.

The passport control officer carefully scrutinized my passport and visa, especially the passport stamps indicating what countries I had visited, but he never asked me the obvious question: "And what is the purpose of your visit, sir?" As I walked away, I just hoped he didn't hear my audible sigh of relief.

So here I was, nervous and fearful but excited as well. I knew one thing: Though some of my relatives had been from here (my father had come from Minsk), it was hardly a homecoming. Hailing a cab, I asked to be taken to the Golden Ring Hotel, where I had made a reservation.

I had no idea what to expect; but I knew precisely what my mission was. I told myself to concentrate on my purpose. I knew that I had to stop thinking that FSB (former KGB) agents were lurking around every corner just waiting to pounce on me and cart me off.

With little interest in an American homicide detective nosing around, the Russians, nonetheless, had few secrets arising from the Moscow subway attack, but they were likely to remain secretive anyway. At one level their secrecy seemed surprising. After all, the United States and Russia were both fighting terror.

It seemed to me that both countries could only benefit from sharing what we knew. But the Russians preferred to pretend that acts of terror simply did not take place on their soil.

But my nosing around might confuse the Russians, especially those at the upper levels, who had been used to speaking only to

U.S. Embassy officials in Moscow or to visiting U.S. government officials. If anyone from an American police force were to visit Moscow and seek information, he would be a police commissioner of a major American city not a homicide detective.

As in Istanbul, I felt that my best strategy was to contact the Israel police representative in Russia at once and ask him to debrief me on details of the attack. Many of these details would have appeared already in the Western media, but the police representative would know which ones were correct.

We arranged to meet for coffee near the Ministry of Interior in central Moscow. There had been uncertainty at first whether the incident had been a suicide bombing; the representative confirmed that it had been. He also gave me a description of the device.

Maybe it was the influence of the Russian spy novels that I had read, but I was convinced that I was being followed all the time. Whether I was or not, I would never know. But I assumed the Russians were monitoring my movements.

For that reason, while meeting with the Israeli police representative, I made sure not to take notes as I ordinarily would have done. I simply did not want the representative to feel uncomfortable. Once our meeting ended, I dashed to the nearest café, where I grabbed a napkin and began writing down furiously everything he had told me. I still have kept that napkin as a souvenir of my Russian adventure.

ASSESSING RUSSIAN SECURITY

My most important work in Moscow for the NYPD was to put together a complete assessment of the Moscow Metro's security vulnerabilities.

For instance, do cell phones work in their system?

If so, that would be vital to know, because someone could then, using a cell phone, activate an explosive in a subway.

And if so, if a passenger should see suspicious activity but not see a policeman or someone of authority in the area, working cell phones would enable the passenger to call for help.

We would then want to check whether cell phones worked in the New York subway system. If they did, what steps might the NYPD take to prevent cell phone activation of explosives?

I also gave my assessment of the police presence in the Moscow Metro.

Were there patrols? Were the police stationary? Were they located on platforms? At entrances to the Metro station? At entrance doors to trains? The answers to these questions suggested that security was at a minimum. I also asked and answered:

Did they do bag and security checks?

Answer: I did not see any at the time.

Were there surveillance cameras?

Answer: Hardly at all. I spotted television monitors only at the bottom of steep escalators watched by matrons to check whether anyone had been hurt because of the elevator's steepness. Oddly, I saw no TV cameras monitoring for suspicious activity.

Were there metal detectors?

Answer: I found none.

Were the police armed?

Answer: Yes.

I concluded that our New York City subway system had far better security than the Moscow Metro.

The Chechen terrorists may have done surveillance on the Metro. They certainly knew when to launch their attack—at 8:32 AM, when the train would be most crowded.

One thing struck me as I wandered around the Russian Metro. None of the passengers were looking at each other. I contrasted their indifference toward possibly suspicious characters with the Israeli obsession with seeking out odd behavior.

On my final day in Russia, Sunday, February 15, as the Russian representative in Israel had promised, I was told that I would be meeting with a senior Interior Ministry official in my hotel that day.

When he arrived, he suggested we visit a famous church that had a metal detector, so that he could detect—so I surmised— whether I was wearing a listening device or concealing a weapon.

The visit to the church and my passage through the metal detector amused me but I decided to play the game.

Of course, the metal detector showed that I was neither wired nor armed. My Interior Ministry "minder" then arranged for someone to take our photograph, probably so that he could put my face in their files.

Inasmuch as I was neither going to record our conversation nor carry anything that I shouldn't, my "minder" invited me to join him at a restaurant, where he proceeded to pour an ample supply of vodka into my glass. I tried to remain on high alert and several times tried to segue our "chitchat" to the subject of the subway attack. Unwilling to say anything of value, he quickly switched topics whenever I broached the bombing.

To boast of the long reach of the NYPD and its proactive stance against world terror, the brass back home told the media of my visit.

My antenna remained on high alert throughout my visit. Strolling along the wintry streets of Moscow in the middle of a snowstorm, I sometimes felt like a man without a country. A New York City embassy would have been nice.

Apart from prying information loose from the secretive Russian big shots, my second most challenging issue was the snow. It was February and the streets of Moscow were covered with sheets of ice. I must have fallen ten times. As I began one of my falls, I thought that it would not be good if I wound up in a Russian hospital with a broken bone.

Terrorist attacks against the Moscow Metro continued in 2010, when suicide bombings were carried out by two women during the morning rush hour of March 29 at two stations of the Moscow Metro (Lubyanka and Park Kultury) within forty minutes of one another. One of the female bombers was baby-faced Dzhennet Abdurakhmanova, a seventeen-year-old widow of a slain Islamist rebel, Umalat Magomedov, killed in 2009.

Some 40 people were killed and another 100 injured. At the time of the attacks approximately half a million people were com-

muting through Moscow's Metro. Early investigations suggested that Chechen separatists had perpetrated the bombings.

As it turned out, my 2004 Moscow trip was the first of several suicide bombing sites that I visited where the main part of my reporting had to do with trains and subways.

CHAPTER 10

Commuter Trains and a Barren Desert: Madrid and Sharm El Sheikh

A month later I was overseas again, reporting on a suicide bombing that sadly illustrated the urgent need for greater security on public transport. This time the incident touched the trains of one of the major cities of the world—Madrid.

The bombings occurred on a Thursday morning (7:30 AM), Israel time, March 11, 2004. From the moment that I heard about the incident, I knew that I needed to get the next plane from Tel Aviv to Madrid.

A total of thirteen explosive devices had been placed on four trains: Ten exploded, two were found and deactivated, and one failed to detonate. One hundred and ninety-one people were killed and over 1,600 injured.

I was at home when I learned of the event by monitoring the Internet. I called the NYPD Operations Desk and asked to be put through to my supervisor, a lieutenant. It was the middle of the night in New York and he was at home sleeping. I woke him up and told him about the Madrid terror attack. He had not yet heard of the incident. As it turned out, the lieutenant had excellent contacts within the Spanish police because at one time he had been stationed at Interpol in Lyon.

At one point he asked me, "When is the next flight to Madrid?" He let me know that I would be part of a four-man team; the NYPD was sending three men from New York. Because of his

contacts with the Spanish, my supervisor was being sent to lead our post-attack investigation; he came from our own Intelligence Division. The other two were from the NYPD Counter-Terrorism Unit.

Since I was much closer to Madrid than the New York team was I was able to get there first. My plane arrived in Madrid around 11 PM on the day of the attack.

My colleagues in New York understood that this attack had important implications for the securing of the city of New York. This was a major terror attack against urban commuters and it could have happened in any city with commuter trains.

If Madrid's train system was vulnerable, so were we. We had to learn as much as we could about what happened—and what didn't happen—before and during the attack.

Unlike my visits to Istanbul and Moscow, where I did not have direct contacts set up in advance with the host country's police, this time team NYPD had those ties. In addition to that connection, I was also able to bring my Israeli contacts to the table.

Fortunately, I was well connected to the various foreign police and intelligence representatives serving in Israel. Under the auspices of the Israel police, the representatives met monthly for security updates, and my unique status at the conference table helped me cement my relations with them. I was the only one to represent a city and not be attached to an embassy, I had another unique feature: I represented the city of 9/11.

However friendly I became with the representatives, each of us had to behave gingerly toward the other, unless our security agencies had a "memo of understanding" (MOU) that allowed each agency's rep to exchange classified information.

Though I did not represent a country, as the rest did, no one questioned my presence at the table. From these meetings I had developed a friendship with Spain's representative in Israel that paved the way for important meetings I was able to conduct with intelligence officials in Madrid.

The NYPD and Spain's Centro Nacional de Inteligencia (CNI) did not have an MOU. But my social connection to the

Spanish representative allowed me to ask him for help in getting in touch with the right people once I got to Madrid. He put me in touch with officials from the CNI.

I was aware that there were no pre-established protocols for a foreign municipal police department officer to speak to a foreign intelligence agency—normally the CIA would talk to the CNI; the NYPD would talk to the Spanish police—so I was careful not to overstep any boundaries.

Unlike the case with my arrival in Istanbul and Moscow, I breezed through immigration at Madrid's Barajas Airport in a matter of minutes. Spain had no visa requirement for U.S. citizens.

I was amazed at how relaxed the airport seemed, considering what had happened that morning. One might have expected that the airport would have turned into a fortress and that Spanish security people would be on high alert, hunkering down at the airport and other sensitive locales.

But that was not the case. I don't know why. When an act of terror happens within our boundaries, both the Israelis and we Americans blanket sensitive places with beefed-up security forces. I could not tell whether Spanish security had been lax prior to the attack at the airport, but it didn't seem on high alert now.

The following morning, March 12, I met three Spanish intelligence officials at the same hotel where two of the four members of "Team NYPD" were staying. The meeting meant a great deal to me: It marked the first time that I felt that my representing the NYPD had been formally acknowledged by a country under attack other than Israel. It was a very professional but cursory meeting, held purely to say, "We know you're here."

By being at the CNI meetings, I was able to perform the highly important task of validating or discrediting open source information, but I knew that I could not probe more deeply, because the NYPD did not have an MOU with the CNI.

One important piece of information the CNI clarified for us had to do with who was responsible for the attack. The media had been running stories suggesting that Euskadi Ta Askatasuna or ETA (in English Basque Homeland and Freedom), an armed

Basque organization, had been responsible. But Spanish intelligence officials indicated that it was way too early to point a finger at any group. It was important for New York to learn of Spain's uncertainty.

If indeed ETA had carried out the attack, that fact would have changed the perspective of our visit. ETA is not an organization of major concern to New York. It was a Spanish group that confined its activities to Spanish targets. We were after terrorists who had their eye on New York. If ETA had been responsible, we would still be interested in the tactical aspect of the attack, because terrorist groups share information and if a method is successful, another group could copy the approach.

It was still possible that some extremist Islamic group had launched the train bombings. Because these kinds of groups had New York as their target, we needed to know everything we could about them.

The Spanish police proved to be very helpful. There was none of the uncertainty I had experienced in Istanbul, and none of the fear and tension of Moscow.

Even in these early hours after the attack, an emotional connection had already emerged between our experience with 9/11 and the Spanish terror that the media had dubbed 3/11. Just as the Spanish had sympathy for our plight in New York, I had sympathy for their new situation: I could see the agony and pain on the faces of officials; twenty-four hours after the attacks, they looked weary. None of them had slept since the attacks.

Following the meeting with Spanish intelligence, team NYPD gathered to discuss our game plan. It was decided that my supervisor, Lieutenant P., would attend the formal meetings with the Spanish police, because of his contacts with them. The rest of the team would assess the Spanish transit system.

A bit of friction developed because some team members wanted to attend the meetings with the Spanish police. I was not surprised that they wanted to attend. The natural instinct of a cop is to be in the middle of everything. If we were going to be successful in our assignment, though, we each needed to accept our

roles. And we three were supposed to prepare an in-depth assessment of the Spanish transit system that we could then compare with our own. We had a great deal of work to do in a short amount of time—photographing the transport system, observing locations at various times. I had no stomach for turf fights.

Inasmuch as I had surveillance and on-site terror scene experience, I would act as a mentor for my NYPD colleagues, explaining what to look for on the trains: Whether the authorities had put extra security personnel aboard post-attack; whether the new personnel were armed; whether there were overt video cameras throughout the transit system; whether one could easily identify a bag of explosives within garbage receptacles near the train; and whether, as the Israelis had done so well, the trash cans were fortified to mitigate the effects of an explosion.

We clandestinely took photos inside the trains and outside of them, careful not to attract attention. We were examining trains for their terrorist vulnerabilities, but trying to act as if we were merely tourists so as not to alarm the locals.

From the details of the attack that we culled from the Spanish police, coupled with a complete workup of their transit system, we were able to provide a great learning tool for New York. The NYPD then implemented immediate changes in the way we policed our transit system.

There was talk that the FBI was furious with our "incursion on its turf," but when asked about this Commissioner Kelly grinned and shrugged (according to one newspaper): "Look, we have a transit system; the FBI does not protect transit systems, they are an investigative agency. We have to protect our subways. We are not fighting a turf battle."

And Mayor Bloomberg made it clear that the Madrid attack had led to immediate changes in the deployment of New York law enforcement, something that the city could not have done so quickly without our detailed, in-depth reports on Madrid.

After the Madrid explosions, he observed: "We clearly are focusing, as you would expect us to do, even more resources on the New York City subway system."

But he cautioned against turning New York into a fortress: "Just because there's one terrorist attack doesn't mean that we're going to let the terrorists win and change our lives. But we have to be reminded that vigilance is something that we cannot afford to drop."

Police officers had increased their visibility in the subway and stepped up sweeps in which officers boarded all the cars of a train at the same time and checked for suspicious people or packages.

As the *New York Daily News* reported, noting the rapid adjustment in law enforcement deployment at the New York subway system: "That is how it works in the new, post 9/11 NYPD, as Police Commissioner Raymond Kelly takes the fight against terrorism around the world."

ENLARGE THE PERIMETER

We learned that the Madrid terrorists had assembled their devices in a van parked a few blocks away from the train station. That was valuable information, for it told us that it was necessary not only to patrol within and immediately around vulnerable sites such as train stations, but also to expand our coverage of those sites out a few blocks. As a result of our reports to them, the NYPD did not just notify merchants and security people immediately around the site about what and whom to look for, but it widened its coverage to include merchants and security people as far as a few blocks away from the site.

We also stepped up our public awareness campaign called, "See Something, Say Something." Civilians in Madrid had actually seen suspicious activity but reported it only after the attack.

As I had been reporting to New York, Israeli civilians had long been alert to their surroundings and did not hesitate to alert security officers to both questionable activity and people. I tried to drill it into the minds of my NYPD colleagues that public awareness and involvement were the centerpieces of Israeli counterterrorism. Sensing the importance of this concept in both Israel and Madrid, New York pushed this message to new heights.

One final point about Madrid:

That Sunday, March 14, when I was in Madrid, ironically New York was conducting a previously scheduled counterterrorism drill. That same day a double suicide bombing had occurred in the Israeli port town of Ashdod. I obviously could not get to the Ashdod bombing site.

The fact that these three events were happening simultaneously in New York, Madrid, and Ashdod, and that I was working on Madrid and Ashdod almost simultaneously, indicated NYPD's and my stepped-up alertness toward terrorism.

Two days later, on Tuesday, March 16, I left Madrid and returned to Israel.

After the February 6 Moscow bombing, I had become the conduit to the NYPD for information about terror attacks in Russia, but I knew that if another Russian terror act occurred, I would need to head back to Moscow. While the Russian police representative in Israel and I had become friendly, I could not expect to get solid information if it became necessary.

MOSCOW II

Then on August 31, 2004, a female suicide bomber killed ten and wounded fifty-one when she detonated a bomb outside the Rizhskaya subway station in northeastern Moscow. The bomber, walking toward the station entrance, retreated upon noticing that police were checking commuters' bags; and then—at least it was first thought—she blew herself up. Her head was later found on the subway station's roof.

Tensions had already been high in Moscow: A week earlier (August 24) nearly simultaneous attacks had occurred against two Russian planes flying out of Moscow's Domodedovo Airport. Eighty-nine people had died in the crashes. Earlier that evening another bomb injured four people at a bus stop on the road to Domodedovo Airport just before the two planes took off. That bomb either detonated prematurely or the bomber got cold feet; but it was meant to blow up a third airplane.

New York was interested in "Moscow II," as I called this latest terror, but not to the same degree as the February incident, because "Moscow II" had happened outside the train station with many fewer casualties than "Moscow I."

The NYPD did not ask me to pop over to Moscow, but it did seek in-depth details of the August 31 event. Not being in Moscow, I had no information for them. When I decided to push the envelope and go back a second time, New York supported my decision. I left for Moscow on September 26, with one goal in mind: To find out what kind of security the Russians had instituted after this latest attack.

Doubting that my forthcoming visit would be any easier than my February one, I braced for the bureaucracy with cautious optimism: If I had managed to get to Moscow once, why not a second time? I realized that once again I would be on my own.

When I arrived at Moscow's Sheremetyevo Airport, I noticed marked improvement in security at passport control since my previous visit; in addition customs officials were performing extensive baggage searches on the majority of incoming passengers.

Without requiring an emergency visa this time, I went through normal Russian channels, avoiding contact with the Israel-based Russian police rep in Israel. I have to admit that the appointment he arranged for me to interview the Interior Ministry official had left me disappointed, given that the official refused to provide pertinent information on the "Moscow I" terror attack.

Once in Russia, I would contact the Israeli police representative, but other than that, I did not plan to make contact with any other officials. I would simply observe what I could this time but not insist upon personal interviews with Russian officials.

I had one key question regarding the August 31 Moscow bombing: Why had only ten people been killed in the attack? After all, the suicide bomber apparently had the element of surprise on her side. Had something gone wrong for her?

Apparently it had. Once in Moscow, I discovered from open Russian sources that in the wake of the first Moscow attack, the

Russians had placed police with hand-held metal detectors at random entrances to Metro stations.

Noticing the police and their metal detectors, the bomber turned around, perhaps to ask her handler, standing some distance behind her, what she should do. It may be that she got cold feet but the handler was determined that the attack be carried out, so he activated her device by remote control, killing her and ten other people (including himself). A key lesson I learned: An explosive device could be activated either by the suicide bomber or by a handler via remote control.

The handler was accidentally killed by a piece of fragmentation from the detonated bomb. It turned out that he was a wanted member of Wahhabi rebels from the North Caucasus Republic of Karachayevo/Cherkessia. His group also carried out the airport bombing. In my opinion, his accidental death showed that justice had been served.

Compared with what I had seen in February, I noted an increased police presence on the trains or stationed at entrances and platforms. One officer seemed to be on every fourth train that I rode on or every fourth platform I was on. I also noticed that since February, select officers were carrying hand-held metal detectors.

When leaving Russia, I noticed that, departing passengers, upon entering the terminal, were scanned by a police officer with hand-held metal detectors and their luggage was screened by an X-ray machine. Passengers were then screened a second time after flight check-in. For sensitive flights such as El Al's, passengers were required to undergo a third screening before boarding. So it was clear that security had been stepped up at the airport.

AN EGYPTIAN BOMBING

Nearly a year after "Moscow II" I had one of my most harrowing and tense experiences. It centered on a terrorist attack at the Egyptian Red Sea coastal resort of Sharm El Sheikh on July 23, 2005.

Deep in the barren and remote Sinai Desert, Sharm El Sheikh was a haven for European tourists eager to escape the cold winter climate back home for sun and snorkeling. It was just after 1 AM, and I was browsing on the Internet when I learned that a series of terror attacks had just taken place in Sharm. Ninety people were killed and 150 wounded, most of them Egyptian.

The first attack had occurred at 1:15 AM when a green Isuzu pickup truck exploded at the Old Market Bazaar; ten minutes later a second green pickup truck rammed the main gate of the 176-room Ghazala Gardens Hotel. At 1:29 AM a suitcase bomb exploded in a parking lot along the boardwalk in Naama Bay, 150 yards from the Movenpick Hotel. Egyptian authorities believed that another hotel, the Iberotel Grand Sharm, was a target, but the presence of security forces outside the hotel stopped the attack.

These attacks occurred on Revolution Day, which falls on the anniversary of the 1962 Revolution, when young officers, among them Muhammad Naguib, Gamal Abdel Nasser, and Anwar Sadat, Egypt's first three presidents, forced Farouk I, the last ruling king of Egypt, to abdicate in a military coup d'état.

I quickly realized how significant the Sharm El Sheikh bombings were for New York, because both cities shared an emphasis on tourism. Here was a real-time model of how a tourist community had coped with terror. Had the Sharm hotels been fortified? Had there been security guards in place? How had the terrorists gotten so close? These were questions I knew New York would want me to address.

Though it was the middle of the night, I knew I had to get to Sharm as fast as I could. But getting the Sharm terror story would be no easy task.

Despite its proximity, getting to Egypt from Israel would be a challenge. While Israel and Egypt had signed a peace treaty in 1979, it remained dangerous in 2005 for an Israeli, or for an American stationed in Israel, to simply "pop over" to Egypt. In spite of their peace treaty, a "cold peace" continued to exist, especially among Egyptians.

Before the Jewish holidays of Pesach and Shavuot, which were celebrated between April and June, the Counterterrorism Department at the Israeli Prime Minister's Office issued a strong recommendation to Israelis against traveling to the Sinai because of fresh intelligence it had received regarding planned attacks. Israeli security agencies had been closely monitoring events in the northern Sinai, including Taba, an Egyptian town that borders the Red Sea coastal town of Eilat in Israel. In 2004 there had been a terror attack against the Taba Hilton and two other northern Sinai resorts, which left thirty-four dead, including thirteen Israelis, and 171 wounded; the hotel had been popular with Israelis, since it was cheaper than Eilat hotels and had legalized gambling.

Because Israeli security agencies had issued advisories against traveling through the Sinai, I did not immediately head to Sharm. While Istanbul and Moscow welcomed Israeli tourists—both had regularly scheduled flights from Tel Aviv—Sharm was not a place where Israelis thought it safe to visit.

While on my annual 2005 mid-August family vacation in the United States, I went into the office for some meetings. It was then that one high-ranking intelligence officer, eager to acquire intelligence on the attacked tourist town, suggested that I go to Sharm El Sheikh.

Noting to him that I lacked Egyptian contacts and that the Israelis would be loathe to turn over their Egyptian sources to me, I told him that I doubted a Sharm trip made sense. Then he proposed what he thought was a clever idea: Why don't I just take my wife and spend a weekend in Sharm, posing as tourists?

Listening with growing anger, I cut him off. This was crossing a line. After fearing the worst for Meryl during 9/11, I had vowed then that I would not put her or our children at any future unnecessary risk.

Thus far, Meryl and the children had been great about living in Israel in what amounted at times to a war zone; but to take her to a dangerous location in a country historically inhospitable to Israel and at times to other Westerners, leaving our children behind, was out of the question.

Rarely did I express strong emotion when addressing a senior police officer, but this time, my voice rising to reflect my anger, I practically shouted: "I will take care of the assignment, but we're not including my wife in this equation." Putting myself in danger was in the fabric of being a policeman; Meryl did not need to be woven into this as well.

Another reason to go to Sharm was that during my August vacation in New York the NYPD Counter Terrorism Bureau asked me to speak on September 7 to an audience of hundreds of hotel security directors, many of them former cops. Never would the NYPD or I have a more appropriate audience or a better platform from which to pass on lessons learned from the Sharm attacks. But to validate my speaking appearance, I had to get there.

If the hotel security directors saw a photograph of me in front of the blown-out Sharm hotels, the attack, despite happening 6,800 miles away, would seem far more real and would impact hotel security at the Sixth Avenue Hilton, the Seventh Avenue Sheraton, and other big New York hotels. Now, I had an even greater incentive to get to Sharm, no matter how difficult the journey.

But, as with Istanbul and Moscow, I lacked a plan that would guarantee my security. Without that, when approaching an Egyptian official at the border, I would open myself up to detention or worse. I pictured the nightmarish scenario at Egyptian Passport Control when I responded to their inevitable question, "So, what are you doing now?"

In the nightmare, I saw myself replying sheepishly, "I am a New York City homicide detective currently living in Israel and I work with the Israel police."

I strongly doubted that the next words I heard would be, "Welcome to my country."

Instead, an Egyptian, inherently suspicious of my Jewishness and of my residing in Israel, would ask: "What are you, a Jewish American police officer, doing at the Border Control in Taba? Why did you come? Are you working with the Israelis or with the New York Police Department?" I've had less imaginative nightmares.

Just as with Istanbul and Moscow I felt that I could not let the NYPD down; I could not fail if only for those who would hear me lecture in September. But without that security plan, I admit that I had no idea what I was doing. Never was the expression "flying by the seat of my pants" more appropriate.

Somehow I had to avoid Egyptian "radar." The drive from my home in Ra'anana south to Eilat takes about four hours. The flight from Tel Aviv to Eilat is one hour. From Eilat, the drive south to Sharm El Sheikh is four hours through the Sinai Desert.

My greatest obstacle lay at Taba. Could I cross the Israeli-Egyptian border at Taba without being stopped? I would soon find out.

I flew from Sde Dov Airport in Tel Aviv to Eilat, the easiest part of my journey. Upon arriving at my hotel on that September 26, the first thing I did was contact the concierge and ask her for the name of a tour leader who could drive me to Sharm for snorkeling. I would again play tourist.

The concierge looked at me as if I had four heads. Apparently it was highly unusual for someone to venture across the border to Sharm. Eilat had great snorkeling; why leave the place and travel to far-off Sharm? Despite her bafflement, the concierge gave me the name and phone number of a tour company that could oblige.

The way the concierge spoke to me, I think she still doubted my snorkeling-in-Sharm story: "You don't look much like a diver." Trying to explain away my looks, I noted that I was not at my fighting weight. I made sure to tell her that I had the cash to pay for Sharm.

TOURING WITH CROCODILE DUNDEE

The tour company driver came to my hotel early the next morning. He looked like Crocodile Dundee: in his late forties, tanned skin that suggested a few good years in the sun, and that Dundee-like wide-brimmed hat that crawled over his ears.

The driver was bound to ask me why I wanted to go to Sharm. Deciding to be truthful, I revealed my real identity to him as his

mouth grew wider in shock. Then I added: "Listen to me. I'm telling you the truth; I'm going to Sharm to get some pictures. This is going to be a terror tour. I'm not going to be diving. I just want to see the sites, get a professional understanding of the place. I work for the NYPD. And this is exactly what I'm doing."

I guess taking one more nut to Sharm was not that scary to him. He didn't even flinch. He then gave me a look as if to indicate that he never believed my snorkeling story anyway! Laughing, he declared: "I don't care what you will be doing in Sharm as long as I get paid." "You will be paid when we arrive back in Eilat," I assured him.

Within twenty minutes or so we arrived at the Israeli-Egyptian border at Taba. I knew I would have no trouble at Israeli passport control when leaving the country, but I tried not to conjure up that nightmarish scenario when I approached Egyptian officials.

I took one look at the Egyptian passport control guy and winced. He gave me a slight smile but he did not seem friendly. He looked over my passport, said nothing, and then told me to step aside. The nightmare had come true! The Egyptian stepped aside apparently to consult with colleagues.

"Oh shit, oh shit," I whispered to myself uncontrollably. Desperately, I turned to Crocodile to ask what was happening. He did not seem fazed.

"Don't worry," he began, and I suddenly got worried. "They do this to me sometimes. About seven years ago there was an article in an Israeli newspaper that said I was a Mossad (Israel Intelligence) agent."

In shock, I tried to understand my plight: I was trying to be stealthy but I wound up hanging out with someone the Egyptians think is a Mossad agent. This is definitely not the way to get into Egypt.

The Egyptian passport control guy, having returned to his post, summoned me to meet with, I assumed, Egyptian security folks in a tiny office off to the side. I tried to read their faces; they did not seem as sullen as my passport control friend. They began asking me questions and I plunged into mild panic. As a seasoned

interrogator, I was not accustomed to being on this side of the table. And I did not know the drill.

"Who are you?"

I told them my name.

"Where did you come from?"

Prevaricating made no sense. I had arrived with an Israeli driver and an Israeli stamp in my American passport. I told them that I had come from Israel.

"What do you plan to do after you cross into Egypt?"

I sensed that full disclosure would earn me scary time in detention.

"I came from New York City."

Not a lie, but not the whole truth. I left out that I was an NYPD homicide detective assigned to gather intelligence in Israel regarding terrorism.

"I want to drive down to Sharm to do some snorkeling."

I was sure one of the Egyptians would get cute and ask me why I didn't stay in Eilat and snorkel there. Their silence chilled me. I still felt their suspicion—or was I imagining it?

One of them pointed to a young Egyptian dressed in a suit and tie, carrying a machine gun: "This guy will go with you. He will be your escort."

I wanted to break into a smile but I feared my interrogators would take it the wrong way. But they had indeed given me the good news I had prayed for. We were going to be allowed to go into Egypt. I would get to Sharm after all.

The slightly less good news was that I would have a "minder" with me every step of the way. What would he say or do once he realized that I wasn't snorkeling but was taking photographs, asking questions, and spending a lot of time at the bombing sites? I had gotten this far. I would worry about that later.

We began the four-hour trek south through the Sinai, heading toward Sharm El Sheikh. The mountains and the Red Sea enveloped us, some of the most beautiful scenery I had ever seen. The ride was bumpy but I didn't pay attention. Too many other thoughts crowded my mind.

I thought about the time in 1979 when I had helped the IDF conduct a Seder at an army base near Sharm. What a different time, what a different trip! Sharm was then still under Israeli control as a result of Israel's conquest of the Sinai in the 1967 Six Day War. The month before my Seder in the Sinai, Israel and Egypt had signed a peace treaty in which Israel agreed to return virtually all of the Sinai to Egypt. As part of the treaty, Sharm remained under Israeli control until the Sinai was returned to Egypt in 1982.

As we drove deeper into the Sinai, no towns, no people for miles around us, just open spaces, I started to worry seriously what I would do if some threat arose. What if those Egyptian security folks at Taba decided to follow us south, pulled in front of our jeep, and told us to get out of the vehicle? Or what if one of those terrorist cells rumored to be hiding in the Sinai happened upon us. In either case, I was unarmed and with no prearranged backup. I would be in a hell of a predicament.

Though I had nailed a perp exiting a robbery, chased after Torah thieves, and escaped Scud missiles, riding through the desolate, unforgiving Sinai made the least sense of anything I had ever done. At this point I was very pleased with my decision not to bring Meryl along.

Nagging at me was whether I would make it to Sharm. Even worse was would I see my wife and children again? Less important but still on my mind was would I give that lecture to the hotel directors the following month?

Arriving in Sharm, I asked Crocodile to take us to the bombed-out hotels. It was time to get the driver's assessment of what might happen if I started taking photos. Did he think that my suit-and-tie "minder" would object if I started taking photos at the hotels?

"Listen to me," he replied, "as long as you take care of him at the end, he'll be fine."

"Excuse me?" I couldn't believe he was suggesting that I bribe the guy.

He repeated, thinking that I had not heard him: "As long as you take care of him, he'll be fine."

Well, if it took "taking care" of him for me to take those crucial photos, I would have to do it back at the Taba border.

I asked the guide to snap photos of me outside one of the bombed-out hotels, trying to pretend that I was simply a curious tourist. I was wearing long jean shorts, casual shirt, and Blues Brothers sun glasses—a tourist!

As Crocodile shot away, my "minder" stood staring into space, seemingly bored and indifferent. Until then he had not uttered a word. Did he speak or understand English? Who could tell? Anyway, I liked his aloofness.

As if I were a spy, I studied distances between the hotels and tried to figure out why the terrorists singled out these targets. Based on what I uncovered, I made a few suggestions to New York: One of the struck hotels, the Ghazala Gardens, functions as a convention center with the potential for large crowds.

I warned New York that terrorists are targeting hotels that have large convention facilities. I strongly recommended that trucks delivering food, linen, and the like to hotels needed to be monitored carefully. The truck used in the Ghazala bombing had tried to pass as a delivery truck in order to get as close to the target as possible.

When I spoke to hotel security directors in September, I stressed the importance of checking delivery trucks, even those regularly scheduled, because the terrorists do countersurveillance and can copy the routine.

Much as I would have liked to know, I could not tell if Egypt had beefed up its security personnel inside or outside the hotels because I had no way of learning how many security guards had been deployed pre-attack; but I did not sense an overwhelming number of guards. I might have been able to tell if the hotels had started fortifying their buildings against further attacks had it not been so soon after the attacks.

While in Sharm I spoke to no one other than Crocodile. No need to draw further attention to myself. Now I had only one concern, getting the camera across the border. If the Egyptian border officials wanted to, they could have taken a look at my photos,

confiscated them, and branded me a spy! Am I exaggerating? Maybe, since I know how the day played out. But at the time I was plenty concerned.

On the way back to Eilat, we stopped for lunch at the Red Sea beachside community of Nueiba, which had suffered through its own terror attack a year earlier, October 7, 2004, the same day as the Taba terror. A car parked in front of a restaurant exploded, killing two Israelis and a Bedouin, wounding another twelve people.

Leaving Nueiba, I remembered Crocodile's advice—to pay my "minder." But I had no idea how much.

"Give him $20 and he'll be happy," he advised.

"Is that it?" I thought the payoff would come closer to $50 or $100.

Crocodile looked at me as if to say, just give him the twenty. I did, and the kid seemed quite appreciative. Nearing the border, I held my breath. Checking us scrupulously, security guards ignored my camera! We were allowed through to Israel, camera, film, and all. What a relief!

Back in New York in September for the speech, I recited my Sharm story to a bunch of colleagues. In retrospect, the whole story came off as quite entertaining, down to the $20 "tip" as a thank you to my "minder."

As dangerous as police work can be, there is always someone who has your back. There are always supposed to be sirens coming to support you. I call that most welcome support the cavalry (I have never forgotten that word since tackling Charlie Jones in the Judaica store!) At least that is the way it is supposed to be. But visiting these foreign bombing sites, I was in the field and on my own, an uninvited guest at times, an "unofficial" investigator on an assignment that was unprecedented for a New York City cop. I had no cover, no pre-set plan; I was just winging it and counting on my instincts to get me by. Fortunately, I always somehow managed.

The whole purpose of my visits to these sites, in Israel and elsewhere, was to elicit lessons that could be transmitted to the NYPD that would help the city curb terror. It's time to take a close look at these lessons.

CHAPTER 11

Lessons Learned

It was all very heady stuff, the adrenaline rush that came when I learned that a bombing had occurred, the reporting from the scene, the drama and danger of those suicide bombing sites, the praise from New York, the media coverage, the promotions.

For all the personal excitement, I had to keep my focus at all times on my ultimate mission: To figure out the lessons that the NYPD could learn from the bombings. I then had to urge New York to employ those lessons to better protect the city from the deadly effect of global terror.

Throughout these pages I have dwelt on the events themselves; my attending a series of twenty-one suicide bombings in Israel as well as my visits to four targets outside of Israel. I have described the challenges of getting to the sites, my debriefings at the site, and my reports to New York. I have deliberately left for now a thorough discussion of the lessons that I learned from these experiences and what New York did upon learning of those lessons.

Not all of my suggestions, when adapted by New York, were visible to the naked eye. But some were. Nor were my proposals meant exclusively for the NYPD; they were as much for New York's residents as for its police force.

LESSON #1

Perhaps the most important lesson I conveyed to New York after one of my early visits to a suicide bombing site (Kfar Saba

in 2003) was the simple fact that a terror attack had occurred and that the NYPD had to pay attention to such events.

Until then it was customary to discount or dismiss terrorist events that occurred in faraway lands as inconsequential in New York. Even after 9/11 it was hard to argue that terrorism in Tel Aviv or London or Moscow carried significant lessons for the NYPD. But here I was, a New York City homicide detective in a faraway land, calling at all hours of the night, reporting events that on the surface seemed only remotely connected to New York and its own security needs. But there was nothing remote about the suicide bombing in Kfar Saba or Haifa or Jerusalem.

If a terrorist could blow himself up outside a railroad station in Israel, another terrorist could decide to imitate that tactic and blow himself up near the Rockefeller Center ice skating rink or some other Manhattan landmark.

The fact that this kind of terror had not yet happened in New York City did not exclude it from happening in the future. That was my message: Guys, we can't relax, because terror was definitely occurring, and seeing it in person was far more powerful and more of a reality than watching it on CNN.

LESSON #2

One highly significant lesson that I was able to convey to the NYPD was this: If terror occurred in New York, we were not helpless. We might not be able to prevent suicide bombings, but we could reduce casualties.

By the time a suicide bomber has carried out an attack, it was too late, too late for the dead victims, too late for wounded, too late to stop the terrorist physically from setting off his explosives.

Terrorists have the advantage over security forces. They possess the element of surprise; they can, under the right circumstances, insinuate themselves into large crowds simply because they are ready to die as part of the attack. And they possess a remarkable devotion to carrying out the most irrational deed imaginable. So catching them in advance or even as they approached a target is hard.

But it is not too late to learn valuable lessons that could reduce the amount of dead and injured in the future, if and when another suicide bomber strikes.

In my visits to suicide bombing sites, I realized fairly quickly that some bombers had inflicted massive casualties, some much less. And the reason for the differing number of injured and dead had to do with the measures that security officers at the target had taken in advance, sometimes weeks before the attempted attack, sometimes seconds.

LESSON #3

This is a no-brainer: The better the security measures, the fewer the casualties; and the worse the security measures, the greater the number of killed and wounded.

That corollary lesson exhibited itself when Hanadi Jaradat, a female suicide bomber struck Maxim, the Haifa restaurant, in 2003. The number of dead (twenty-one) and wounded (sixty) was especially high, because of the security guard's failure to detect the explosives she was "wearing."

For whatever reason, the guard's metal detector was not at the restaurant entrance, but elsewhere in the restaurant. Had the woman realized she would have to go through a metal detector, she probably would have exploded her device on the spot, probably killing the security guard and a few people nearby; but instead, she was able to enter the restaurant, causing the high casualty rate. It was anguishing for Israelis to learn that the suicide bomber had sat in the midst of her future victims, calmly eaten a meal, and then paid the bill! She then stood in the center of the restaurant and blew herself up!

There were also the more positive experiences. It intrigued me that only one person (the security guard) died in the Kfar Saba train station attack in 2003. At first, I could not understand how this happened. Had the station been suddenly closed? Were there only a few people outside the station when the bomber blew himself up?

Then I thought of a session I had attended prior to the attack, run by a private security agency that trained security guards to work at sensitive locations. Thanks to the Kfar Saba security guard's training at that session, his professionalism resulted in only one death—sadly, his own.

The guard had established an aggressive presence outside the railroad station, confronting the terrorist, not permitting him to move one step further toward the train station. The terrorist had no other choice than to explode his device at a time and in an area where few people had gathered.

What I took away from that training experience was an appreciation of the professional level of these guards. These were men in their twenties who had recently completed a three-year stint in the Israeli army in combat roles. They were skilled and not particularly well paid. However, their dedication is unquestioned.

LESSON #4

Another lesson I acquired was the absolute necessity to take steps to fortify public places. From my visit to Istanbul I learned that lesson firsthand and vividly. Terrorists had hit two synagogues. One had been fortified in advance of the attack; the other was not. The fortified synagogue suffered fewer casualties than the unfortified one.

Israel required effective security measures because terrorists had been continually targeting its public places: Malls, theaters, coffee houses, railroad stations, bus stations, and the like. New York City had been spared from such constant attacks. Still, I felt there was no time to lose. I strongly urged the NYPD to create a playbook of lessons learned should terrorists begin zeroing in on New York City's public places.

Based on my reports and those from other foreign liaisons, the playbook would be in place at the proper time. Faced with a spate of terrorist attacks in New York, the NYPD would not have to start from scratch. And it would have a roadmap for becoming proactive. Merely responding to terror events was clearly not

enough. I was pleased to find that the New York authorities had adopted my idea at once.

The playbook was a compilation of reports generated by me and other foreign liaisons attending overseas attacks. Sometimes, after getting information from one of us, changes in day-to-day operations were implemented immediately (for example, expanding the security perimeter of public transportation stations and developing a presence of police officers with heavy weaponry patrolling the city and subways).

Following 9/11 the idea that it might be possible to reduce casualties at a suicide bombing event seemed either far-fetched or irrelevant. Other than the World Trade Center attack, New York had been spared attacks that would have made the issue of reducing casualties very relevant.

Commissioner Ray Kelly's mandate to me had been to do what I could while in Israel to protect New York from terror. This directive lacked specifics and so I interpreted what he meant.

I doubted that the commissioner imagined that I might on my own prevent attacks in New York. That would certainly be a part of my mandate, but my key role was to learn lessons from Israeli suicide bombing sites that the NYPD could then integrate into its playbook aimed at reducing terror casualties, once an event occurred.

As I scoured suicide bombing sites, I kept in mind that, while the Israelis were the most experienced nation in terms of counterterror, there were security measures that had worked well in Israel but would not work in New York. Therefore I felt a special obligation to look for the lessons that New York could apply to itself.

LESSON #5

One vital lesson was to focus on the one measure that had proven the most effective in reducing suicide bombing casualties: The placement of professional security guards outside public places.

New York City, with its massive population of 8.3 million, was far too large to possess the manpower required to place

professional security guards at all public places and to guard each and every individual. Israel, however, could do it. The total population of Israel was less than that of New York City—7.4 million. New York might have been able to establish a security guard force that matched the quality of Israeli security guards, but the city lacked the automatic staff replenishment that Israel drew upon.

Every year Israel "graduated" a fresh class of twenty-one-year-olds from the Israel Defense Forces, trained in security work and willing to work cheaply as civilian security guards for a few years. While Israeli security guards had accepted an average wage of $8 an hour as the norm, New York guards of this caliber would expect at least $30 an hour.

The job of the Israeli guards did not on the surface seem particularly dangerous. A guard had to be on the alert for suicide bombers, but, with thousands of Israeli targets around the country, the odds were low that a security guard might actually confront a suicide bomber. To be sure, Israeli guards were killed or wounded in suicide bombings; but they were few and far between.

Israelis suggested to me that the NYPD should place security guards at every mall, department store, restaurant, and theater at Times Square, indeed at all public buildings. I listened politely, but I explained that such a strategy was unrealistic. We understood how valuable Israeli security guards had been at suicide bombings and how many lives they had heroically saved. But as long as New York remained quiet, armed security guards with metal detectors would not be placed at all public places. I did feel, especially after the Maxim and Kfar Saba incidents, that it would be worthwhile for New York to institute random security checks at especially sensitive public locations.

LESSON #6

I knew New York was unlikely to respond positively to a proposal for random security checks at all public sites. The politicians would worry what armed security guards posted at all Broadway theaters would do to the city's tourism. The libertarians would

ponder whether random security checks violated someone's civil rights.

For all the differences between Israel and New York City—in terms of size, the amount of continuing terror, and the availability of professional security guards—there was much that I could pass on to New York that could prove useful.

LESSON #7

The suggestion that I passed on that was the least visible but was directed at both the NYPD and its citizens was the need to maintain a constantly high state of alert for suspicious people and objects.

This is not a lesson that is easy to get across to New Yorkers. Their default response to anything out of the ordinary—a suspicious person, a brawl in the street, the largely naked "Singing Cowboy" frequenting Times Square—is not to take notice of such events, because almost anything goes in New York and nothing seems out of the ordinary. Still, the message had to be taught.

My suggesting that New Yorkers stay on high alert was buttressed whenever I could find a connection between a terrorist carrying out an attack abroad and at the same time referencing the United States, perhaps even New York City specifically.

Anything that established a possible connection between a suicide bomber in Israel and the city of New York was a first-rate piece of evidence. In trying to track down would-be terrorists, I was always looking for the minute, granular nexus between two places.

The mere fact that an American flag appeared in an advertisement near the site of a bombing (Petach Tikva attack, Christmas Day, 2003), or that a suicide bomber wore a T-shirt on which was printed U.S. Army (Tel Aviv, January 2006), brought the connection home.

So did the discovery of the note referring to 9/11 that a terrorist left at a suicide bombing site in Haifa (March 2003), or the fact that a suicide bomber had attacked a location adjacent to the

U.S. Embassy in Tel Aviv frequented by its personnel and other American citizens (April 2003).

For terrorists, sending a message to their victims was vital. The selection of what to wear—a T-shirt with U.S. Army written on it—was not coincidental to the suicide bomber. Nor was it coincidental that the Petach Tikva suicide bomber had chosen a target that was near an advertisement containing an American flag.

The T-shirt, the note, the American flag helped me get my message across: We have to be vigilant. We can't let our guard down. Every time I called New York from a bombing site, I always felt that I was making a world event more localized.

What messages were the terrorists trying to convey? Perhaps, the message was we will hit Israeli targets, and we will hit American targets as well. I wanted New York to take into account that as the suicide bomber is attacking a target in Israel, he is also thinking about his hatred toward the United States.

Sometimes the connection between a terrorist event in Israel and one planned to take place in New York was not abstract. Let's say that a suicide bomber in Israel had come from Hebron in the West Bank. Once we knew that he had been thinking about 9/11 when he blew himself up, or positioning himself near an American flag, we would want to check if he had a relative or friend living in New York or its surroundings who might be planning a similar attack in New York. If that friend or relative existed, we would track him down immediately.

Looking at police patrolman and crowds of citizens on New York's streets, you would not necessarily sense a state of high alert on their faces. But the alertness could have still been implanted in their minds, triggering the right response in the event of someone or something suspicious.

Of all the lessons that I learned while visiting suicide bombing sites in Israel, and flying off to foreign locales that had just been struck by bombings, unquestionably one of the most crucial was the need for everyone—the NYPD and citizens alike—to be on heightened alert for anyone acting suspiciously and for any unattended objects that appeared suspicious.

I knew what could happen when citizens were not alert. Take the time when a suicide bomber managed to walk on to a bus carrying mostly ultra-Orthodox Jews in Jerusalem from the Western Wall to their homes in Mea She'arim in August 2003. Once in the bus, he walked to its center, able to maximize casualties when he blew himself up. Because Haredi Jews (or, as they are known in Hebrew, *Haredim*), when on a bus, make a habit of not staring at others for modesty reasons, and would certainly not look at a non-Haredi Jew, the suicide bomber was able to hide in the crowd, get on the vehicle, move toward the center, and blow himself up.

This behavior of theirs told me that, while the Haredi Jews were religiously observant, they were not observant of their surroundings, fervently believing that G-d would protect them. As is evidenced by attacks on the general Israeli population, alertness and vigilance help minimize casualties. As a result of the Haredi passengers avoiding eye contact, the bomber was able to inflict a larger number of casualties. Twenty-one people were killed. The lesson to be learned from the behavior of the *Haredim* was this: For those who are not vigilant, who do not pay attention to every detail in their surroundings, the price could be very high.

All suicide bombing sites were gut-wrenching for me, but the bus carrying *Haredim* tore at my heart. As I had witnessed at the Maxim bombing, I still vividly recall seeing mangled strollers everywhere and I immediately thought of my own kids and how easily it could have been their strollers. That image haunted me for years. It is no wonder that whenever I heard of events for children, I thought less of the joys the event would bring to parents and children and more to it providing fodder for a terrorist.

The need for constant high alert was a lesson that I drilled home on every possible occasion, if only because it was abundantly clear that one could guarantee saving lives if security forces and citizens were on constant high alert.

The corollary of this lesson was that the less the public was alert, the greater the likelihood of high casualties in terror attacks.

When I moved around in Moscow after the attack there in early 2004, I sensed that the Russians were acting as if nothing

had happened. I saw no police presence, no wariness by civilians. I did not get the sense that the trains had recently been bombed.

I reported my Moscow findings to New York, noting that in Israel, checking identification and using hand-held metal detectors had proven effective in inhibiting terrorists and spotting explosives. But such steps had to be instituted aggressively and consistently and this was not apparent in the Moscow Metro, which remained very vulnerable.

Indeed, the NYPD seemed on a higher state of alert than Moscow or Madrid, even after the train bombings there. What with our Train Order Maintenance Sweeps program aimed at deterring reconnaissance of the transit system and the omnipresence of our Transit Operational Response Canine Heavy Weapons program, we looked like we were on a post-attack alert.

New York found my Moscow reporting compelling. In that report I had provided a lesson to be learned: I had made the strongest case possible for bag checks at important sites in New York, namely, that bag checks decrease casualties in terrorist bombings.

After Madrid, Team NYPD stressed the value of the public's participating in terror awareness, which resulted in New York's revving up its public awareness program "See Something, Say Something."

It was the London bombings on July 7, 2005 (52 dead and 700 wounded), that prompted New York to begin its random bag checks within the NYC transit system.

On July 21, New York decided to institute random bag checks, setting off a major legal battle with the New York Civil Liberties Union. Two weeks later, responding to the NYPD's new policy, the NYCLU filed a lawsuit to stop the practice. Explaining the lawsuit, Donna Lieberman, the NYCLU Executive Director, observed: "Our very real concerns about terrorism do not justify the NYPD subjecting millions of innocent people to suspicionless searches in a way that does not identify any person seeking to engage in terrorist activity and is unlikely to have any meaningful deterrent effect on terrorist activity."

Filed in federal court, the suit argued that the NYPD was violating the Fourth Amendment rights of commuters to be pro-

tected against unreasonable searches and seizures. But NYPD attorneys argued, undoubtedly partly on the basis of my Moscow report, that bag checks could save lives.

Finding that "the risk of a terrorist bombing of New York City's subway system was real and substantial," U.S. District Judge Richard M. Berman ruled on December 2 that random bag searches were constitutional: They were not as intrusive as alleged by the NYCLU. Justice Berman noted that "the threat of terrorism is great and the consequences of unpreparedness may be catastrophic," arguing that it would be folly not to allow random searches.

The proposal to go on a high state of alert depended little on financial or human resources. It only required the NYPD brass as well as New York City officials to issue constant reminders to its citizens in speeches and advertisements, in short, to engage in a media barrage.

The NYPD began a series of programs: One was called, "See Something, Say Something." Another sponsored continuing announcements at every subway and train stop. Yet another ran television and radio commercials. Still another, called NYPD Shield, offered a series of NYPD briefings for private security managers aimed at protecting New York City from terrorist attacks. The program shared best practices and lessons learned, and it offered training and promoted information sharing. It was in the framework of the NYPD Shield program that I spoke to New York hotel directors in September 2005.

With the awful memories of 9/11 fading, with an absence of bombings in the city, it was easy for New Yorkers to become lethargic. Accordingly, in my reporting back to the NYPD I advocated the importance of mounting campaigns that would make the public more alert.

It was clear, especially after Madrid that passengers on public transport had to elevate their state of awareness. A distinct lack of public alertness had allowed the Madrid terrorists to place their bomb-filled luggage on luggage racks and elsewhere on the commuter trains, and then disembark. Nobody said anything or seemed alarmed that people got on with bags and then left without them.

LESSON #8

Part of elevating the state of alert that police and citizens should feel was the need to widen the perimeter that would ordinarily be set up to prevent terrorism against major landmarks in the city.

Prior to Madrid, we focused our efforts at "hardening" or fortifying the target itself, keeping an eye out for suspicious people or suspicious packages entering the premises. But after the Madrid attack, Spanish security officials discovered that the terrorists had parked a van as far as a few blocks away from the site of the attacks and had assembled their devices at that spot. Hence there was a need to widen the security perimeter, to make sure that suspicious activity near potential targets was quickly identified and reported to the proper authorities.

Initially the NYPD went on the assumption that somebody would either assemble an explosive device at home or bring the device into a densely populated site such as Grand Central Station or Penn Station and assemble it within sight of the planned attack. However, after learning from the Spanish police that the devices used in their train attacks had been assembled by the terrorists a few blocks away from the point of entry into the location of the attack, we saw the value of widening the police perimeter.

Here is what we advised the NYPD to do:

Instill a new vigilance, a higher state of alert, in the NYPD to be on the lookout for anyone acting suspiciously and, specifically, trying to put an explosive device together. Certainly continue to protect landmarks, but broaden that perimeter to include watching out for the bad guys getting themselves ready for the attack.

I was pleased to see a quote in the *New York Times* on June 22, 2005, from Paul J. Browne, the deputy police commissioner and chief spokesman for the NYPD: "If our people weren't there [Madrid and other foreign cities where attacks occurred], we would have had to wait months to get granular details like this and put them into effect."

LESSON #9

After the great cooperation we received from the Spanish police, we understood even better how important it was for us to strengthen our own links with intracity agencies in New York. Before Madrid, too many New York City agencies guarded their intelligence too carefully and were not sharing security information among themselves.

Madrid gave us a new reference point: The terror attack had happened—against a major European country, against a major landmark, against a transport system. What we were able to convey to our own people within the NYPD was that terror incidents like Madrid were real; they were not the stuff of fiction just because they happened thousands of miles from American shores. And we had to make sure that all of us in counterterror had the same information.

All of us in the counterterror field had to share information much more freely than we had before—and urgently.

Without exaggerating, it seems fair to say that it was the NYPD that instilled the need for new and urgent interagency cooperation with security agencies along the entire Northeast Corridor. Information was exchanged in regularly scheduled briefings with twelve transit and police agencies from Washington, D.C., to New York City and with AMTRAK, the government-controlled provider of intercity passenger train service in America, the Long Island Railroad and the Port Authority Trans-Hudson (PATH) rapid-transit railroad that linked Manhattan with New Jersey.

You might say that we also reinforced our perimeter in our relations with these agencies both in terms of cooperation and conversation. This was a huge step forward.

LESSON #10

Profiling will not work in most situations.

From my visits to suicide bombing sites I realized that putting New York City on high alert was not enough to curb the

effects of terrorism. Alert for whom? That was a crucial question. A police officer as well as a citizen had to know who might be suspicious. Until then the conventional wisdom had been that all suicide bombers looked and acted alike.

The corollary was this: As all terrorists look and act alike, it is easy to pick one out in a crowd. I learned from my visits to bombing sites that the opposite was true.

I had been at suicide bombings where a Palestinian Arab terrorist had disguised himself as an ultra-Orthodox Jew, another had dyed his hair, still another had trimmed his hair into a buzz cut (something I noticed while standing only three feet from the bomber's detached head!), hoping to pass themselves off as Israeli teenagers, all done to blend into the crowd.

Sometimes a disguise just didn't work: In the suicide bombing at French Hill in Jerusalem in 2003 a civilian, who happened to be a security expert, detected a suicide bomber dressed as an Orthodox Jew before the attacker detonated his bomb. Maybe it was the way he carried himself, or his body language, or the way he was wearing his yarmulke and *tzitzit*. Something just did not seem right. All of a sudden the word "profile" was out the window.

To New York's credit, it was already security conscious. After 2002 we had established a formal program called "Operation Nexus," whereby supply companies and store owners were encouraged to notify the police of suspicious purchases or requests.

As a result of my findings, I was able to demystify the notion that a potential suicide bomber would always come from a poor, downtrodden background, that the bomber could be easily recognized by his or her dress. Quite the opposite, I argued: A suicide bomber could, through stealth and cleverness, easily blend into a large crowd—all the more reason for law enforcement and citizens alike to be on high alert and to employ gut instincts to sense anyone suspicious.

I am happy to say that New York took my advice to engage the public in the security effort in the most serious manner. In spite of the fact that there hasn't been any successful terror attack carried out against New York in nine years—since September 11,

2001—police awareness—and public awareness too—had grown more intense. To the NYPD's credit, many planned attacks were thwarted before they were carried out. It is only natural, when there is a lull between these attacks, that people tend to forget what needs to be done to provide maximum security. But all of us in the NYPD worked hard to keep that intensity high.

LESSON #11

It is of great importance for the public-at-large to return to normal as quickly as possible. The return to normal sends a powerful message to terrorists: You can't defeat us!

Every Israeli, upon hearing the news of a suicide bombing, reaches for his or her cell phone and tries to contact loved ones. Then they quickly return to normal patterns of behavior.

Israelis believe that a suicide bomber had not truly succeeded unless a prolonged disruption in Israeli life occurred as a result of the bombing. The Israelis would not allow that to happen. And so even as they cleaned up the bomb site, others made sure to ride the buses, go shopping, visit restaurants, or even take in a movie.

All of the observations that I gave to the NYPD regarding the crucial role that security measures played in mitigating casualties were, in my opinion, my greatest contribution to the NYPD. Unfortunately, all of what I have monitored and reported on is real. These events did happen—and they could happen to you. That is not meant to be alarmist. But it does seem worthwhile to offer a "how to" manual (see the next chapter) that will help you, the reader, if and when you are confronted with a terror attack in the making.

CHAPTER 12

How to Identify a Terror Attack: A Manual

Thus far this book has recounted my life and career, showing that, extracting the proper lessons from suicide bombings, it is possible to take precautions and thus reduce casualties should a bombing occur.

Much of what I have talked about has to do with the way security forces deal with suicide bombings. I have not yet discussed in great detail what an individual or a private institution can do to minimize the impact of a suicide bombing or other terror attack.

This chapter provides advice for the individual and institutions. It will be presented in the form of a manual, a how-to set of rules that, if taken seriously, should minimize death and injuries at a suicide bombing.

The goal of the manual is to give individuals and institutions the sense that they are in control of the situation, to empower them, to give them the resources and the knowledge that will allow them to function under emergency situations, with specific reference to suicide bombings.

I want to emphasize that I have no magic wand that, if waved properly, will prevent suicide bombings. That is the mission of the intelligence community. My personal mission was helping New York City prevent terror and, if it did happen, keeping casualties to a minimum.

PROTECTING THE GENERAL POPULATION

The manual begins with the general population—the average person living day by day, traveling to work five or six mornings a week, visiting malls, walking the streets. A very basic question for this person is: What can you do to ward off the horrible effects or even thwart a suicide bombing?

SITUATION #1: THE UNATTENDED OBJECT

You are walking on a crowded sidewalk, let's say Fifth Avenue in New York City, and you spot what appears to be an unattended object leaning against the wall of a nearby building.

What makes an object look suspicious?

It is unattended.

It seems out of place. An unattended suitcase in Yankee Stadium or in a movie theater is out of place.

Visitors to these venues do not usually bring their luggage with them and then leave it unattended. An unattended item that does not fit the venue should raise suspicion. Unattended luggage at an airport, where you expect luggage to be, should also be treated as suspicious. For that matter, any unattended items left in a public place should be considered suspicious.

If any of these situations occur, what should you do?

WHAT ARE YOUR OPTIONS?

1. You can run away without alerting anyone that there is a suspicious object nearby. This may seem the best course of action for you personally; but fleeing might cause harm to many people after you have left the scene. Then you will have to deal with your conscience.

2. You can approach the object and touch it to make sure it's not a bomb. This is not advisable and is probably the worst thing you could do.

3. You can try to find out who the owner is by asking people near the object. This should be done quickly as your first course of action, but do not take too much time because, if it is indeed an explosive, time is wasting.
4. You can seek out someone in charge.
5. You could call 911 and inform the person answering the call that you may be looking at a suspicious object. The police, specifically a bomb squad, can then be sent to the site of the unattended object.

SITUATION #2: THE SUSPICIOUS PERSON

You are in a crowd of people, whether outside on a sidewalk, or in a mall, sports stadium, or bus stop. Suddenly you look at someone in the crowd, and for one reason or another, the person looks suspicious to you and you get a bad vibe about him or her.

Here are examples of suspicious activity to be aware of and report:

- A person loitering for long periods of time without any apparent purpose
- Concern over the authenticity of credentials/identification passes
- Someone recording, videotaping, photographing, or sketching things that just don't make sense (i.e., that have no tourist value), such as transit system tunnels, bridges, highway overpasses
- Overheard conversations in which an individual(s) make alarming statements
- A person or people found in areas that are off-limits to nonemployees (e.g., rooms with access to electrical systems, ventilation areas, emergency stairwells)

What makes a person look suspicious?

The subject is alone, excessively nervous, perspiring, wearing bulky clothing that is inappropriate for the season's temperature/weather conditions.

Indications that the person is in disguise, such as wearing a bulky hat, scarf, or some other clothing article to hide his face or body, or is wearing a uniform that does not seem to "fit" the individual. The person may be carrying something that doesn't seem right under the circumstances.

Someone is wearing a religious garb but doesn't seem natural in it. Perhaps you notice someone inside a synagogue wearing a *tallit*, a prayer shawl, but not wearing it right or fidgeting with it; or someone in a church who is inappropriately attired.

At a Baptist church in Lexington, Kentucky, a Middle Eastern looking man went into the church during Sunday services carrying a backpack. Both his looks and backpack drew attention, and he was politely questioned about the pack and then was asked to remove it from the church. The man arose and left the church not to return. His strange behavior was passed on to local authorities. The man could have been innocent or doing a dry run. Regardless, the church acted properly to protect its congregants.

A person has something protruding in an unusual way under clothing (e.g., wire running through a sleeve or a toggle switch).

The person checks to see if something hidden under clothing is still there.

Someone giving off the smell of chemicals or excessive perfume/cologne.

A person exhibiting signs of nervousness. Nervousness should not be enough to arouse suspicion. All of us look nervous at one time or the other. Another element besides nervousness must be present.

Perhaps he or she is swearing or has trouble looking into people's eyes, or walks strangely because of something hidden in clothes, or the person's gait is not natural, or someone is extremely focused or in a "trance."

The person makes repeated attempts to avoid police or security.

The person could also raise suspicion by asking you certain questions: When do the largest crowds gather at this spot? Do the police come by here often? Is there any security in the building?

You have to understand that your personal safety may be in question, not only if you are inside a sensitive building, but also if you are standing in line waiting to get into that building. Let's say you are at a baseball game, and you are one of fifty people waiting in line to enter the stadium. You must be as alert to your surroundings waiting outside in line as when you are inside the stadium. You have to keep in mind that the terrorist's goal is to maximize casualties. Bottom line: When large crowds gather one should not be totally relaxed.

Persons who sell items or provide services need to be alert for suspicious people. As America tragically learned, if someone asks to take flying lessons but mentions that he or she does not want to learn how to land, that should send up a red flag.

Or, if someone enters a store and asks to buy large amounts of items that could be used for improvised explosives, such as hydrogen peroxide, that should be a red flag.

Other red flags: Someone checks into a hotel for a long time but has no luggage or pays in cash. Or someone buys a one-way plane ticket and pays in cash.

Someone doing surveillance might appear suspicious, standing in front of a church or some other public institution for an inordinate amount of time. He would be suspicious if he is taking photos, videotaping places that might reveal the amount of security outside a building, the best time to launch an attack, or the best location to stand when setting off an explosive.

You should not assume that every potential terrorist looks like the Middle Eastern terrorist stereotype. There is no uniform stereotype. Because it is easy for a potential suicide bomber to wear a disguise, there is no point in deciding that someone "looks" suspicious only because of what he or she is wearing. The terrorist will not come from central casting. There is no "look" to a suicide bomber; therefore behavior characteristics must be considered.

Conventional wisdom had it that potential bombers fit a stereotype: Middle Eastern male, eighteen to twenty-eight years old, unmarried, religious. But we need to demystify such notions: A terrorist can be white, black, Hispanic, or Asian. A terrorist could have been born Jewish, Christian, Buddhist—or Muslim and then radicalized.

A terrorist can be a foreigner or someone homegrown. In short, your mind has to be open. There are no rules; bombers no longer fall into a gender or age range. They include the religious and secular, the professional and lay person; and they can come from the local population or be foreign visitors.

WHAT ARE YOUR OPTIONS?

1. You can ignore your suspicions. Clearly, your goal is to survive a suicide bombing, not to be hurt, and so your natural instinct would be to flee the scene.
2. You could observe the person for a while to see what he or she is up to.
3. You could carefully engage the person in conversation to see if he has some legitimate explanation for why he is in this location.
4. You could call the authorities, even if you don't feel comfortable doing so. For instance, if you are about to enter a building that has a security guard, you can alert the guard that someone standing outside looks suspicious.
5. If you are outside a building with no security guard, you could look for someone of authority, a police officer, anyone who can take charge of the uncertain situation.
6. You should be on extra alert when in or near major landmarks in a city. In New York, examples would be Grand Central Station, Penn Station, the Empire State Building, and the Statue of Liberty. These heavily trafficked, highly symbolic locations would appeal to a bomber.
7. You should also be on extra alert when passing a spot that has a large number of children or elderly, a school or a nursing home.
8. Other sensitive spots at which you would want to be on high alert would be financial institutions on Wall

Street, trains, buses, religious institutions, and of course airports.

SITUATION #3: THE SUSPICIOUS AUTOMOBILE

What might make you think an automobile was suspicious?

It might be parked at an especially sensitive location for a long time, or in a no-parking area that is heavily crowded.

The car may seem weighted down, with the rear of the vehicle sagging.

The license plate might look improvised or mismatched (e.g., a truck with passenger license plates).

Someone might be sitting in a car for a long time, perhaps watching for something for no apparent reason.

The car contains objects that look suspicious: Polyvinyl chloride pipe that could be used as an explosives container, chemicals, wires that protrude from certain areas, batteries, or timers.

WHAT ARE YOUR OPTIONS?

1. You can ignore the situation, walk away from the car, and hope that it is not wired to explode soon after you leave. That's not very thoughtful!
2. You can try to find out from people in the area if the car belongs to one of them. We recommend this as your first course of action.
3. You can approach the car and try to open it. Don't do that!
4. You can call 911. This should be the second thing you do after not finding anyone who claims ownership of the car.
5. If someone gets into the car and drives off before the authorities show up, you can try to assemble as much information about the car and driver as possible: Its license plate, the make and model of the car, any tell-tale markings such as a broken taillight. What did the driver look like? What was he or she wearing? Share this information with proper authorities!

On May 1, 2010, a real-life suspicious car-related event occurred arising from the actions of an alert vender who notified a mounted NYPD police officer that a box with smoke was pouring from the back of a Nissan Pathfinder. The suspicious car was parked on 45th Street between Seventh and Eighth avenues in Times Square, New York, one of the busiest and populated locations in the city. The NYPD undertook a rare immediate evacuation of Times Square. The device contained such explosive elements as propane tanks, a form of explosive powder, gasoline, and a timing device. The device failed to explode so no one was injured.

SITUATION #4: SUSPICIOUS BEHAVIOR BY A COWORKER

If you hear a colleague at work mouth off against the country you are in, keep in mind that someone bold enough to make incendiary statements might be prepared to take violent action. This person should definitely be considered suspicious.

The perfect example: The mass shooting at Fort Hood, Texas, on November 5, 2009, in which Major Nidal Malik was reported to have killed thirteen people and wounded thirty. According to news reports, Malik had argued some time before the shooting that Muslims had the right to rise up and attack Americans.

If someone at work engages in erratic behavior such as becoming religious overnight, he or she should be regarded as suspicious, especially if he is making radical Islamic references. You may not feel the person's behavior is worth reporting to authorities right away, but it's something to which you should pay attention.

WHAT ARE YOUR OPTIONS?

1. Keep the person under observation.
2. If the person becomes very suspicious, speak to someone in Human Resources as well as notifying the proper security authorities so that they can follow up on the person.

PROTECTING INSTITUTIONS

What should institutions do to deal with suspicious situations? Perhaps most important of all: If you are an executive or an administrator at an institution, do not rely solely on the police or the government to help you minimize casualties in case of a terror attack. You must take responsibility for securing your own location.

What can you do to "harden" or fortify your facility?

WHAT ARE YOUR OPTIONS?

You can pick some of these options to implement—or all of them. The more sensitive your location, the more measures you should install.

1. **Make Sure Professional Security Personnel Are in Place**

You must have trained security personnel (preferably armed) in place to keep anyone suspicious from doing damage outside or inside your location.

It is essential to hire a professional, well-trained security staff. Ideally, your most competent security person is somebody with prior military or law enforcement experience, someone trained by professionals who has implemented this training in real life before becoming a security professional. Remember: Five and dime security gets you five and dime safety.

If the building hires someone with military experience, that person should have had field experience and not just done office work.

Those who qualify as proper security guards include off-duty retired correction officers, police officers, even former firefighters. If someone seeking employment in security does not have this background, the person should at least be licensed by the state as a security

professional; he or she must seem sharp and aggressive and know the job well.

It is crucial that the location's security manager be a professional with security training and background. If the manager doesn't have that training, then you are fooling yourself.

In a perfect world, all public locations should have armed security guards at all entrances with X-ray machines and metal detectors. Bags should be screened. It is vital that those checking bags know how to do the best possible check: Looking inside bags for suspicious items and feeling the weight of bags (overly heavy bags could mean the presence of explosives and fragmentation).

The sophistication of the screening technology should depend on the sensitivity of the location. The greater the sensitivity, the more sophisticated the screening devices should be.

Technology is fine, but the burden rests with the security guard. The guard must not rely purely on the technology to detect suspicious people or objects. Metal detectors, for instance, can detect fragmentation, but not explosives.

An X-ray machine hopefully would detect unusually formed items as a gun or knife or tiny pieces of metal used for fragmentation in an explosive device. An explosive trace detector machine, augmenting the X-ray device, would be able to pick up traces of explosives, and not just metallic items. In order to make certain that all of these items are discovered, only highly trained security personnel should be operating these machines.

If somebody has a metal detector and nothing beeps because there is no fragmentation yet the person is carrying an explosive, the suicide bomber will have easy access to inside the location.

The fact is that even at its most sophisticated, screening technology cannot detect all explosives. This means that security guards working the metal detector must rely on their instincts—that "gut feeling."

Ideally, people going into a building should identify themselves by showing a driver's license, passport, or work ID. A record should be kept of all guests on the premises.

If it is not practical for guards to personally interact with everyone entering a facility, an electronic card access system should be deployed. Lost or stolen cards should immediately be reported and purged from the system, and this requirement must be strictly enforced.

What about profiling as a tool for detecting potential suicide bombers? I strongly believe that it can't be taught. I suggest relying on all the other suggestions given in this chapter.

Deciding purely on the basis of a person's racial makeup whether he or she might be a suicide bomber or some other kind of terrorist is often an unwise screening method. Security personnel, aware of how good a job the Israelis do in their profiling, can be seduced into believing that profiling can be done at all times. What's not understood is that the Israelis have an easier time profiling than do others because they have a known enemy: The surrounding Arab states with their terrorist elements. Therefore, any Arab showing up at a public location and acting the slightest bit suspicious puts Israeli security personnel on the highest alert. For Israelis, therefore, it's quite easy to say one person is suspicious, another is not. Still, even within Israel, terrorist organizations have ways to defeat profiling by deploying non-Arab nationals to carry out suicide bombings, such as the two British nationals who carried out the Mike's Place bombing.

For all other security personnel operating around the world, profiling, however seductive, has little chance of success given that would-be terrorists can use disguises, blend into crowds, and be home-grown. A terrorist can try to pass himself off as Joe next door or the star quarterback of the local football team.

To identify a terrorist, security personnel outside the Middle East have to rely on other suspicious signs: The person's behavior or inappropriate dress.

If security personnel around the world decide to engage in profiling, it is best that only trained professionals do so. Do not ask an untrained and inexperienced college student to do profiling. It's very important that the security person have a prior law enforcement or military background if profiling is going to be employed.

2. **Make Sure the Building's Occupants Are on Full Alert**

Hiring security personnel is not enough.

You must raise the level of alertness of those people occupying your building: Workers in office buildings, tenants in apartment buildings, must become your eyes and ears in looking for suspicious people and items. This means giving these people formal training. The more people who are alert for suspicious activity, the greater your chances of limiting the damage that a terrorist attack can cause.

You should have some sort of plan if an emergency does happen. Practice evacuation of the facility; the frequency of these drills is to be determined by how sensitive your location is.

3. **Certain Dates Should Trigger a Heightened Sense of Alert**

Of great importance for personnel in charge of security at an institution is to be keenly aware of dates that bear significance for potential terrorists, dates that relate both to national and international events.

Any one of these events might trigger a sense of revenge among would-be terrorists. It could be a Western attack against Iran's nuclear facilities; an Israeli confrontation with Arabs on the Temple Mount in Jerusalem; or a targeted killing of a high-level terrorist.

4. **"Harden" Your Locations**

You must "harden" or fortify your location as much as possible. Fortification of schools should be a top priority.

Terrorists could strike at institutions in a number of different ways: Explosives could be placed in a vehicle, with the terrorist trying to get as close to the target as possible and then set off the explosive device. Or, an item containing explosives could be left inside the location and set off by remote control or timer.

Suicide bombers could seek to penetrate the location and detonate the explosives they are wearing at a point where there would be maximum casualties. Once inside a location, a terrorist could indiscriminately shoot into large crowds. They might also engage in knife attacks against individuals.

The least likely kind of terrorist attack would be a chemical or biological assault, because that requires the most sophistication.

"Hardening" or fortifying a building includes doing background checks on all employees; when appropriate, it includes doing searches of people coming into your building.

Security personnel should install a good camera system that photographs both inside and outside a building to determine if someone is engaging in surveillance near the building.

Monitors and recordings should be viewed by professional personnel on a regular basis and any unusual or suspicious activity should be relayed to law enforcement.

When and if possible, building managers should put in place physical barriers, such as planters or cement blocks that can block an explosive-laden vehicle from getting close to its intended target. The barriers will almost certainly minimize casualties and building damage.

All exterior windows of a building should be covered with blast-resistant film to mitigate shattering in case explosives are used in an attack.

If the building, especially a sensitive one, has a garage, cars entering should be checked, including trunks, to make sure that they are not carrying explosives.

Security and building maintenance officials need to be aware of the building's heating, ventilation, and air-conditioning systems, since terrorists might try to place chemical or biological agents inside of them. Make sure access to these systems is limited and controlled.

All exterior doors and operable windows should be alarmed and have motion sensors.

Panic buttons should be installed in key locations, especially in a school's classrooms.

A gate or fence should be installed along the perimeter of a school (as Israelis require at their schools) or of any other building where applicable.

Youngsters should be taught safety practices against terrorism from an early age, especially not to pick up anything from the ground. It just might be an explosive. In Israel such instruction begins in kindergarten. It's never too early.

CHAPTER 13

Chasing The Demons

I continued to do my job and do it well. But I was not aware of the price that I would pay for spending years observing the results of terrorism, the horror of it.

My four years of monitoring and reporting on suicide bombings in Israel and elsewhere around the globe—2003 through 2006—had been the most dramatic, most satisfying, and the most taxing of my life.

When I took up the assignment early in 2003 I never thought of an exit strategy. Much would depend on what I thought of the job, but even more would depend upon the pace of suicide bombings in Israel and the constant level of high alert.

During those four years, waking up every morning wondering if I would be running to a suicide bombing site that day or learning details of an attack that was thwarted, I simply did not think of how this would all end. But by the fall of 2006, signs increasingly appeared that, in retrospect, suggested that I might be nearing the end of my Israeli assignment.

FEWER SUICIDE BOMBINGS

For one thing, the number of suicide bombings had been dropping: There had been eighteen in 2003, ten in 2004, five in 2005, and two in 2006.

Despite the drop in attacks, the number of attempts to dispatch suicide bombers was actually growing; but Israeli security forces, vastly improved, kept the would-be bombers at bay: The Israelis raised the state of the public's alert to the highest level as

well as building fences, establishing roadblocks, and most important, stepping up their intelligence capabilities.

Looking back, the declining number of suicide bombings raised the question, at least in my eyes, of what further value I could be to the NYPD in Israel.

Events were happening to me on a personal level that changed my approach to the assignment. The most important was Gil Kleiman's retirement early in 2006. We had become great friends; we had worked together professionally, and we had shared many good moments during the down times.

But now I had lost my "partner." I was not concerned that Gil's absence from the police force would impair my ability to do my job. The point was mainly that without him at work as an anchor, as someone who could help me relax during these fitful times, I wondered whether I wanted to continue on my own.

SHWARMA I

There was a bombing in Tel Aviv on January 19, 2006. In this attack, which occurred at 3:45 PM, only the bomber died, because of a malfunction in his vest. Thirty people were injured. The attack was carried out at a restaurant called Shwarma Rosh Ha'ir in southern Tel Aviv.

I noticed the bomber's body, sliced neatly in half. This even cut was due to his posture at the time of the bombing: He was leaning over a sink when he exploded the bomb.

After that, there had been no terrorist attacks until March 30, when four Israelis were killed: A suicide bomber hitchhiker, disguised as an ultra-Orthodox yeshiva student, blew himself up in a private car near the entrance to Kedumim on the West Bank. I did not visit this bombing, because the West Bank for the most part did not fall under my NYPD mandate.

SHWARMA II

Then on April 17, 2006, nine people were killed and another forty wounded in a suicide bombing over the Passover holiday at

the same Shwarma Rosh Ha'ir restaurant in Tel Aviv that had been struck three months earlier. Islamic Jihad took responsibility for both attacks. One of those killed was sixteen-year-old American, Daniel Wultz, of Weston, Florida. He died of his injuries on May 14.

The April 2006 suicide bombing proved, in retrospect, a turning point in my assignment. But I could not know it at the time.

I learned of the attack while en route with Gil Kleiman in my car to meet another Israeli police officer for lunch. Gil had just retired. I got beeped, learned that the Shwarma place had been hit again, and told Gil that I had to get there. I needed ten minutes to drive there. I felt awkward.

By now Gil was retired and recovering from PTSD; if we had happened to be together in the past and heard about a bombing, there would have been no question of our going to the site together. But this was different. Do I ask him to go with me? Do I leave him behind?

I asked him to come with me. He wanted to go but felt uncomfortable showing up at the site afflicted with PTSD. I was being selfish: I wanted Gil with me as in the old times. I was thinking more of myself than of my friend, and I apologized to him. He did come with me, but once I gained access to the site, he disappeared, realizing that these scenes were no longer places for him.

The terrorists had obviously felt "cheated" in January when their explosive device malfunctioned, killing only the suicide bomber. Heading back to finish the job was one of the patterns of suicide bombers, and I needed to shout this from the rooftops to New York.

Learning the lesson of the first incident, restaurant owners paid fresh attention to securing the place: At the January attack the restaurant did not have a security guard posted at its entrance and the bomber had entered easily, but by this time, security was increased and a security guard had been stationed at the entrance. This time the guard was a hero and stopped the bomber from getting into the restaurant. Most of the fatalities, including the guard, were people sitting outside. The guard was one of the April fatalities.

With the April repeat I thought back to the assaults on the World Trade Center both in 1993, and how the terrorists also felt "cheated" by killing only six people.

WHERE ARE YOU, JOSE RODRIGUEZ?

A month or so after Shwarma II (April 17, 2006) I received a message from the NYPD. It had come across the name of someone named Jose Rodriguez, who was suspected of having information regarding an act of terror planned against New York. The NYPD wanted me to try to locate him. There was some suspicion that he was in Israel.

This request, while it veered from the normal pattern of my Israeli assignment, was as important to New York as my visits to suicide bombing sites. Locating Rodriguez might mean preventing a terrorist bombing from actually taking place. I interviewed four people across Israel who happened to have the same name.

I came up with zero as far as one of them being the Jose Rodriquez that New York was looking for. Reporting this fact to the NYPD, I eliminated Israel as a connection to this investigation. The point was not that I had come up with nothing to help New York in this case; rather, the importance was that I was in Israel if and when the NYPD needed me to search out actual terrorists.

TURNING POINT

I've mentioned that the April 2006 suicide bombing was a key turning point in my assignment. I had been an eyewitness to many gruesome scenes of carnage, but, conscious of the need to do my job, I had somehow been able to keep those scenes from searing my brain with lasting images. For that reason, I had always been able to contribute, to provide constant intelligence on how better to protect New York City. I had always felt I was making a difference. I had been operational and active for twenty-four years, always in the thick of things, always on the edge of my seat, ready to go.

But by 2005, and especially 2006, as Hamas and Hezbollah, the Islamist political and paramilitary Lebanese-based group, found suicide bombings against Israelis more difficult to execute, they employed other forms of terrorism, especially rockets fired from the Gaza Strip and from Lebanon onto Israeli communities. The kind of intelligence I had been able to cull from suicide bombing sites was not transferable to these rocket attacks; it was not relevant at this time for New York City's needs.

Determining who was firing these rockets was the job of the army. Most important, no direct connection existed between the rocket attacks and the issue of protecting New York City from terror. It seemed almost out of the question that terrorists would start firing rockets from New York or Connecticut on to Manhattan!

This situation left me a spectator, still living and working in Israel, but forced to the sidelines by a change in Palestinian terror tactics. I still continued efforts to cultivate and nurture my Israeli contacts for intelligence that might shed light on possible terror attacks in New York, but now this activity represented only a portion of what I had been doing in Israel.

PERSONAL DESCENT

With too much time on my hands, too much opportunity to think about what I had experienced and witnessed in Israel, I began to feel overwhelmed, burnt out. The nightmarish visions that I had kept at bay began haunting me.

I believe that my personal descent had to do with my having experienced terror events on my own without a partner. During my twenty years in New York I had a partner to talk with and deal with the ups and downs of the job. But the foreign liaison program did not assign two police officers as partners in one country.

Throughout 2006 I continued to monitor my beeper and sit in front of the computer to check if terror attacks had occurred in Israel or elsewhere. It was not as dramatic as racing to a suicide bombing scene, but at least I still felt my work was of value to the NYPD.

The Second Lebanon War in response to Hezbollah attack-
ing and killing civilians by sending rockets into northern Israel
had started on July 12, 2006. I was scheduled to take my family
back to the United States for a vacation in a few weeks, when
someone in Commissioner Kelly's office called and asked me if
I wanted all of us to come home right away; in all candor I was
tempted for a moment.

I knew diplomats and embassy staff from various countries
who had sent their families home during both the Second Gulf
War (March 2003) and the Second Lebanon War. But one of the
lessons that Meryl and I had integrated into our thinking was that
if you run and back down from terror, the terrorist wins. It was
important for us to take a stand and not run away. We felt we were
showing support and strength.

So, Meryl opted to stay with me, though the stress levels were
unbearable at times and her memories of the planes striking the
World Trade Center were evoked every time she saw war planes
overhead.

I began to feel increasingly burned out. No specific event
triggered this feeling. In the past the pressures of getting to a
suicide bombing site quickly, of sweeping all the details, and of
reporting to New York as soon as possible had been mitigated
by my adrenaline high as well as by the continuing praise I had
received from the NYPD, the commissioner, and the media. I
knew that, while I was on that roller coaster, I had been obsessed
with my work, as I waited for the beeper to go off, not taking a
day off, morbidly curious over whether this might be a day when
I would have to look at dead bodies and listen to the screams of
the seriously wounded.

During these current quiet times, I remained obsessed, the
only difference being that I had plenty of time to dwell on my
obsessions. For the past five years or so I had been coolly clinical
at these suicide bombing sites, the way a detective has to be at a
crime scene, the way a doctor must be in surgery.

But I realized, as 2006 wore on, in a kind of out-of-body
experience, that my career, my obsessions, my uncertainties had

become my entire life and there was nothing I could do about it. The grisly images grew into sharper focus, and my spirits dampened. The images were mostly of human flesh, blood, body parts, and mangled strollers.

The signs that I was personally suffering from a serious psychological ailment that actually had a medical name attached to it stared at me; but I ignored those signs for as long as I could, trying to convince myself that I was too absorbed in my work to take time off and give them the attention they may have deserved. Meanwhile, my health was deteriorating. My blood pressure was sky high and my doctor put me on medication.

I grew obese, ballooning from 250 pounds in January 2003 to over 300 pounds four years later. Always big, I had never been so heavy. Frustration over the pressures that I had once lived with calmly but now were taking over my life, drove me to eat—and eat and eat.

A social drinker my whole career, I began doing the wrong kind of drinking. Any American cop will tell you—and himself—that the social drinking that he or she engages in leads to positive bonding. What we all liked about our trips to D.J. Reynolds, one of our favorite local bars, was the camaraderie that developed over a few beers.

But, instead of the joyous social drinking that was a constant for cops and that helped us all to unwind, I now looked to drinking as something that I needed to do by myself, hoping that it would help me deal with my new demons.

I did not drink that often, but when I did, I drank too much. I began using alcohol as a crutch. It became a way to numb myself. I developed the same rationales as other alcoholics did. I could control the amount of my drinking. Even if I had taken one too many, I would know how to keep from injuring myself or anyone else. I never thought that I needed Alcoholics Anonymous. But I knew that drinking was no longer fun.

With the obesity and the drinking, and the continuing pressures from the job, I could not enjoy anything. I could not free my mind of my work; I could never turn it off.

I might be at an event with my wife and children and I could not enjoy the moment. While we were in the United States in August 2006, Meryl and I took the children to Disney World in Orlando, Florida. But I was simply not there. I was too preoccupied with dark thoughts of events that I had witnessed and that might be recurring at this very moment thousands of miles away.

I was disassociating from enjoying life. And still, knowing what I was going through, even though my situation was difficult for the family, Meryl understood and supported me. She knew more about terror than 99 percent of the American police. We were both learning about the effects it had on first responders like me.

In retrospect, I assumed she thought I would "get better," that the job would end one day, that with a lessening of terror in Israel, I would return to normalcy. That's what she had hoped for, but it was going to be a struggle to get back to a good place. I needed some help, perhaps even medical. Though I had no specific physical pain, I still felt that it was time to visit a doctor. I had not been to one for a general checkup in several years.

In the fall of 2006 the doctor ran a series of tests, and found nothing of any worrisome nature, but he did warn that if I did not take off weight, I would face serious medical issues. He did not elaborate, and I didn't need him to. That visit was a wakeup call and I got the message. The doctor made me look in the mirror. That was crucial. He brought me back to Earth.

My conclusion, apart from believing that I had to lose weight, was that I had to end my assignment in Israel soon.

When I was deep into my malaise, what I think of as my dark period, I began to confide in Gil, who had been burdened with many of the same emotions that I had endured, and for many of the same reasons. After all, for as many suicide bombing sites that I had visited (twenty-one in Israel), Gil had gone to more.

After the Stage Club bombing in Tel Aviv in February 2005, Gil began describing his own situation as Post-Trauma Stress Disorder, that affliction which so many American soldiers had experienced after war. But, similar as our symptoms were, I refused to

describe what I had as PTSD. I wouldn't allow myself to have it. I didn't feel like I deserved it. Later, part of the evidence that I was recovering was my willingness to acknowledge that indeed I had suffered from this illness.

One reason I thought I didn't "deserve" to be tagged with a disease was my recollection of NYPD detectives, including myself, in the 1980s and 1990s routinely going to crime scenes. My own personal deterioration made me think of the cops in NYPD's Crime Scene Unit because of their constant exposure to unnatural deaths.

EVERYONE HAS SEEN SHIT

"Dear God," I thought, "If these guys, with their almost daily contact with horrific scenes of both death and injuries, don't have PTSD, or they're not claiming to have it, how dare I claim to have it? Many of us had been at 9/11. Everyone has seen shit."

I myself had seen hundreds of bodies; I must have been to hundreds of crime scenes. I saw every conceivable kind of death from a newborn with Sudden Infant Death Syndrome to an elderly person dying peacefully in her sleep, to people who had been run over by trains.

I had seen it all: Suicides, murders, shootings, stabbings, and too many autopsies to count. I even came across a beheading in New York: A "jumper" committed suicide and was beheaded on his way down when he collided with sharp metal support rails in the midtown Marriot Hotel's atrium. He was a very considerate "jumper." His last booming words were: "Look out below."

Yet the burnt corpses and the screaming injured could tug at my heartstrings in a more profound way than could victims of a robbery, or jealousy, envy or greed.

Perhaps my psychological tailspin had to do with the fact that terror was such an indiscriminate crime, that the only motive of the suicide bomber was hatred. The bomber seemed more vicious than the greedy thief or the vengeful wife who turned on her husband for his having an affair.

It was only when I spent time during 9/11 and at suicide bombing sites that I understood what the term "crime against humanity" actually meant. The suicide bomber I experienced was a killer who based his violence on a radical Islamic ideology that arrogantly proclaimed that nonbelievers such as Jews and Christians, because they were "infidels," did not deserve to live.

As much as I had tried to convince myself that I was not suffering from PTSD, I knew deep down that witnessing suicide bombing sites could have affected me emotionally in ways that did not happen to the cops at New York crime scenes or autopsies.

From April 2006 there were no suicide bombings in Israel until January 29, 2007, when three people were killed after a bomber blew himself up in a bakery in the southern resort town of Eilat after trekking through the Sinai Desert. I decided to skip the Eilat suicide bombing, since it was a four-hour drive and I would have arrived too late to be able to elicit information obtainable only at the scene.

Somehow the bomber sneaked into Israel, perhaps arriving from the Gaza Strip. Hitchhiking to Eilat, he was picked up by a reserve lieutenant colonel in the IDF who decided that the man's lack of Hebrew and his long black coat on a warm sunny day and his heavy bag made him suspicious. Dropping the passenger off in a residential section of the Red Sea resort, the army officer reported the man to the police. Zeroing in on the potential bomber two minutes after the officer's warning, the police arrived on the scene where the bomber was walking. Though he may have wanted to target one of Eilat's major hotels, the bomber apparently panicked, went into a nearby bakery, and exploded his device.

The episode strengthened my view that what keeps down casualties in a suicide bombing is public awareness. Sure, the very fact that he got into Israel with his explosives was a breakdown in intelligence; but from then on, enough people had became suspicious of him so that only three people were killed, not fifty.

Though I had not been at the scene, I was able to convey my findings and analysis to New York. It was my last report on a suicide bombing to them from Israel.

I remained in the assignment, looking into any possible connection between people and potential terror cells in Israel and New York City; waiting for the next attack, and arranging for Israeli police and the NYPD to exchange visits for cross training, including my bringing the NYPD bomb squad to Israel. The tension that I had always felt remained; but my life became far less dramatic.

There were no suicide bombings the rest of 2007. From conversations that I had had with my NYPD colleagues in recent months, they knew it was time for me to turn over my assignment to someone else.

In October 2007 I ended my assignment in Israel but not before I trained my NYPD replacement and introduced him to my network of contacts. I then took four months of vacation time that I had accrued.

WHAT IS NEXT FOR ME?

The first opportunity to look into a future that did not include the daily monitoring of suicide bombings came when I traveled to New York and, a few days before Christmas 2007, talked with Commissioner Kelly about my future career options. Hearing of my plan to retire, the commissioner asked to meet with me. Why, I was not sure.

Senior officers let me know that Commissioner Kelly wanted to discuss the possibility of my staying longer with the NYPD. He wanted to know whether there was any specific area in the department that I would consider. They stressed that it was not every day that a police commissioner—one regarded as perhaps America's finest—called a homicide detective in for a meeting to discuss his future. It meant a lot to me that Commissioner Kelly cared and appreciated my work in Israel. I had received encouragement and support from him personally throughout my assignment.

Some colleagues suggested that I take up another foreign assignment, maybe in a less violent locale, but quite frankly, I was not up for it; mostly I thought of simply retiring from the police force. But I wanted to hear what the commissioner had to say. Had

I truly wished to continue with the NYPD, I would have welcomed using my expertise to train other officers in best practices in counterterror; and/or going back to being a homicide detective in New York. As a First Grade detective, I would have most likely gone back to work in some investigative capacity, remaining within the Intelligence Division.

But at the time of my meeting with the commissioner, though I had given thought to how much longer Meryl, the children, and I would stay in Israel, I felt strongly that this was not the right time for us to pick up and leave. Life in Israel was the only one my children knew. When we arrived in Israel, Zach was three years old and the twins were seven months.

Invited into his office, I thanked him for the incredible five-year opportunity that he had given me. Bringing up my future, he asked if there was something else that I wanted to do in the department. I thanked him for the offer but explained that my family and I wanted to remain in Israel, at least for now. Had I not been married, had I not had children, I might have reconsidered retirement and jumped at Commissioner Kelly's offer to take up a new assignment in New York; but I told him, "Thank you but I have to say no. My kids are happy and settled in Israel. I don't want to change their environment now."

I left the meeting feeling very good about what I had contributed to New York. I was ready to start the next chapter.

I realized that my Israeli posting had been my dream assignment; there could not be another one in New York or anywhere else, at least not for me. I could have tried to resurrect the "good old days" of the 1990s, when I had truly enjoyed the day-to-day police work and the day-to-day camaraderie, but I decided that there was nothing else that I wanted to do at this near-retirement stage of my police career.

Besides, Meryl and I, at this and all other times when decisions of this nature arose, put the children first. We had our priorities—and they were named Zach, Jake, and Talia. It seemed like the right time to retire from the NYPD and focus on my family life.

I RETIRE FROM THE NYPD

In January 2008 I had served twenty-five years with the NYPD, five years more than the twenty required for my full pension to be paid. I was forty-five years old and ready to move on to the next phase of my life.

Meanwhile, the NYPD's foreign liaison program was shifting under my feet. When I became the third New York detective to take up a foreign posting in early 2003, and the first to Israel, the program was experimental. We were all flying by the seats of our pants. It was not clear how long any of us would stay abroad.

Because I was in a so-called "hardship" post (Israel was considered a war zone), New York would have welcomed me home anytime. Indeed, several other liaisons had found being away from their families and New York too much to endure. They returned after only a few months on the job. One location had four different liaisons during my posting in Israel.

When I had first taken on my assignment in Israel, I was guaranteed to be there for three months. Three months turned into a year, a year into three years, and three into five years. But by the fall of 2007, after seeing the tremendous success of the international liaison program, the NYPD decided to standardize it, so that each of the eleven foreign liaisons served for two years, with an option for a third year. I had already served nearly five.

January 28, 2008, was my retirement day. After twenty-five years and twenty-five days as a New York policeman, I was ending my career with a sense of relief, but a great deal of uncertainty; I did feel that I was in the right place (Israel) with a family that supported me through thick and thin.

I was feeling better these days. Time had proved a great healer. I was now in the best shape of my life, ironically, even better than I had been as a twenty-year-old rookie in the Academy. I joined a gym and made sure to visit it six days a week. It proved a great release. I took off 100 pounds between 2007 and 2009, not by engaging in a crash diet, but as more of a "way of life" change.

But what was I going to do with the rest of my life? At first I wasn't sure. I wanted to continue to make a difference, as my father had always advised me to do. But did that mean I should go pick tomatoes at a kibbutz?

I preferred working with Americans to improve their approach to countering terrorism. I was in a unique position: Knowing what was possible and not possible to do in fighting terror in the United States and knowing the Israeli counterterror experience as well. Looking at my curriculum vitae, I knew where my strengths and expertise lay. I thought the private sector offered the brightest prospects. And so Gil Kleiman and I, still best friends, began working together as consultants to U.S. first responders.

We were both well enough upon retiring to talk publicly about our past assignments, feeling lots of pride in the jobs that we had done, seeing ourselves as proactive early-warning systems in the continuing struggle to keep terrorists at bay.

With that in mind, we began passing on to law enforcement groups and other American first responders the lessons that we both had learned regarding terror in Israel and around the globe. We consult for all law enforcement and first responders such as homeland security officials, firemen, and emergency medical service staff. While pointing out Israeli best practices, we make sure to indicate how those best practices can be adapted to American realities.

I knew that I wanted to contribute to society after retirement and my consulting work made me feel that I was indeed contributing.

I make no pretense that my recovery went smoothly. It was hard enough for me to adjust to my post-NYPD life, but during one six-month period I was hit with the loss of a brother-in-law, someone almost like a brother and best friend to me, and my father, so my ascent to full recovery was slower than I had hoped for or imagined. Losing these two people was not easy, and I had to dig deep for the inner strength to forge on.

My sister Adina's husband, Frank Kutnicki, was a role model for me and my mentor from the time I was twelve years old; he

taught me how to enjoy life and value its simple things. He died of a heart attack on February 20, 2008, at the age of fifty-four. He and Adina had dreamed of retiring to Israel. By 2010 she was living in Israel with their two sons and their families.

Then, on October 2, 2008, my father, the most influential person in my life, passed away at the age of ninety; he was a remarkably good man with clear blue eyes and a gentle soul. With his death, I recalled the love and support he had given to his seemingly wayward son, a nice Jewish boy who had chosen to become a cop. By being true to myself and to my Jewish values, I made my father proud. He could not get over the fact that my career led me to recovering stolen Torahs and to residing for years in Israel.

REMAINING IN ISRAEL

Our decision to stay in Israel after my NYPD retirement was one that Meryl and I made mostly for our children. Because of the special place that Israel had in our hearts, we wanted to give our children the opportunity to experience living in our Jewish homeland. The decision did not come easily—for me personally. The one thing I wasn't prepared for when I got here in early 2003 was how much I would miss New York, my friends, and family.

It was a quirk of fate that I had stayed in Israel for so long. Had Commissioner Kelly not sent me to Israel when he did, I am convinced that I would have retired from the NYPD back in 2003. After all, I had served the required twenty years to be eligible for full retirement benefits. I had even sought out the NYPD's Pension Section to find out how much my retirement benefit would be, as most officers do when approaching their twenty-year anniversary. My appointment was scheduled for the end of October 2002. I ended up canceling it when I found out that Commissioner Kelly wanted to see me that same day.

I had a strong sense that the police commissioner would ask me to stay beyond my twenty years and serve as the NYPD liaison in Israel. Since I very much wanted to take the Israel assignment, there was no point in keeping the date with the Pension Section.

All the time I was in Israel, from 2003 until the present, I was torn between living in the Jewish state or the United States. I knew that had there been no 9/11, had I not been given the post in Israel, I would have retired early in 2003 and at some point tried life in Israel with the family. I don't know if we would have stayed in Israel for more than a few months, though, because I was a true New Yorker to the core.

So why am I still in Israel? While I love and miss New York, I still believe that Israel is the perfect place for my children. In addition to its being the place where our ancestors made history and so many of our grandparents' generation arrived after escaping the Nazis, Israel offers our children identity, community, and independence. Israeli society is in many ways geared for children. So, as the parents of three children, that feature alone makes it easy for Meryl and me to live here. Meryl and our children feel the Jewish state is their home, but I will always consider the USA as my home.

When the sirens wail signaling the sadness of Israel's Memorial Day for its fallen soldiers then immediately following that, when martial music blares and firecrackers go off, signifying Israel's Independence Day, our enthusiasm for living here is reinforced.

It may sound like an outright contradiction, but I cannot imagine my kids growing up anywhere other than Israel. We hope the children will agree with that decision. For the time being, the rash of suicide bombings that I monitored and reported on has become a thing of the past, not part of a continuing dark tale that continues to the present. That tranquility has helped in my recovery.

I have learned to abandon my old obsessions, and I have chased away the demons. I am at the gym every morning; exercise has become a way of life. I'm doing my best to make drinking a thing of my past, though it admittedly is a difficult vice to fight.

How can I tell that I am improving? I am having fun watching my boys play basketball and am getting a kick out of teaching them some of my moves from earlier days. I love watching my daughter's dance performances and feel so proud when I catch her eye while she is on stage.

How vividly I recall that period when I could not get to such events, or if I attended, how distracted I had been, unable to focus on her performance. At times, while at a basketball practice or a dance performance, I whisper to myself, "Oh my God, I missed all this."

Still, I know that I cannot completely rid myself of my obsession with terror. I am both happy and sad about this.

Let's be frank, those suicide bombing scenes entered into my mind, resided there on hold for a time, then entered my consciousness with the shock of a bolt of lightning. Fortunately, I stopped denying that my experience had left me intact. I am told that part of dealing with PTSD is recognizing that there is no instant "cure" for my obsession. But the obsession is not overbearing anymore, and I can use what I learned to help many others.

I find great support from my family and friends. Looking back to those times when I could not interact with any of them, I now realize what I had given up, lost for a while, and desperately wanted back. I was fortunate that the support my family and friends have shown me throughout has never dissipated.

Most important, I believe in myself, in the Morty Dzikansky who talks about the past with pride in his contributions, but with a smile and laughter that are now more and more a part of my personality.

INDEX

A

Adler, Mona, 62, 66–67
Allee, William, 56
Al-Qaeda, 61, 114, 165
Al-Rantiss, Abdel Aziz, 133
Appelbaum, Dr. David,
138–139
 young paramedic (David's
 daughter—Nava's sister)
 139
Appelbaum, Nava, 139
Arafat, Yasser, 87
Austin, Stuart, 147
Averbach, Steve, 131

B

Bachety, Mike, 24
Baz, Rashid, 42–43
Berman, Richard M., 203
Blair, Tony, 160
Bloomberg, Michael, 84, 134–
135, 179
Boyd, Markieth, 22
Bradley, Ed, 151
Browne, Paul J., 204
Bush, George W., 160
 Administration, 114

C

Cogswell, Ed, 121
Cogswell, Terry, 9–12

D

Daschle, Tom, 83
Drug Enforcement
 Administration (DEA), 93
Dzikansky children, 126, 149,
 186, 230, 233, 237–239
 Jake, 86, 90, 92, 152–153
 Talia, 86, 90, 92
 Zachary, 57, 59–60, 63, 65,
 74, 92, 114–115
Dzikansky, Meryl, 19, 31, 57,
 60–63, 65–66, 68, 72, 74,
 86, 90, 92, 114–115, 126,
 140, 146, 148, 153, 186,
 228–230, 233, 237–239
 mother, 91
Dzikansky, Mordecai:
 A to Z Luggage robbery,
 22
 Ari Halberstam case, 42–43,
 57, 75
 assigned to Bedford-
 Stuyvesant, 21

begins Israel liaison assignment, (January 3, 2003), 103
chasing drug dealers, 20
childhood, 1
CIA, 121, 177
Dykan, Reva and Jeff (Morty's American cousins), 104
FBI, 120
Meir Kahane case, 24–29
mother, 2, 6, 65
NYPD offer to work in Israel, 87–92
Post-traumatic Stress Disorder (PTSD), 231–232, 239
promoted to First Grade Detective (February 23, 2004), 148
"Prostitute/Serial Killer" case (June 29, 1995), 45–47
remaining in Israel, 238
retires from NYPD in January 2008, 234
Sar-El program (1991), 30
Shoshana, Navah, Adina, (sisters), 2
"singing detective" case (November 15, 1993), 41
teenage years, 3
Torah thefts cases, 35–40, 47–57
Tupac Shakur case (November, 30, 1994), 43–45

visits to Israel (1971), 2, 29–30, 93
Dzikansky, Jekuthiel, 1, 12, 32, 40, 115, 148–149, 237

G
Ganor, Boaz, 136
Gibbons, Bob, 37–38
Gunaratna, Rohan, 136

H
Hecker, Harvey, 8
Harkins, Walter, 38–39, 46
Hennessey, Eddie, 44, 47
Hoffman, Bruce, 136

I
Israel terror attacks (2000–2003), 89
Israeli-Arab conflict, 87–88

J
Jaradat, Hanadi, 140–141, 195
Jones, Charles, 54–57, 192

K
Kahane, Meir, 23, 25–28, 43, 75
Kelly, Raymond, 27, 84–87, 94, 113–114, 121, 126, 146–151, 180, 196, 228, 233
Kleiman, Gil, 96–97, 102, 104, 114–115, 123, 125, 138–139, 141, 144, 146–147, 149, 155–156, 225–230, 236

Post-traumatic Stress
Disorder (PTSD), 155-
156, 225
Koppelman, Irwin, 79
Kutnicki, Frank, 236

M
Malik, Nidal, 216
Markowitz, Howard, (Meryl's
father), 62, 65–66
McCabe, Brian, 22, 57–58, 64,
67–68, 150
Miller, Judith, 151
Morgenthau, Robert, 39

N
Nichols, Terry, 75–76
Norris, Ed, 26
Nosair, El Sayyad, 27

O
Operation Defensive Shield
(March 2002), 89

P
Parker, Mitch, 53–54
Peres, Shimon, 136–137
Perez, Renaldo, 41
Pinero, Rafael, 149
Pollock, David, 38, 50–51, 54

R
Random bag checks
lawsuit to prevent such
checks, 202
Renow, Alex, 41

Ribowsky, Shiya, 79
Rivera, Wendy Hoffman, 46
Rivera-Duffy, Irma, 72
Rodriguez, Jose (May 2006),
226

S
Schlesinger, Alvin, 27
"See Something, Say
Something" public alertness
program, 131, 180, 202–203
Seidemann, Joel, 39–40, 150
"Shield" NYPD partnership
with private security, 203
Shomrim Society, 5, 13, 17, 46,
168
Sicilia, Barbara, 24
Slater, Robert, 130
Smith, Moira, 73
Stevens, Richard, 48–52
Suicide bombings in Israel
Beersheba, (August 31,
2004), 151
Eilat, (January 29, 2007),
232
Haifa, (March 5, 2003),
112, 199
Haifa, Maxim, (October 4,
2003), 139–142, 195, 201
Jerusalem, (November 21,
2002), 95
Jerusalem, French Hill
(May 18, 2003), 129–132,
206
Jerusalem, (June 11, 2003),
132

Jerusalem, Café Hillel,
 (September 9, 2003),
 137–139
Jerusalem, (August 19,
 2003), 134–135, 201
Jerusalem, (January 29,
 2004), 146
Jerusalem, French Hill,
 (September 22, 2004), 152
Kfar Saba, (April 24, 2003),
 193–195
Netanya, Park Hotel,
 (March 27, 2002), 88
Netanya, Sharon Mall, (July
 12, 2005), 156
Netanya, Sharon Mall,
 (December 5, 2005), 156
Petach Tikva, (Christmas
 Day, 2003), 142, 199–200
Rishon LeZion, (September
 9, 2003), 136
Tel Aviv, Mike's Place,
 (April 30, 2003), 118–126,
 154–157, 199–200, 219
Tel Aviv, (November 1,
 2004), 152–153
Tel Aviv, Stage Club,
 (February 25, 2005), 153–
 156, 230
Tel Aviv, Shwarma I attack,
 (January 19, 2006), 199,
 224
Tel Aviv, Shwarma II
 attack, (April 17, 2006),
 224–225

Suicide bombing outside Israel
 Casablanca attack, (May 16,
 2003), 158–159
 Istanbul synagogues attack,
 (November 15, 2003),
 150, 157, 159–162, 165,
 167–168, 170, 176–178,
 185–187, 196
London, attack, (July 7,
 2005), 202
Madrid attack, (March 11,
 2004), 175, 202–205
Moscow I attack, (February
 6, 2004), 147, 150, 165–
 173, 194, 202, 204
Moscow II attack, (August
 31, 2004), 181–182
Sharm el Sheikh attack,
 (July 23, 2005), 185–192
Suicide bombings in
 Israel—statistics
 (2002), 88
 (2002–2003), 89

T
Tabib, Avi, 122
Taubenfeld, Goldie, 134
Taubenfeld, Shmuel, 134
Tege, Michelle, 136–137
Terror attacks in Israel
 (September 1979 to June
 1980), 3
Terror attacks in United States
 World Trade Center attack
 (September 11, 2001), 119

Fort Hood attack,
 (November 5, 2009), 216
Times Square car bomb
 attack, (May, 1 2010), 216

W
World Financial Center, 61
World Trade Center bombing,
 (1993), 37, 226
 (September 11, 2001), 60–
 63, 65–68, 71, 73, 75, 80,
 84, 130, 197, 226, 228
Wultz, Daniel, 225

Z
ZAKA, 130

OTHER BOOKS IN OUR
BARRICADE CRIME SERIES

The Jews of Sing-Sing
Ron Arons
Besides famous gangsters like Lepke Buchalter, thousands of Jews committed all types of crimes--from incest to arson to selling air rights over Manhattan--and found themselves doing time in Sing-Sing.
$22.95 • Hardcover • 1-56980-333-1

The Mafia and the Machine
Frank R. Hayde
La Cosa Nostra reaches right into the heart of America. Nowhere is that more evident than in the "City of Fountains," where the Mafia held sway over the political machine.
$22.00 • Hardcover • 1-56980-336-6
$16.95 • Paperback • 1-56980-443-5

Black Gangsters of Chicago
Ron Chepesiuk
Chicago's African American gangsters were every bit as powerful and intriguing as the city's fabled white mobsters. For the first time, Ron Chepesiuk chronicles their fascinating stories.
$22.00 • Hardcover • 1-56980-331-5

The Silent Don
Scott Deitche
A follow-up to Deitche's best-selling *Cigar City Mafia*, *The Silent Don* exposes the life of one of America's most powerful and feared mob bosses, Santo Trafficante Jr.
$22.00 • Hardcover • 1-56980-322-6
$16.95 • Paperback • 1-56980-355-2

Blood & Volume
Dave Copeland
Ron Gonen, together with pals Johnny Attias and Ron Efraim, ran a multi-million-dollar drug distribution syndicate in 1980s New York. But when the FBI caught up, Gonen had to choose between doing the right thing and winding up dead.
$22.00 • Hardcover • 1-56980-327-7

Gangsters of Harlem
Ron Chepesiuk
Veteran journalist Ron Chepesiuk chronicles the life and crimes of Harlem's gangsters, including "Nicky" Barnes, Bumpy Johnson, and the notorious Frank Lucas.
$22.00 • Hardcover • 1-56980-318-8
$15.95 • Paperback • 1-56980-365-X

Cigar City Mafia: A Complete History of the Tampa Underworld
Scott M. Deitche
Prohibition-era "Little Havana" housed Tampa's cigar industry, and with it, bootleggers, arsonists, and mobsters—and a network of corrupt police officers worse than the criminals themselves. Scott M. Deitche documents the rise of the infamous Trafficante family, ruthless competitors in a "violent, shifting place, where loyalties and power quickly changed."
$22.95 • Hardcover • 1-56980-266-1
$14.95 • Paperback • 1-56980-287-4

I'll Do My Own Damn Killin'

Gary W. Sleeper

A detailed look into the life of notorious casino owner Benny Binion, which looks into his life in Dallas before his infamous Las Vegas days.

$22.00 • Hardcover • 1-56980-321-8

Thief!

William "Slick" Hanner & Cherie Rohn

The true story of "Slick" Hanner and how he gained insider access to the Mafia, starting out as a Chicago street tough and workin his way to a friendship with Tony Spilotro, the Outfit's notorious frontman.

$22.00 • Hardcover • 1-56980-317-X

Gangster City: The History of the New York Underworld 1900–1935

Patrick Downey

From 1900 to 1935, New York City hosted more than 600 mob-land killings. No other book delivers such extensive detail on the lives, crimes, and dramatic endings of this ruthless cast of characters, including Jack "Legs" Diamond and the sadistic Dutch Schultz.

$23.95 • Hardcover • 1-56980-267-X
$16.95 • Paperback • 1-56980-361-7

Il Dottore

Ron Felber

By day, he was Dr. Elliot Litner, respected surgeon at Mount Sinai Hospital; by night, Il Dottore, a sex and gambling addict with ties to New York's reigning Mafia Dons. But when Attorney General Rudolph Guiliani stepped in, Litner had to decide where his loyalties lay: with La Cosa Nostra, or the Hippocratic oath.

$24.95 • Hardcover • 1-56980-278-5

Murder of a Mafia Daughter

Cathy Scott

Not until college did Las Vegas native Susan Berman learn her father had been a notorious leader of the local Mafia. Her life took an even more bizarre turn when the wife of her college friend, real estate heir Robert Durst, disappeared, leaving Durst a murder suspect. When Berman was found dead, shot execution-style, investigators wondered if she knew more about Durst than he could afford.

$23.95 • Hardcover • 1-56980-238-6

The Life and Times of Lepke Buchalter

Paul R. Kavieff

Lepke Buchalter had a stranglehold on the New York garment industry, rising from small-scale push-cart terrorism to leadership of Murder Inc.'s staff of killers-by-assignment, until an obscure murder ended his reign as America's most ruthless labor racketeer.

$22.00 • Hardcover • 1-56980-291-2

The Purple Gang

Paul R. Kavieff

This is the hitherto untold story of the rise and fall of one of America's most notorious criminal groups. The Purple Gang was a loosely organized confederation of mobsters who dominated the Detroit underworld and whose tentacles reached across the country.

$15.95 • Paperback • 1-56980-281-5
$22.00 • Hardcover • 1-56980-417-9

The Violent Years
Paul R. Kavieff
A follow-up to Kavieff's best-selling *The Purple Gang*, this book delves deeper into the Prohibition-Era gangs of the Detroit area.
$22.00 • Hardcover • 1-56980-210-6

The Rise and Fall of the Cleveland Mafia
Rick Porrello
From obscurity, the Cleveland Mafia rose rapidly to power and position, taking its place as the third most powerful operation in the country. But the city's crime syndicates nearly decimated themselves during the Sugar War—"Big Ange" Lonardo's vendetta-driven play to control the lucrative bootleg liquor production racket.
$15.00 • Paperback • 1-56980-277-7
$22.00 • Hardcover • 1-56980-058-8

Lucky Luciano
Hickman Powell
Written by a top investigative reporter who covered Luciano's trial from beginning to end, *Lucky Luciano* is a detailed account of Luciano's intriguing life.
$23.95 • Hardcover • 1-56980-163-0

Mala Femina
Theresa Dalessio with Patrick W. Picciarelli
Theresa "Terri Dee" Dalessio was a Mafia daughter, pregnant teenager, barkeeper, heroin addict, murder wit ness, and twice-divorced mother of three. For a start.
$24.95 • Hardcover • 1-56980-244-0

Jailing the Johnston Gang
Bruce E. Mowday
Pennsylvania's Johnston Gang, led by Bruce Sr. and his brothers Norman and David, ran a prolific burglary ring during the 1960 and 1970s. But in 1978, fearing that younger members of the gang were going to rat them out, the brothers killed four teenagers and nearly killed Bruce Sr.'s own son.
$22.95 • Hardcover • 1-56980-363-3
$16.95 • Paperback • 1-56980-442-1

Human Sacrifice: A Shocking Exposé of Ritual Killings Worldwide
Jimmy Lee Shreeve
Human sacrifice still goes on today, and uncomfortably close to home. Jimmy Lee Shreeve paints a horrifying picture of ritual killings around the world.
$15,95 • Paperback • 1-56980-346-3

Balls: The Life of Eddie Trascher, Gentleman Gangster
Scott M. Deitche with Ken Sanz
For 50 years, Eddie Trascher stole from mob-owned casinos, scammed gangsters, and was one of the top bookies in the country. He capped his career as an informant for Florida enforcement to get inside the Trafficante Mafia family.
$24.95 • Hardcover • 1-56980-366-8

A Cop's Tale: NYPD The Violent Years

Jim O'Neil and Mel Fazzino
Focusing on New York City's most corrupt years, the 1960s to 1980s, this book delivers a rare look at the brand of law enforcement that ended Frank Lucas's grip on the Harlem drug trade, cracking open the Black Liberation Army case, and the author's experience as the first cop on the scene at the "Dog Day Afternoon" bank robbery.

$24,95 • Hardcover • 1-56980-372-2

Gangsters of Miami: True Tales of Mobsters, Gamblers, Hit Men, Con Men and Gang Bangers from the Magic City

Ron Chepesiuk
Chronicling gangs and gangster history using profiles this book traces the notorious smugglers of the Prohibition era, famous mobsters like Al Capone and Meyer Lansky, the Cuban mafia, the Colombian cartel, and the current street gangs that have come to plague Miami after the advent of crack cocaine.

$23.95 • Hardcover • 1-56980-368-4